Changing Contours of Microfinance in India

This book brings together empirical evidences and theoretical perspectives to provide a comprehensive overview of the microfinance sector in India. The chapters in the volume:

- focus on the application of information and communication technology (ICT) solutions in microfinance institutions to strengthen the savings movement and widen credit access to the poor and marginalised sections of society;
- present case studies on self-help group (SHG) movements, federations and SHG–Bank Linkage programmes;
- propose measures for strengthening regulatory and governance structures of the microfinance sector; and
- identify linkages between overall financial inclusion and the contribution of microfinance institutions (MFIs).

The volume will be indispensable for scholars and researchers of microeconomics, South Asian economics and development economics as well as professionals and aspirants in the microfinance, rural banking and financial inclusion sectors.

Jayadev M. is Professor at the Indian Institute of Management Bangalore, Karnataka, India.

Diatha Krishna Sundar is Professor at the Indian Institute of Management Bangalore, Karnataka, India.

Changing Contours of Microfinance in India

Edited by Jayadev M. and
Diatha Krishna Sundar

Routledge
Taylor & Francis Group

LONDON AND NEW YORK

First published 2016
by Routledge
2 Park Square, Milton Park, Abingdon, Oxon OX14 4RN

and by Routledge
711 Third Avenue, New York, NY 10017

*Routledge is an imprint of the Taylor & Francis Group,
an informa business*

© 2016 Jayadev M. and Diatha Krishna Sundar

The right of Jayadev M. and Diatha Krishna Sundar to be
identified as the authors of the editorial material, and of
the authors for their individual chapters, has been asserted
in accordance with sections 77 and 78 of the Copyright,
Designs and Patents Act 1988.

British Library Cataloguing in Publication Data
A catalogue record for this book is available from the
British Library

Library of Congress Cataloging-in-Publication Data
A catalog record has been requested for this book

ISBN: 978-1-138-66570-5 (hbk)
ISBN: 978-1-315-61977-4 (ebk)

Typeset in Sabon
by Apex CoVantage, LLC

Contents

Figures

Tables

Preface

This book is an outgrowth of the seventh International Conference on E-Governance (ICEG-2010) held at the Indian Institute of Management Bangalore (IIMB), in Bangalore, India, from 22 to 24 April 2010. This conference was organised on behalf of International Congress of E-Government (ICEG), a professional society that was established in 2003 with the aim to address the growing need for furthering knowledge in e-governance. ICEG organises conferences and seminars, and plans to publish periodicals and start a research centre of excellence. The International Conference on E-Governance is a signature event that brings together thought leaders, policy makers and practitioners of e-governance. ICEG-2010, the seventh conference in this series, was organised at IIMB with three themes: public health and ICT, microfinance and ICT, and e-government and m-government. This book is primarily an outcome of selected papers on the theme of microfinance that were presented in the conference. The second half of 2010 witnessed several changes in the microfinance sector due to the crisis in Andhra Pradesh and other regulatory changes. To include contemporary issues, a few papers were invited for this volume. This book is an edited volume comprising of thirteen selected papers in the revised form, that cover four main aspects of the microfinance sector – regulation, self-help groups (SHGs), technology and other microfinance services. These selected papers highlight the emerging trends in microfinance, such as the increasing role of technological interventions using mobile and information and communications technology (ICT), societal empowerment through SHG and bank linkage policies, improvements in microfinance services provided to the poor and the role played by SHGs in post-disaster reconstruction.

Abbreviations

AI	artificial insemination
ALW	A Little World
AML	anti-money laundering
AP	Andhra Pradesh
APR	annualised percentage rate
APSWAN	AP State Wide Area Network
ASS	Annapurna Sewa Sansthan
ATM	automatic teller machine
B2B	business-to-business
B2C	business-to-citizen
BPL	below poverty line
C2C	citizen-to-citizen
CAM	computer-aided manufacturing
CASA	current and savings account
CB	commercial bank
CGAP	Consultative Group to Assist the Poor
CIC	credit information company
CMIS	Chief Minister's Information System
CRI	critical rating index
CRM	customer relationship management
DA	development alternatives
DCCB	district central cooperative bank
DRDA	District Rural Development Agency
DWCRA	Development of Women and Children in Rural Areas
ERP	Enterprise Resource Planning
FICCI	Federation of Indian Chambers of Commerce and Industry
FINO	Financial Inclusion Network and Operations
FSI	financial services industry

G2B	government-to-business
G2C	government-to-citizen
GL	general ledger
GMSS	Gramin Mahila Swayamsiddha Sangh
GoP	Government of Pondicherry
GRC	governance risk and compliance
GSM	Global System for Mobile Communications
GSMA	Global System for Mobile Communications Association
HR	human resource
HRDO	Human Resource Development Organisation
ICEG	International Conference on E-Governance
ICT	information and communication technology
ID	identification
IGA	income-generating activity
IRDA	Insurance Regulatory and Development Authority
IVR	interactive voice response
JLG	joint liability group
JMVP	Janani Mahila Vikash Parisada
KB	Khushhali Bank
Ksh	Kenyan shilling
KYC	know your customer
LPA	loan portfolio audit
MFB	microfinance bank
MFI	microfinance institution
MFIN	Microfinance Institutions Network
MFP	microfinance provider
MIS	management information system
MITRA	mobile information technology for rural advancement
MMBF	Maneswar Matrushakti Block Level Federation
MMU	Mobile Bank for the Unbanked
M-PESA	M is for mobile; 'Pesa' is Swahili for cash
MSM	Mahil Sangharsh Manch
MUDRA	Micro Units Development and Refinance Agency
MYRADA	Mysore Resettlement and Development Agency
MZMS	Mahbubnagar Zila Mahila Samakya
NABARD	National Bank for Agriculture and Rural Development
NBFC	non-banking financial corporations
NBP	National Bank of Pakistan
NER	north-eastern region
NFC	near field communication

NREGA	National Rural Employment Guarantee Act
NREP	National Rural Employment Programme
NRLM	National Rural Livelihood Mission
OBC	other backward castes
OLTP	online transaction processing
PACS	primary agricultural credit societies
PCC	per capita credit
PCI	per capita income
PKR	Pakistan rupee
POS	Point of Sales
PRADAN	Professional Assistance for Development Action
PSL	priority sector lending
RBI	Reserve Bank of India
RDO	Rural Development Organisation
RLEGP	Rural Landless Employment Guarantee Programme
RoE	return on equity
ROI	return on Investment
RRB	regional rural bank
RSP	rural support programmes
SAPO	South African Post Office
SBI	State Bank of India
SBLP	SHG–Bank Linkage Programme
SBMS	Shakti Block Mahila Sangathan
SBP	State Bank of Pakistan
SGSY	Swarnajayanti Gram Swarozgar Yojana
SHPI	self-help promoting institution
SKDRDP	Shri Kshetra Dharmasthala Rural Development Project
SMART	It is an electronic wallet that allows you to do bills payment, reload of airtime and money transfers using a SMART mobile phone (Philippines)
SME	small- and medium-scale enterprises
SMS	short message service
SNAKS	Samsthan Narayanpur Kalanjia Sangamitra
SNEHA	Social Need Education and Human Awareness
SPSKK	Savitribai Phule Sawadhan Kendra Karanja
SRC	Swiss Red Cross
SS	Saheli Samiti
SSP	social security pension
ST/SC	scheduled tribe/scheduled caste

SWIFT	Society for Worldwide Interbank Financial Telecommunication
TCO	total cost of ownership
TMX	True Money Express
TRAI	Telecom Regulatory Authority of India
TRC	training resource centre
UID	unique identification number
UML	Uganda Microfinance Limited
UN	United Nations
UP	Uttar Pradesh
UPSLRP	UP Sodic Land Reclamation Project
USAID	United States Agency for International Development
USSD	unstructured supplementary service data
VCS	Village Coordination Sangam
VRC	Village Resource Centre
WU	Western Union
ZMF	Zero Mass Foundation

Contributors

B. Anjaneyulu is a graduate in general and advance management. With a career of nearly two decades within the development sector, he has previously worked at mid- and senior-management levels in different organisations involved in livelihood promotion and microfinance and has been engaged in training, technical support and consultancy services.

Veena Yamini Annadanam is Senior Analyst and Leader of Micro-Save's Social Performance Management (SPM) Practice Group. She is a development practitioner with experience of working with microfinance institutions (MFIs) and banks in India, Kenya, Colombia, Indonesia and Cambodia.

G. Trivikrama Devi is a commerce graduate and has a master's degree in social work. As a senior Quality Assessment Officer she has worked with self-help groups (SHGs) and their federations at the field level and later in assessment (ratings) and their federations. She was also involved in the development of the self-assessment tool for SHG federations. She was part of a variety of studies such as 'SHG Federations in India – A Status Report', CGAP study 'Cost of Promoting SHGs: Value for Money?' and 'Lights and Shades of SHGs' for USAID and GTZ.

Shubham Goswami is Assistant Professor at the School of Management, Sir Padampat Singhania University, Udaipur, India. His research interests include technology adoption, information systems, ICT for development, enterprise systems and electronic marketing.

Melody Kshetrimayum is Senior Research Fellow at the Tata Institute of Social Sciences, Mumbai, India. She is currently working on informal credit institutions and empowerment of women. Her areas of interests are informal credit institutions, informal women groups and microfinance.

Naveen Kumar K is member of faculty at the National Institute of Bank Management (NIBM), Pune, India. He received the National Doctoral Fellowship from the Indian Council for Social Science Research (ICSSR), New Delhi, and from the Institute for Social and Economic Change, Bangalore, to pursue his PhD in economics. He has been involved in teaching, training, research and consultancies in the area of rural and development banking.

Sunil Kumar is Fellow, Indian Institute of Management, Lucknow, and member of faculty at the Bankers' Institute of Rural Development, Lucknow, India. His areas of interest include risk management, investment and treasury management, commodity derivatives and microfinance.

Jayadev M. is Professor at the Indian Institute of Management Bangalore, Karnataka, India. Previously, he has been affiliated to the Indian Institute of Management Lucknow and a leading public sector bank and he was with the faculty of Investment Banking at the academic staff college of a public sector bank. With interests in finance and banking, financial markets and risk management, he has recent research studies in credit risk, mergers and acquisitions in banks and credit delivery system. He has been associated with a research project on microfinance in South Asia in collaboration with Birmingham University, United Kingdom, and has published papers in several professional journals.

D. H. Malini is Assistant Professor in the Department of Management Studies, School of Management Karaikal Campus, Karaikal, Pondicherry, India. She holds a doctorate in management from Sri Krishnadevaraya University, Anantapur, Andhra Pradesh, India. Her current research interests include marketing management and financial services.

Swetha Muralidharan is pursuing a course in Company Secretaryship Professional Programme from the Institute of Company Secretaries of India (ICSI) and has completed her undergraduate degree in commerce specialising in corporate secretaryship. She specialised in insurance and risk management studies as a part of her MBA programme at Pondicherry University, India.

Umar Rafi is Consulting Practice Director at Oracle Financial Services. His areas of expertise include Islamic finance, risk management and enterprise IT architecture. He has worked in the financial services sector in South Asia, the Middle East and Canada as well as in the IT sector in Silicon Valley, United States. He is currently completing his coursework for a PhD in Islamic finance from the International Centre for Education in Islamic Finance (INCEIF), Malaysia.

Lavneet Singh is Researcher at University of Canberra, Australia. He also works as Research Fellow at CSIRO, Royal Brisbane Hospital, Brisbane, Australia, working on a bowel cancer research project.

Jaspal Singh is Junior Research Officer at Cost of Cultivation Scheme, Ministry of Agriculture, R.B.S. College, Agra, India. He did his PhD in agricultural economics and is involved in multidisciplinary projects in collaboration with external research partners.

Manoj K. Sharma is Managing Director at MicroSave and a development finance and SME specialist with experience in Bangladesh, India, Indonesia, Nepal, Kenya, the Philippines, Sri Lanka and Papua New Guinea. His areas of interest include assistance to start-up microfinance institutions, product development, market research and urban microfinance.

Rajeev Sharma is Director, Faculty of Management & Computer Application, R.B.S. College, Agra, India. He is also Fellow Member of the Institute of Chartered Accountants of India.

Diatha Krishna Sundar is Professor of Operations Management, Chairperson of Production & Operations Management Area, and Chairperson, ERP Center at the Indian Institute of Management Bangalore, Karnataka, India. Prior to this, he served as a faculty member at the Indian Institute of Technology Kharagpur. With eighteen years of research and teaching experience, he is consultant to many national and international manufacturing and service (IT) organisations as well as government departments in the areas of operations strategy, supply chain management, IT strategy, e-governance and ERP implementation. His interests include e-business management, enterprise resource planning, supply chain management and manufacturing strategy. He has published more than seventy research articles in international journals, international conference proceedings and book chapters.

Suraj Theruvath works at Tata AIG General Insurance Company Limited. He specialised in insurance and risk management studies as part of his MBA programme at Pondicherry University, India.

Raghuram G. Rajan is the current Governor of the Reserve Bank of India. He has been the Chief Economic Adviser to India's Ministry of Finance and Chief Economist at the International Monetary Fund. He received his PhD from MIT Sloan School of Management, United States. His research interests are in banking, corporate finance and economic development, especially the role of finance. He co-authored *Saving Capitalism from the Capitalists* with Luigi Zingales (2003) and *Fault Lines: How Hidden Fractures Still Threaten the World Economy* (2010), for which he was awarded the Financial Times-Goldman Sachs prize for the best business book that year.

Anand Sinha served as Deputy Governor of the Reserve Bank of India (RBI). He was RBI's alternate representative in the Basel Committee on Banking Supervision (BCBS), Bank for International Settlements, Basel. He also represented RBI on the Committee on Global Financial Systems (CGFS), BIS and represented India at the G20 Working Group on 'Enhancing Sound Regulation and Strengthening Transparency' set up in the aftermath of the Global Financial Crisis.

Veerashekharappa is Associate Professor at the Centre for Economic Studies and Policy and Institute for Social and Economic Change, India, and also Visiting Professor at University of Social Science and Humanities, Ho Chi Minh City, Vietnam. His area of interest is largely in the finance sector, including banking, rural credit and microfinance.

Graham A.N. Wright is Founder and Group Managing Director of MicroSave. Prior to establishing MicroSave, he helped develop, test and implement a sustainable rural savings and credit programme for BURO, a large and influential MFI in Bangladesh. He also provided long-term technical assistance to a rural finance system setting up self-help 'Savings and Loan Groups' linked to strong cooperatives in a remote mountainous area of the Philippines.

Introduction

Jayadev M. and Diatha Krishna Sundar

The first microcredit summit was held in Washington in 1997. Since then, the microfinance industry had grown exponentially, and the United Nations declared 2005 as the year of microcredit. The donors, academics and non-governmental organisations as well as the politicians were happy with the outcomes of this institutional access of credit to the poor and the needy. Many organisations, in whatever form, joined this movement with a social motive of credit accesses, poverty removal and women empowerment. Several new agents and investors considered this as potential opportunity to make huge profits.

To increase the outreach, sustain the microfinance movement, and to bring cost effectiveness, technology applications have become necessary. Automation helps in providing multiple products through single delivery system, and also for capturing transactions. Information and communication technology (ICT) applications build ecosystems that increase outreach of microcredit services, minimise service and delivery costs and build up effective control systems. Several experiments on ICTs have taken place in different parts of the world. In this context, the seventh International Conference on E-Government (ICEG-2010) has extensively focused on ICT applications in microfinance, public health and e-governance. The conference was held during 21–24 April 2010 at the Indian Institute of Management Bangalore. Overwhelming response was received from academics, medical doctors, microfinance institutions, National Bank for Agriculture and Rural Development (NABARD), technology companies, students and voluntary organisations. Apart from papers presented in the technical sessions, there were invited talks from the industry experts, policy makers and others.

This book is primarily an outcome of selected papers presented in the conference on microfinance theme. Chapter 1 presents the brief review of recent microfinance developments in Indian industry and analyses current issues and challenges to be addressed. Graham and others discuss how important it was for the Indian microfinance institutions (MFIs) to heed to the early signs of problems. The three cases discussed show the importance of understanding the local sensitivities, appropriate training of field officers and avoiding methods of collection that could be seen as coercive. Thus, the regulation seeks to address these specific aspects of lending when the MFIs were unable to follow the self-regulation principles. In India, the MFI sector is benefitted in view of the priority sector targets of the commercial banks.

Chapter 3 is the speech delivered by Anand Sinha, former Deputy Governor of Reserve Bank of India. This chapter emphasises need for strengthening of governance in microfinance institutions with a proper regulatory framework and also through industry level self-regulation mechanism. Improving the governance is essential to achieve the goal of inclusive finance.

Shubham Goswami's chapter examines the impact of mobile technology on microfinance with respect to poverty alleviation and socio-economic empowerment in rural areas. The chapter suggests future directions and measures to reach low-income customers in developing countries through mobile technology.

Umar Rafi provides status of microfinance banking in Pakistan and application of ICT solutions. He also presents ideas for future applications of ICT.

Another study of SHGs pertains to Etah village in Uttar Pradesh by Singh, Singh and Sharma. They show that income and employment have been generated through the SHGs, which were involved in agricultural, allied, glass beads, bulbs, carpet and tailoring activities.

The critical role of mobile enabled SHG microfinance management system and software like computer munshi by NGO PRADAN are the steps forward in role of the information and computer technology to expand the services. The key weakness of SHGs is the maintenance of book of accounts. However if external help is taken then the incentive within the group to learn the same goes down. Thus wherever literate members are available effort should be encourage the SHG members to maintain basic books which can then be transcribed by the computer munshi. The idea is to create efficacy and increase self-determination.

A study on impact of federations on the functioning of SHGs conducted by Andhra Pradesh Mahila Samatha Society (APMAS) in 2007 by Sunil Kumar, informs that there are 69,000 SHG federations in the country with 22 at the apex level, 2571 secondary federations and 66,310 primary federations. The primary reason for federation of SHGs is to harness the potential of the larger group and thus be able to advocate issues and garner more funds Veerashekharappa studies the impact of SBLP in credit delivery in the state of Karnataka in India. Bank linkage is provided by commercial banks, regional rural banks or cooperative banks.

Theruvath and Muralidharan discuss a case study of NGO Social Need Education and Human Awareness (SNEHA) and the role of the SHGs, promoted by it and other international agencies in the reconstruction of tsunami-hit Karaikal in Pondicherry, India. With the financial help of international financing agencies, SNEHA an NGO created SHGs called Sangams. These 110 Sangams with 1,800 members in 10 villages were further organised into Village Coordination Sangams and District Fisherwomen Federation, through representative participation. At the district level, the facilitation for the fishing activity was provided through construction of dry fish platforms, purchase of auto carrier for fish vending, cooking vessels for renting. Thus a federation of sangams helps in increasing the level of the activity as well as builds the principle of democratic representation at the grass-roots level.

Melody Kshetrimayum's study aims at finding out the contribution of microfinance in poverty alleviation. It examines the changes brought about by microfinance activities from the experiences of the NGO functionaries and the women members.

Naveen K. Shetty's chapter presents empirical evidence saying that microfinance intervention has contributed in widening the access to credit, savings, micro-health insurance, self-employment and micro-enterprise development, and training and awareness in the member group as compared to the control group households. On the economic front, microfinance-plus services, in general, enabled the households to improve their income, assets, expenditure, employment and housing conditions. Further, the microfinance-plus services have also enabled the households to improve their housing conditions, which was particularly true for member group households in the study area. Furthermore, the empirical result reveals that microfinance-plus services have supported small-scale self-employment or micro-enterprise development among the member households. It is important to note that the innovation in microfinance has played a crucial role in inculcating savings and thrift habits among their members, particularly poor women. The study finds that participation in the microfinance programme also resulted in various skill enhancement trainings and awareness programmes, networking with various institutions and empowerment of poor women. Thus, the study concludes that the microfinance-plus services not only uplifted the poor from 'income poverty' but also from 'knowledge poverty'.

The final chapter sets the road map for financial inclusion a speech delivered by Dr Raghuram Rajan, Governor of Reserve Bank of India. This chapter emphasises on role of technology in meeting the financial inclusion goal. It also underscores the importance of institutions and policy changes required in this direction. Finally, the chapter emphasises on the need for financial literacy for achieving the millennium goal of financial inclusion.

The other papers and invited presentations made in the conference are as follows:

Mr Anal Jain, advisor Sa-dhan (The Association of Community Development Finance Institutions), emphasises that the current issues of the microfinance sector are multiple lending and over-indebtedness, strengthening of internal systems and processes and minimisation of operating costs. Jain expresses that the technology solutions are needed for addressing of these issues. To address the problem of multiple lending and over-indebtedness, a credit bureau is required. Although technological solutions are currently applied in microfinance sector, the challenges for extensive usage are poor literacy rates among rural population and doubts about robustness of biometric solutions. Jain envisaged on UID and 3G connectivity as the two potential opportunities before microfinance sector for spreading the technological solutions.

Mr D. Krishnan, Principal Consultant and Advisor, National e-Governance Division, discussed in detail about mobile banking applications in India and policy initiatives taken by the government of India. He also emphasised on the role of various stakeholders in extensive usage of mobile banking. The main stakeholders are UIDIA, NPCI, TRAI and mobile service providers. Mr M. V. Patro, General Manager of NABARD, has discussed the significant contribution of NABARD for microfinance sector and reviewed the initiatives taken by the NABARD for extensive usage of ICT solutions.

Ms Totsie Mamela Khambula, Managing Director of South African Post Bank (SAPO), has reviewed various initiatives taken by South African post office to address the issue of financial inclusion. The biometric solutions and payment systems introduced by SAPO and challenges for these systems and emerging opportunities in South African market were emphasised in the presentation. Mr John Wentzel, Chief Operating Officer of South African Post Bank, has emphasised on potential opportunities for post offices in addressing the issue of financial inclusion and discussed in detail how post offices can leverage their network for providing multiple financial services and low cost banking to underprivileged.

Vijay Pratap Singh Aditya and others have documented a case study on mobile-based framework (MITRA) for provision of microfinance services in Dungarpur District of Rajasthan. This field-based technology application is for monitoring, transacting and real-time interaction system for addressing service gap for SHGs modeled grass-roots financial institutions. This technological solution aims at strengthening the financial service delivery allowing 'financial independence' of the SHG federations would go a long way in developing self-sustaining decentralised financing institutions.

Aruna Kumari Devarakonda's paper suggested antiphishing strategy based on voice and image. This paper presented a two-factor authentication solution, which aims to protect users against e-mail phishing attacks. Main key words used are a user ID and password which is given by the user with his unique voice identity and an image sent by the bank. An e-mail that a bank sends to user contains a pre-selected image which the phisher couldn't have, that the user chose when setting up the account. This proves to the user that the e-mail came from the bank or business, not a phisher, and that it is safe to use the provided link. The user is asked to provide his or her user ID, password and unique voice ID. This voice ID is already trained to the system of the bank. This is verified with the voice ID given during the login time. When the received password along with unique voice ID is accepted, user is allowed to access the website.

Hanumanthappa and others' paper discusses applications of data mining in e-governance. This paper, a case study of agricultural bank loans, sets out to make a comparative evaluation of classifiers in the context of banking to maximise true positive rate and minimise false positive rate of defaulters. Suresh and others discuss credit risk management in private sector banks and its relevance to microfinance sector in India.. Pavan Rama kumar and others reviews delivery model schemes pertaining to micro-insurance, and discusses issues for massification of micro-insurance industry in India. Monalisa Das's paper highlights the contribution of micro-finance organisations for social growth and bringing economically backward into the mainstream of economy. This paper makes colloquia of emphasising activities of microfinance and institutional support they are getting in the upliftment of upper poor, very poor and ultra poor. The whole write-up also tries to cover the gap in knowledge by using secondary research to critically examine how information technology is used in normal finance functions and trying to project how such uses can be applied to microfinance footprints towards establishing self-reliant poor resisting poverty. Dinuja Perera documents the evidence on women participation in microfinance and delinquency of microfinance institutions in Sri Lanka. The researcher intended to identify the women participation in microfinance in Sri Lanka and assess how far their involvement has mitigated the risk of microfinance institutions becoming delinquent. In this study, it is concluded that microfinance institutions are mitigating the risk of delinquency by maintaining their portfolio quality with women-driven microfinance. Roberto Moro Visconti says that microfinance institutions (MFIs) in developing countries are less affected by the worldwide turmoil, due to their segmentation and resilience to external shocks. If contagion is milder, the biggest risk is probably that of becoming out of scope, being unable to collect the much needed foreign capital at competitive costs. Recession has a big impact on corporate governance mechanisms, altering the equilibriums among different stakeholders and increasing the risk of investment returns. This paper highlights the importance of governance in microfinance.

Lakshman Gugulothu discussed that microfinance bill has flaws and the issues to strengthen MFI regulations. Seema Sahai's paper also discussed innovations in microfinance sector with OTF model and recommended that market forces need to be duly regulated to ensure that microfinance does not cost poor heavily.

The technical session ended with a presentation made by Atyati technologies, a software solution provider to microfinance sector.

We take this opportunity to thank all the experts and industry professionals for accepting our invitation and making presentations on innovative ideas for future. We also thank the paper/chapter-contributing authors for their timely support in making the conference a successful event and making this edited volume an accomplished one. We thank Dr Raghuram Rajan, Governor, RBI, and Sri Anand Sinha, former Deputy Governor, RBI, for permitting us to include their speeches as part of the edited volume.

Chapter 1

Microfinance in India

The way forward

Jayadev M.

Microfinance is providing financial services to low-income individuals who lack access to the conventional banking sector. The early-stage microfinance institutions (MFIs) were non-profit organisations, with a social mission to alleviate poverty, by helping the poor to develop vocational and business management skills and by giving them small, uncollateralised loans, usually a working capital. From this modest, of course revolutionary, beginning in South Asia and many Latin American countries in 1970s, microfinance now encompasses a number of organisations and regulated entities across the globe, which offer a burgeoning array of credit, savings, housing finance, remittance and insurance products to serve the people at the bottom of the pyramid. Microfinance has gained significance as a movement for women empowerment, and for transforming the poor to work their way out of poverty. Microfinance clients are predominantly engaged in income-generating activities in the informal economy in emerging countries, as a means to self-reliance in the face of high, systemic unemployment.

Despite the vast expansion of banking system in the country, the last-mile connectivity has always been a distant dream for formal banking system. There are two important factors[1] for banks not lending to poor. First is adverse selection; banks cannot easily determine which customers are likely to be more risky. The second is a moral hazard; banks are unable to ensure that customers make full effort required for their investment projects to be successful. Moral hazard also arises when customers try to abscond with the bank's money. These problems are much more serious in enforcing contracts in regions with weak legal systems. Microfinance has the potential to fill the critical gap left by formal financial institutions in providing financial services to low-income groups. It is argued that microfinance can facilitate the achievement of the Millennium Development Goals, as well as national policies, that target poverty reduction and women empowerment, supporting vulnerable groups and improving standards of living. While launching the International Year of Microcredit in 2005, the UN secretary general Kofi Annan stated that, 'Sustainable access to microfinance helps alleviate poverty by generating income, creating jobs, allowing children to go to school, enabling families to obtain health care, and empowering people to make the choices that best serve their needs'.[2]

The objective of this chapter is to provide a brief review of recent developments in the Indian microfinance industry, and to discuss the current issues and challenges. The first section gives the status of microfinance activity in India; recent developments are discussed in the second section and the final part of this chapter reviews current issues and challenges to take microfinance activity way forward.

Microfinance in India: retrospect

In the Indian context, microfinance movement gained momentum in 1992, with the introduction of SHG (Self-Help Group)–Bank Linkage Programme by National Bank for Agriculture and Rural Development (NABARD). Subsequently, several non-governmental organisations, societies and non-banking financial companies (NBFCs) have entered the microfinance sector. Currently, three popular models of microfinance[3] are being operated in India. These are SHG–bank linkage model, NBFC–MFI model and trusts and societies.

The SHG–Bank Linkage Model: The SHG–Bank Linkage Model was pioneered by NABARD in 1992. Under this model, women in a village were encouraged to form SHGs. An SHG is a group of about fifteen to twenty people from a homogenous class, who join together to address common issues, where members regularly contribute small savings to the group. These savings, which form an ever-growing nucleus, are lent by the group to members, and are later supplemented by loans provided by banks, for income-generating activities and other purposes for sustainable livelihood promotion. Banks provide loans to SHGs in certain multiples of the accumulated savings of the SHGs. Loans are given without any collateral and at interest rates as decided by banks. Banks find it comfortable to lend money to the groups as the members have already achieved some financial discipline through their thrift and internal lending activities. The peer pressure in the group ensures timely repayment and becomes social collateral for the bank loans. This model accounts for about 58 per cent of outstanding loan portfolio of microfinance sector.[4]

MFI–NBFC model: This model accounts for about 34 per cent of the outstanding loan portfolio.[5] Under this model, NBFCs encourage villagers to form joint liability groups (JLGs) and give loans to the individual members of the JLG. The individual loans are jointly and severally guaranteed by other members of the group. Many of the NBFCs operating this model started off as non-profit entities providing microcredit and other services to the poor. However, as they found themselves unable to raise adequate resources for the rapid growth of the activity, they converted themselves into for-profit NBFCs. Others entered the field directly as for-profit NBFCs, seeing this as a viable business proposition. Significant amounts of private equity funds have consequently been attracted to this sector. The third model is trusts and societies, accounting for the balance 8 per cent of the outstanding loan portfolio.

Irrespective of the type of model adopted, microfinance activities have shown significant growth on all parameters, such as terms of loan portfolio, client outreach and average loan size. On an average, the yield to MFIs on the loan portfolio is around 30 to 32 per cent and most of the MFIs have recorded a higher recovery rate of 95 to 98 per cent. The total client outreach of microfinance activity, both SHGs and MFIs, has grown from 48 million in 2006–07 to 93.90 million by the end of 2011, with a compounded annual growth rate of 8.8 per cent. The NBFC–MFI channel was seen to be fast catching up with Self-Help Group– Bank Linkage Programme (SBLP), with the latter growing at only about 8 per cent, compared to the MFI channel, which grew at 18 per cent.[6]

The following are well-stated facts of microfinance sector by several studies and reports[7]:

1   It addresses the concerns of poverty alleviation by enabling the poor to work their way out of poverty.
2   It provides credit to that section of society that is unable to obtain credit at reasonable rates from traditional sources.
3   Microfinance customers are mainly women; thus it enables economic empowerment of women when routing credit directly to them, thereby enhancing their status within their families, the community and society at large.

4   Easy access to credit is more important for the poor than cheaper credit which might involve lengthy bureaucratic procedures and delays.
5   Microfinance loans are uncollateralised as the poor are often not in a position to offer collateral to secure the credit.
6   The tenure of the loans is short, normally not more than twenty-four months. The frequency of repayments is greater than for traditional commercial loans.
7   Microfinance sector offers small size of individual loans; thus transaction and operating costs are very high.
8   The loans are mainly utilised for income generation, repayment of old debt and meeting domestic obligations like marriage, health and education.

Studies[8] have shown that microfinance plays three critical roles in development. First, it enables the very poor households to meet their most basic needs and protect/hedge against risks. Second, concomitantly, it is associated with improvements in households' economic welfare. Third, by supporting women's economic participation, it helps to empower women and promote gender equity.

Recent developments

Although microfinance industry has made significant growth in the last decade, there has been a sudden decline in the prospects of the sector, especially post-September 2010. With large-scale entry of NBFCs in the microfinance sector, and active funding from private equity, investors viewed this sector as very lucrative providing high short-term profits and substantial capital gain through equity sale. These motivations led to explosive field force. MFIs are very strict, and often barbaric, in collection of debts. This has led to huge number of suicides by farmers, especially in the state of Andhra Pradesh. Perhaps, the lack of stringent regulatory framework may be the reason for failure of governance. The state government has been sensitive to this social turmoil and has reacted quickly, and sharply, by putting in place helplines and village-level vigilance committees to oversee the microfinance activity. To address these issues with proper statutory framework, the state government came up with the Andhra Pradesh Micro Finance Institutions (Regulation of Money Lending) Ordinance 2010. The ordinance enforces registration of MFIs, and imposes restrictions on further lending if loan outstandings are significant. It also emphasises on display of interest rates and monthly repayments against the practice of weekly repayments. Overall, the operational freedom of the MFIs is restricted.

The Andhra Pradesh episode highlights serious deficiencies in the microfinance activities. The important among them are serious compromise on customer needs and capabilities and excessive focus on growth without building up internal controls and systems; irrational exuberance by investors made top management to focus on achieving higher valuation of equity and higher rates of return than the social objective of lending to the poor. Excessive reliance on single products and herd mentality are detrimental for the industry's survival. According to Reddy,[9] the trust the Reserve Bank of India (RBI) placed in the commitment of MFIs was misplaced. Given the track record, the RBI should have insisted on enforceable regulation and not been content with an advisory role.

Subsequently, RBI also realised that there is need to provide regulatory strength to microfinance activity, which was otherwise considered as social and for-profit motive. RBI constituted a committee under the chairmanship of Y H Malegam to study issues and concerns in the microfinance sector. The committee made detailed analysis of the sector and the current concerns and made recommendations to evolve a proper regulatory framework. Significant among are listed here[10]:

1 Creation of a separate category of NBFCs operating in the microfinance sector, to be designated as NBFC-MFIs
2 Imposition of a margin cap and interest rate cap on individual loans
3 Requirement of transparency in interest charges
4 Lending by not more than two MFIs to individual borrowers
5 Creation of one or more credit information bureaus
6 Establishment of a proper system of grievance redressal procedure by MFIs
7 Creation of one or more 'Social Capital Funds'
8 Continuation of categorisation of bank loans to MFIs, complying with the regulation laid down for NBFC–MFIs, under the priority sector.

Based on the recommendations of the Malegam Committee, the RBI has issued detailed guidelines, permitting bank lending to eligible microfinance companies as priority sector advance, which is statutory requirement for banks. Such eligibility is linked to core features of microfinance, such as lending of small amounts to borrowers belonging to low-income groups, without collaterals, with flexible repayment schedules and with particular emphasis on measures to curb over-indebtedness. Margin caps and interest rate caps have also been stipulated to ensure protection of borrowers. Subsequently, the RBI created a separate category of NBFCs dealing in microfinance – NBFC–MFI, and issued comprehensive guidelines covering, inter alia, fair practices in lending such as transparency in interest rates, non-coercive methods of recovery, measures to contain multiple lending and over-indebtedness.[11]

The Government of India has come out with the Microfinance Institutions (Development and Regulation) Bill 2011. The objective of the bill is to provide access to financial services for the rural and urban poor and certain disadvantaged sections of the people, by promoting growth and development of MFIs as extended arms of the banks and financial institutions, and to regulate MFIs. MFIs and other entities, engaged in providing microfinance services, both existing and new ones, except banks and cooperative societies, will be brought under the regulatory purview of the RBI. The bill provides for a new category of MFIs, namely, 'Systemically important microfinance institution', deploying a particular amount of funds for providing microcredit to a minimum number of clients as may be specified by the RBI. The bill provides for setting up of Microfinance Development Council, to advise the central government on formulation of policies, schemes and other measures required in the interest of orderly growth and development of the microfinance sector and MFIs, to promote financial inclusion. The bill also provides for setting of state advisory councils for microfinance at the state level. The bill bestows wide-ranging powers to the RBI for registration, direction, regulating, inspection, fixing caps on margins and interest rates, setting repayment schedules, maintaining books of accounts, fixing rating norms, capacity building, building information system and so on of MFIs. The bill envisages setting up of the Micro Finance Development Fund with RBI, for receiving grants, receiving donations and granting loans and other financial support for various purposes. To address the grievances between clients of MFIs and MFIs, with powers to issue directions to MFIs, the bill provides for appointment of microfinance ombudsmen.

The Government of India is committed to revival and the development of microfinance sector. The union finance minister, in his 2011 budget speech, expressed that 'The Micro Finance Institutions have emerged as an important means of financial inclusion. Creation of dedicated fund for providing equity to small MFIs would help them maintain growth and achieve scale and efficiency in operations'. The government accordingly created, 'India Micro Finance Equity Fund' of Rs 100 crore with Small Industries Development Bank of India and Women's SHG Development Fund, with a corpus of Rs 500 crore, to empower women and promote their SHGs.[12] In May 2012, the union cabinet cleared the microfinance bill, empowering RBI to regulate the MFIs.

The way forward

Undoubtedly, the microfinance sector has made significant contribution in poverty reduction and improving the livelihood of rural people. This needs to be strengthened. Some key issues that can take MFI activity forward are discussed in this section:

Pricing of credit: At present, microfinance facilitates easy access of debt. Often, the effective interest rate is not less than 24 per cent, which is at least 9 percentage points higher than the interest rate charged by mainstream banking institutions. For long-run sustainability of microfinance, MFIs have to make efforts to reduce interest rate on loans, either by accessing low-cost social capital or by reducing operating expenses. MFIs employ large number of field-level persons for credit delivery, monitoring and recovery, which are highly labour-intensive activities. Unless the portfolio volumes are substantially large, reduction in operating expenses is a challenging issue. Recently, RBI has done away with the 26 per cent cap on lending rates due to the dynamic nature of the cost of funds for microfinance companies; however, it has imposed cap on margins.[13]

Strengthening of the SHG model: The SHG model is a group-based lending activity that promotes the culture of savings. The theoretical expositions[14] of group-based micro-lending emphasises on social collateral; this can help institutions to effectively circumvent the problems of adverse selection and moral hazard, which are the two main characteristics of imperfect credit markets and may reduce the costs. SHG model is also far away from the profiteering approach of NBFC-type MFIs; hence the problems of governance, board enthusiasm and higher rates of return are conveniently avoided, and a healthy culture of group savings will be promoted.

Credit bureau: Microfinance sector requires a credit bureau that produces transparent, reliable and valid information reports which are useful to know borrower credit history and to minimise multiple borrowing and delinquencies. Active participation of all stakeholders and international agencies, like Consultative Group to Assist the Poor (CGAP), are needed to build a database which has integrity and quality. Recently Microfinance Institutions Network announced the launch of its credit bureau.[15]

Social versus financial objectives: The initial years of micro-lending activity was driven by virtues of poverty alleviation and social capital formation, group participation and group members' accountability. In the later years, there was a transformation into a commercial model with shareholder maximisation, and the corporate lifestyles of managers made it a pure for-profit commercial organisation. Undoubtedly, self-sufficiency and financial sustainability are essential for survival of microfinance activity. Of late, there has been a mission drift, with MFIs deviating from original social mission in pursuit of conflicting unstated mission of racing for huge profits. This has shown the need for educating the front-line staff about organisational culture values, social mission and the purpose of existence. They should not be get swayed by the performance targets, which are more short-term oriented.

Technology: Globally, payment delivery systems based on smart cards, mobile phones and other technology applications are increasing the outreach of financial services. Technology provides microfinance organisations in India the opportunity to innovate at a much faster pace and to create products that are closely linked to the needs of the consumer. There is a need to create an enabling ecosystem which will encourage and foster innovation by leveraging the best available technological platforms. Still, a wide gap exists in the application of technology for credit delivery, monitoring and recovery of loans.

One of the successful applications of technology in India is the Financial Inclusion Network and Operations (FINO).[16] FINO is a provider of electronic technology services, and operates through a network of around 10,000 bandhus (bandhu means a friend in Hindi, who serves as human automatic teller machines in areas that often have no electronic teller machines). Each bandhu is equipped with a small hand-held biometric device that he or she takes into the field and uses to transact with clients, who access banking services through smart cards. Other functions like balance transfers, deposits and withdrawals can all be done through the smart card system. Although FINO may not be panacea to all problems of microfinance, it can promote low-cost delivery system. Such applications are needed for cost-effective technology to support multichannel delivery system with speed and integrity. Standardised systems, structures and processes are needed along with comprehensive management information system, capable of meeting all management information requirements, which is reliable and fast. MFIs need to ensure that financial innovation should be focused and result in faster, safer and cheaper access to financial services, particularly for the large sections of population that are still excluded from the formal financial system.

Control systems and risk management: Like other financial institutions, MFIs also encounter all generic risks such as credit risk, liquidity risk and operational risks. As the MFIs do not have any market investments, the market risk is ruled out. But other risks are embedded in the portfolio of activities. MFIs have to identify the sources of risks, to recognise and quantify the impact of such risks on profitability of the organisation. MFIs have to develop relevant control system and their boards have to review and monitor their operations on a periodic basis. CGAP framework, in this direction, is worth considering.

Responsible finance: Studies show that multiple borrowing is growing among members, which, in turn, is leading to over-indebtedness and eventually to delinquencies. Chasing customers and sometimes poaching from other segments of microfinance and loading with more debt are frequently observed practices of MFIs.[17] MFIs need to be more mindful of borrower needs and capabilities. In this context, responsible finance is the most relevant aspect. They require selection of borrowers with diligence and to be more human and ethical in their recovery methods.

Governance: The crisis in microfinance sector also highlights the serious deficiencies in the governance framework of some MFIs. The main reason for fallout of microfinance was that MFIs indulged in other undesirable practices such as commercial lending and generous compensation and incentive structure for senior management and directors. The listing of MFIs' shares on stock exchanges, and sudden spurt valuations, created an impression that MFIs are for making huge profits at the cost of farmers' suicides.

Especially in the case of 'for-profit' MFIs, the corporate governance issues were exacerbated. Governance system represents not only a legal but also an ethical and moral framework. It is maximising shareholders' wealth legally, and ethically, on a sustainable basis, without being unfair to other stakeholders. Governance is based on the basic tenets of transparency and accountability. Transparency in decision making provides comfort to all stakeholders, and account-ability, which follows from transparency, fixes responsibilities for actions taken or not taken. Together, they safeguard the interests of the stakeholders in the organisation.[18] The board has a challenging task of balancing the interests of various stakeholders; equity hold-ers, donors, borrowers and society. Strong governance could play an important role in balancing seemingly exclusive, but potentially complementary, objectives from a long-term perspective.

The gap in the regulation is being addressed by Microfinance Institutions (Development and Regulation) Bill 2011. Further, there is also a need for self-regulation to build robust and efficient MFIs. The microfinance industry should come forward with a code of con-duct framework and adhere to it. Strengthening of self-regulatory mechanisms also paves way for better governance.

Beyond microfinance

Microfinance alone is not the panacea for problems of poverty and rural empowerment. The poor require considerable support in terms of input supply, training, technical support, market linkages and so on. Institutional development and capacity-building services are essential, in addition to providing credit. MFIs should also expand their services in the fields like micro-insurance, and integrated financial solutions are needed to meet the financial requirements of poor. Several initiatives have been taken by the government, which is closely associated with microfinance and related activities.

National Rural Livelihood Mission (NRLM)[19]: The Ministry of Rural Development has decided to re-design and re-structure the ongoing Swarnajayanti Gram Swarozgar Yojana into National Livelihood Mission. The idea has been conceived as a cornerstone of national poverty reduction strategy. The objective of the mission is to reduce poverty among the rural people who live below poverty line (BPL), by promoting diversified and gainful self-employment and wage employment opportunities, which would lead to an appreciable increase in income on sustainable basis. In the long run, it will ensure broad-based inclusive growth and reduce disparities by spreading out the benefits from the islands of growth across the regions, sectors and communities. The mission has been designed to achieve the specific 'Outputs' and 'Outcomes' by 2016–17. These are mainly formation of new SHGs involving BPL families, revolving fund support for SHGs and providing skill development training. NRLM is putting collaborative efforts with district-level authorities and panchayat raj institutions. The training and capacity building, deployment of multidisciplinary experts and other initiatives will enhance the creditworthiness of the rural poor. The periodic interaction of the mission with public sector banks, and other financial institutions, to enhance the reach of rural poor to the un-banked areas, is likely to ensure their financial inclusion.

Financial inclusion: The RBI's approach to financial inclusion is aimed at connecting people with the mainstream financial institutions. RBI had chosen the bank-led model for financial inclusion – leveraging on technology. The goal of financial inclusion is better served through mainstream banking institutions, as only they have the ability to offer the suite of products required to bring in effective/meaningful financial inclusion. Other intermediaries and technology partners, such as mobile companies, have been allowed to partner with banks in offering services collaboratively. RBI's strategy is to create an ecosystem comprising a combination of branch and information and communication technology (ICT)-based business correspondent outlets for evolving an effective financial inclusion delivery model. In November 2009, banks were advised to draw up a road map for providing banking services, through a banking outlet, in every village having a population of over 2,000. The newly formed financial stability development council has been mandated to focus on financial inclusion and financial literacy.

Micro-insurance business: In order to facilitate penetration of insurance among rural people, regulations of the Insurance Regulatory and Development Authority (IRDA) are encouraging a new class of distributors called micro-insurance agents, whereby MFIs, NGOs and SHGs have been allowed to take up distribution of micro-insurance products. Composite products are created, where multiple risks faced by low-income families, such as life, health, accident, dwelling and livestock, are covered under a single policy, through a tie-up between life and general insurers. The number of micro-insurance policies has grown from 9.37 lakhs in 2007–08 to 36.50 lakhs by 2010–11.[20] A sizeable portion of the group micro-insurance has been supported by government-sponsored social security schemes; around 3.6 million individual life policies are mostly self-funded, which indicates that the target segments are willing to purchase insurance if the right kind of supply is made available.

To sum up, financial inclusion and extension of financial services to all is a challenging task for mainstream banking institutions. MFIs have the potential and brighter future ahead in this arena, provided they recognise the fact that sustainability in this sector is relevant with borrowers' lives and livelihoods. MFIs have to be sensitive to borrowers' requirements and to be ethical in their lending practices. Long-term sustainability depends more on following effective governance and adopting best self-regulatory practices.

Notes

1 Beatriz, Armendariz and Jonathan Morduch (2005), *The Economics of Micro Finance*, MIT Press, Cambridge, MA; and London, England, p 14.
2 Microcredit Summit E-News (Jan 2004), Volume 1, Issue 6.
3 Malegaon Committee Report on Microfinance (2011), Reserve Bank of India.
4 Report of the Sub-Committee of Central Board of Directors of Reserve Bank of India to Study Issues and Concerns in the Micro Finance Sector (2011), Reserve Bank of India.
5 Report of the Sub-Committee of Central Board of Directors of Reserve Bank of India to Study Issues and Concerns in the Micro Finance Sector (2011), Reserve Bank of India.
6 Srinivasan, N. (2011), *Micro Finance: State of the Sector Report*, Sage Publications, New Delhi.
7 Srinivasan, N. (2009, 2010 and 2011), *Microfinance India: State of the Sector Report*, Sage Publications, New Delhi.
8 For example, Banerjee, Abhijit, Esther Duflo, Rachel Glennerster and Cynthia Kinnan (2009), *The Miracle of Microfinance: Evidence from Randomized Evaluation*, Working Paper Series No. 31, Institute of Financial Management and Research, Centre for Micro Finance, Chennai.
9 Reddy, Venugopal Y. (2011), Microfinance in India: Some Thoughts, *Economic and Political Weekly* Vol. XLVI, No. 41, pp 46–49.
10 Malegam Committee Recommendations (Jan 2011), Report of the Sub-Committee of the Central Board of Directors of Reserve Bank of India to Study Issues and Concerns in the MFI Sector, Reserve Bank of India.
11 RBI Circulars on Micro Credit (14 Feb 2011), Master Circular on Micro credit', RPCD. FID.BC.No. 53 / 12.01.001/ 2010–11.
12 Union Finance Minister's Budget Speech 2011, available at: http:// indiabudget.nic.in/ub2011–12/bs/bs.pdf

13 Non Banking Financial Company–Micro Finance Institutions
   (NBFC–MFIs) – Directions – Modifications, 3 August 2012, Reserve
   Bank of India.
14 Besley, Timothy and Stephen Coate (1995), Group Lending, Repayment
   Incentives and Social Collateral, *Journal of Development Economics*,
   Elsevier, vol. 46(1), pages 1–18, February.
15 http://www.mfinindia.org/content/mfin-launches-credit-bureau-mfi-clients,
   Accessed on 19 August 2012.
16 www.Fino.co.in
17 Kamath, Rajalaxmi, and R. Srinivasan (2009), *Microfinance, Small,
   Ostensibly Rigid and Safe*, Indian Institute of Management Working
   Paper.
18 Sinha, Anand (23 April 2012) *Strengthening Governance in Microfinance Institutions (MFIs) – Some Random Thoughts*, Keynote address
   by deputy governor, Reserve Bank of India, at FICCI's Workshop on
   'Strengthening Microfinance Institutions (MFIs): Good Governance
   and Strategic People Practices', Mumbai.
19 Available at: http://pib.nic.in/newsite/erelease.aspx?relid=52423.
20 IRDA Annual Report 2010–11.

References

The Millennium Development Goal Report (2005). New York: United
   Nations.
Nair, S. Tara (31 July 2010) Commercial Microfinance and Social Respon-
   sibility: A Critique, *Economic and Political Weekly* Vol. XLV, No. 31,
   pp. 32–7.
Shylendra, H.S. (20 May, 2006) Microfinance Institutions in Andhra
   Pradesh: Crisis and Diagnosis, *Economic and Political Weekly* Vol. XLI,
   No. 20, pp. 1959–63.
Sriram, M.S. (2010) Commercialization of Microfinance in India: A Dis-
   cussion of the Emperor's Apparel, *Economic and Political Weekly* Vol.
   XLV, No. 24, pp. 65–74.

Chapter 2

Rebuilding the microfinance industry post–Andhra Pradesh crisis

Graham A.N. Wright, Manoj K. Sharma, B. Anjaneyulu, Veena Yamini and G. Trivikrama Devi

Three dress rehearsals ... and then the full drama

In the four years prior to the Andhra crisis, Indian microfinance had three dress rehearsals for the final drama now unfolding. In Indian microfinance circles, these are known as the 'three Ks', and each provided an important lesson and warning for the Indian microfinance industry which studiously ignored all three.

The first rehearsal was in Krishna District in 2006, when the district collector, responsible for the administration of the whole district, shut fifty offices of leading microfinance institutions (MFIs) including Spandana, Asmita and Share, and instructed clients not to repay their loans. This was done, essentially, on the basis that MFIs were charging usurious interest rates, making enormous profits at the cost of the poor; co-opting the government self-help groups and being coercive in their collection methods. The intervention and active support of the Reserve Bank of India (RBI) prevented prolonged closure of the MFIs' offices. The MFIs promised to reduce interest rates and introduce a code of conduct. This was done, but as soon as the controversy died down, interest rates soon began to rise and the code of conduct largely remained only on paper.

The second rehearsal was in Kanpur (and other cities of Uttar Pradesh) in 2009, where a local MFI, Nirman Bharti, defaulted on the loans it had received from various banks and other financial institutions amid significant portfolio problems. The underlying problem was that Nirman Bharti had not developed the processes, systems of internal control and management information system (MIS) to manage the rapid growth driven by the priority sector lending-based flood of debt financing.

In fact, as early as April 2009, MicroSave had raised the red flag while conducting a loan portfolio audit (LPA) of one of the large MFIs. The MIS was clearly inadequate for the scale of operations, and (probably, as a result) the reporting of non-performing loans was inconsistent at various levels. New field officers were being provided with two days of training followed by two to three weeks of exposure shadowing another field officer before being given the responsibility of managing a thousand clients or more. These were clearly serious issues when the institution is dealing with a portfolio of nearly USD250 million and has to manage nearly a thousand branches. Nirman Bharti's reaction was a combination of denial and a demand for a different consulting company to perform another LPA in the expectation that it would be less rigorous, and thus less critical, than the one conducted by MicroSave.

The third rehearsal was in Kolar District in Karnataka in 2009/2010, where a repayment strike instigated by the Anjuman committee, a local Muslim group, paralysed repayments for many months, affecting most of the major southern MFIs. The underlying reasons for this strike were complex; one study concluded that 'Client information from seven of the nine MFIs operating in the town shows that at least 33 per cent of them have more than one loan and around 20 per cent have three or more loans'. Furthermore, problems in the local silk-reeling industry had reduced flows of income, which reduced the debt repayment capacity; there was pressure from clients' husbands to cut back on attending weekly meetings and finally the use of agents by MFIs to drive sales; all created an environment that was highly risky for traditional, zero-tolerance, group-based lending operations.

These three rehearsals were clear enough warnings of each and every component of the Andhra Pradesh crisis. But the larger MFIs were too busy focusing on rapid horizontal growth and sales to pause to examine the political and reputational risks that were written on the wall in large, neon, flashing letters. By the beginning of 2010, the government and RBI were already showing clear signs of disquiet with the way the MFIs were conducting their business, as well as their impact on the self-help group (SHG) movement that a variety of government agencies had so carefully nurtured.

The full production drama

The main allegations against the MFIs in Andhra Pradesh are that they are charging opaque and usurious interest rates as well as using strong-arm techniques for collections and, thereby, are accused of profiteering at the cost of poor women. What started as a concern about the reported suicides by some harassed MFI borrowers soon grew into a major crisis, which has grown as a virus for the entire sector. The government in the state of Andhra Pradesh has issued an ordinance requiring MFIs to register with local government offices, which will also monitor any incidents of harassment/complaints from MFI clients. In case the complaint is found to be prima facie tenable, criminal cases will be lodged against MFI staff members. Loan repayments are to be made monthly at the gram panchayat office – thus effectively taking away the convenience of small weekly repayments at meetings in clients' own villages, and levelling the playing field with the SHGs.

So what is likely to happen in the long term?

Clearly the microfinance, or better said 'microcredit', industry in India is undergoing a major shake-up. MFIs are busy trying to reorganise their operations to comply with the ordinance in Andhra Pradesh, and this is likely to accelerate a trend that has occurred throughout Latin America and Africa already. MicroSave has been suggesting that the long-term future of mono-product group-based microcredit is questionable – and that there is a pressing need to reinvent it as individual-based microfinance that leverages m-banking platforms to offer a wide range of financial services. Furthermore, it is clear that RBI would like the banks to be more directly involved in lending in the villages through banking correspondent–based systems, offering a range of services, and is likely to keep refining the regulations until this is commercially viable for the banks. This being the case, it is possible that MFIs eventually end up as the agents of banks in rural areas, selling products and managing clients/repayments and other services.

Interest rate cap

An interest rate cap of 26 per cent is likely to lead to demise of many smaller MFIs without the capital base to build the scale to breakeven at that rate. It will also lead to large-scale financial exclusion for the poor in not only remote rural areas but also urban and metro cities like Delhi and Mumbai. One of the fallouts of interest rate caps would also be that MFIs would tend to focus on higher-ticket-size loans. This could lead to the poorer amongst the existing clients being excluded from the provision of microfinance (or microcredit as it is presently) and they will have to go back to informal sources of credit, at much higher interest rates.

Another potential negative fallout of a ceiling in interest rates would be the propensity of MFIs to push consumer products with the loans; it will enable direct cash inflows to the MFIs in terms of commissions. Some banks seem to be focusing on 24–30 per cent as the maximum acceptable interest rate, reflecting important pragmatism. For example, on 12 December 2010, the *Hindustan Times* reported T. M. Bhasin, chairman and managing director, Indian Bank, saying, 'There is no bar in lending to MFIs, but we have decided to sign a contract before lending to them, ensuring that they cannot charge interest above 30%.' Similarly, Small Industries Development Bank of India has written to MFIs asking for plans to reduce rate of interest to 24 per cent. In the current crisis, the role of players like Dia Vikas Capital, Maanveeya Holding (Oiko Credit), and other MFIs will enhance, as their capital supply lines are independent of Indian banks.

The worst-case scenario

The worst-case scenario is that the microfinance industry may continue its downward spiral. In early December 2010, Microfinance Institutions Network (MFIN), the network of larger non-banking finance companies and MFIs (NBFC–MFIs) reported that MFIs were not in a position to collect about Rs 7,200 crore outstanding loans in Andhra Pradesh, and had missed the opportunity to lend about Rs 1,200 crore since October when the ordinance was introduced. The future for microfinance does not appear to be as projected just a couple of months ago.

Equity and valuations

Large MFIs, waiting to tap the capital markets, will be unable to do so in the near future and get any decent valuations. The government is on record that it will consider tabling the bill after taking into consideration the recommendations of the Malegam Committee constituted by the RBI in the wake of crisis.

The upside

On the positive side, capping of interest rates (informally) will lead to a relook at the whole model of microfinance, and will, in the long run, enhance the use of technology to reduce operating costs. MFIs and banks will experiment with different forms of agent models, and these could form the basis of reducing costs and cross-selling products such as savings and insurance – enabling delivery costs to be shared across different products. Risk management will be given the importance that it deserves, especially in the larger MFIs.

The current crisis will also lead to some emphasis on brand building and differentiation, in order to allow MFIs to compete to meet clients' needs for financial services on a more comprehensive and holistic basis. The joke in the field (not far from truth) at the moment is that clients know MFIs only by the day on which they make collections, namely, 'Monday MFI', 'Tuesday MFI' and so on. As part of their response to the crisis, MFIs are likely to have to move closer to what MicroSave has been calling third-generation microfinance, harnessing technology and collaborative arrangements to offer a range of financial services to their clients. This would provide an opportunity to reconnect and rebuild relationships with their clients and to move the incentives for repayment away from group liability–based 'sticks' to the 'carrots' of maintaining ongoing access to a broad range of valued financial services. To do this effectively, MFIs will need to choose their position on the basic perceptual map or positioning triangle, and choose combinations of price, quality products and customer service on which to differentiate themselves in competitive markets.

What should MFIs do?

Transparency of interest rates

First and foremost, MFIs need to respond to the accusations that their pricing is not transparent – a common charge that is echoed around the world in microfinance, and points to a clear and present need to change. Clients do not always understand annualised percentage rate

(APR), as typically informal sector interest rates are expressed as 'X% of loan outstanding at the beginning of the month', or 'Rs X per Rs 100 outstanding'. Often clients are only interested in how much they have to repay each week. So pressing for expression of interest simply on an APR basis may add little real transparency for clients. Other elements of the typical MFI's loan package that obfuscate real effective interest rates include grace periods, the number of weeks over which the loan is to be repaid and requirements/'encouragement' to prepay the loan (most of which would be addressed by a move to declining balance-based interest rates). Clearly there is a need for an industry standard way of pricing, and a real commitment to helping clients to understand the real cost of their loans.

Transparency of operations and governance

MFIs in India have a very real credibility problem when it comes to transparency of operations and governance – and continue to underestimate how damaging this can be. Discussions with bankers repeatedly show that the price of loans advanced to MFIs depend greatly on perceptions of their transparency and governance. However, MFIs, large and small, continue to ignore this sacred tenet. MFIs in India, and indeed elsewhere in the world, need to establish outstanding levels of transparency and governance, in all parts of their business – financial and operational. They deal with a sensitive segment, the poor of the country, and should not only do well but should also be seen to be doing so.

Improved analysis and dissemination of social performance

MFIs often collect data about the nature of the clients they serve, but this typically remains on loan application forms, unanalysed, in branch offices. This data could provide important insights into how MFIs are indeed reaching the very people that the Government of India is so keen to have served. Analysing and acting on social performance on the basis of client satisfaction and loyalty makes business sense – not just because it can be used to describe how the MFI is performing to external stakeholders, but also because it enhances the client responsiveness of the MFI. MicroSave has been concerned about the rate of growth of Indian MFIs and their loss of relationship with their clients for several years now.

The concrete steps that MFIs can and should take are to are as follows:

1   Follow stricter policies around *client protection* principles and do no harm. Maintaining transparent and fair pricing/interest rates, addressing multiple borrowing/lending and ensuring appropriate collection practices are the starting points (and the bare minimum). Understanding clients' perspectives of what client protection actually entails is also essential.
2   Take steps towards ensuring *client delight* through offering a range of high-quality, client-centric and flexible financial products in a manner that is appropriate and suitable for clients.
3   Develop a strategy that makes sense for the company, the management and the mission – not copy-paste from others.
4   Improve communication on benefits of social side of microfinance with the stakeholders such as government officials and media.
5   MFIs need to grow and expand at a rate sustainable and manageable; this enables valuation of human resources also. MFIs should grow as credible institutions and an integral part of society, rather than becoming loan disbursal machines and treating the clientele accordingly.

Meeting these challenges will not only help MFIs meet their mission and social performance needs, but also clearly make business sense and enhance risk management (including strategic and reputation risks).

Establish a credit bureau?

The Indian MFIs that comprise the membership of MFIN (an industry association) are proposing to establish a credit bureau, which, they believe, will allow them to mitigate the risk of over-indebtedness. However, even with the national unique identification number, a credit bureau may struggle to deliver information that is valuable in terms of reducing over-indebtedness for two important reasons. First, MFIs effectively lend to a household, not an individual, and it is from the household income and expenditure flows that the repayments will be managed. In the event of one member of the household being blacklisted on the credit bureau, another can easily step in and join another MFI(s). The second point is that the informal sector will not participate in the credit bureau; the vast majority of poor households' loans come from informal sources. So the database will only show a small proportion of the debt burden of the households registered.

Move to third-generation microfinance

Ultimately MFIs need to provide a suite of products to their clients to reduce their vulnerability and enhance their ability to earn income. This cannot be done by delivering a mono-product, group-based lending. This provides a tremendous opportunity to use banking correspondents to offer the full range of financial services (savings, credit, remittance and insurance) and thus real financial inclusion of the poor of India. High-quality saving services, so often demanded by clients in focus groups held by MicroSave in the villages across India, would allow poor people to build financial assets to help manage their household budgets and loan repayments through the lean seasons and household crises. Micro-insurance products, to reduce households' risk or to provide a long-term savings mechanism, could also be accessed through the banking correspondent. Clients would repay loans to secure ongoing access to a wide range of valued financial services rather than because their group and a credit officer were pressurising them to do so – moving to a carrot- from a stick-based incentive. MicroSave calculates that loans of Rs 20,000–25,000 are adequate to cover the costs of conducting a cash flow analysis of, and reference checks on, the borrower's business and household, and thus to offer a cash flow–based individual loan. Mobile phone technology could take care of loan reminders, collections and initial follow-up, thus allowing staff to focus on origination, appraisal and monitoring of client relationships and the few cases (hopefully) of delinquency. Coupled with an agent-based network, this could be the answer to a low-cost model that India needs at the moment.

What should the government do?

Recognise and build on the success

The microfinance industry in India has grown by leaps and bounds and has managed to achieve in a decade what banks could not do in more than sixty years since India's independence. The banking industry has supported the growth of the microfinance sector in

India, and its ready provision of the funds needed for the growth of the sector has enabled the horizontal expansion. In a country still looking for greater penetration of financial services, it is well known that banks find it very difficult to extend credit for enterprises in the informal sector with credit needs of Rs 200,000 to Rs 500,000. Microfinance institutions should be encouraged to fill this gap while maintaining levels of transparency and realistic pricing.

Enforce transparency

Transparency is a pre-requisite in any business, and more so in the microfinance sector, as it deals with millions of poor. The RBI, which has till recently fought shy of closely regulating the sector, should take up the challenge. Reporting standards should be developed for MFIs, and to the extent possible, common reporting formats and measures for sharing of information should be adopted across banks.

Regulate for responsible lending

Group lending, in its present form, is a methodology that can only go so far. MFIs should be encouraged to provide a wider range of products, not only limited to credit. Even in terms of credit, a wider range of products should be encouraged. Providing artisans and farmers access to appropriate and cost-effective credit products should be made eligible for priority sector lending. The challenge, of course, will be to have appropriate audit/end-use verification measures in place. In terms of recovery practices, strong-arm tactics cannot be tolerated; however, action should be taken against errant MFIs, and not against the industry as a collective. The RBI has the option of regulating the microfinance sector comprised of NBFC–MFIs on its own, or through banks, or a combination of the two. RBI should probably enhance its own capacity to regulate and supervise NBFC–MFIs, and also entrust greater responsibility to banks extending credit to MFIs.

Use priority sector lending

Managing the explosive growth of MFIs could play an important role in ensuring that these organisations develop in a client-responsive and sustainable manner – rather than focusing exclusively on sales and gross numbers. Priority sector lending (PSL) requirements played a key role in encouraging the unsustainable growth rates of MFIs. They should be amended to temper the incentives for rapid growth and to encourage competition. One such approach might be to limit the amount of lending per MFI that can be counted towards PSL requirements, as has been done in the case of direct agriculture credit eligible for PSL. This would both reduce the scope for MFIs to leverage PSL debt to attract aggressive private sector equity and encourage banks to lend to a wider range of MFIs, thus enhancing competition amongst them. Furthermore, as in the case of banks, MFIs should be encouraged to set up operations in remote areas. Access to priority sector funds should be contingent on MFIs' presence in remote unbanked areas, transparency and provision of a wide range of financial services – not only credit.

Develop union-level legislation

The applicability of money-lending legislation of various state governments and efforts to regulate the sector through a plethora of state-level legislations will harm the industry, and the poor in the country. Different state-level legislations would lead to the promotion of state-specific entities as pan-India institutions will find it difficult to navigate through myriad legislations. This will ensure survival of smaller institutions and will preclude the options of economies of scale in the provision of credit and other financial services to the poor. Hence MFIs, in all regulatory formats, should be exempt from state-specific money-lending and other legislation.

Interest rate caps

Similarly, attempts to cap interest rates in microfinance will be detrimental for the poor and will set back the agenda for financial inclusion by decades. Clients in remote areas, in difficult terrains such as sparsely populated hills, and in high-cost urban settings will be denied access to quality financial services. If the regulator is concerned about super-profits being made by some of the MFIs, it should look at capping return on equity (RoE) rather than capping interest rates. The effects of interest rates on financial inclusion have been well documented, and are almost universally detrimental to the well-being of the poor.

Enhance and encourage banking correspondence

RBI should also facilitate movement from microcredit to full and comprehensive financial inclusion through the banking correspondent model. As of now, attempts are being made to enhance access to savings through e/m-banking channels. Such a model will continue to struggle to break even unless a more comprehensive range of financial services are made available. Microfinance institutions have developed expertise in low-ticket-size group lending; this can be very easily expanded to cover trade-specific individual loans, savings, remittance and insurance. Such an approach by MFIs, at least for some products, acting as agents of banks will leverage the outreach and networks already created and will also be a step forward in bringing down costs.

Recognise, and hold accountable, an industry association

The microfinance industry collectives have also been struggling to maintain focus in a sector experiencing such rapid growth. Industry associations go into overdrive at the time of crisis, but lose their pre-eminence once the crisis is resolved. A clearer and more proactive role has to emerge for industry associations – or probably a singular industry association. Coming up with codes of conduct, which remain voluntary, on paper and not adhered to by members in practice is clearly inadequate. A few MFIs have, in the past, adopted grossly unfair and unacceptable practices, which have been topics for gossip, but on which no collective action has been taken. This will have to change or else the entire sector will have to face the consequences – as has been demonstrated by the turn of events post Andhra Pradesh crisis. The RBI needs to recognise and hold accountable a credible, well-resourced industry association.

Be open and honest about the SHG movement

The events of the recent past should not encourage the illusion that the SHG model is the way, truth and light for financial inclusion in India. People involved in the sector admit that the SHG model is struggling, and will crumble unless rapid efforts are made to re-engineer it. It is time for an open and honest review of SHGs – analysing why MFIs had the space to lend to SHG members when MFIs were charging 24 per cent (or more) and SHGs were charging just 3 per cent. The National Bank for Agriculture and Rural Development (NABARD), as the custodian of SHGs, should conduct rigorous analysis of the model and arrive at ways and means of strengthening it. Given NABARD's deep involvement and ownership of SHGs, it can be safely said that the staff and officers of NABARD are aware of the problems and challenges, and are capable of addressing them. Indeed the Society for Elimination of Rural Poverty, a programme started by the Government of Andhra Pradesh, has already started sincere efforts to do this.

Clients' perspective

Clients historically admired and appreciated MFIs before the Andhra crisis, because of their products and delivery systems, which offered:

1   easy access to collateral-free loans;
2   convenient, doorstep delivery;
3   quick processing of loans with little documentation;
4   lower interest rates compared to moneylenders and others.

Even for SHG members with loans through the bank linkage programme, MFIs were an attractive option, as they provided larger loan amounts in a short span of time. For most members, the loans they received from/through the SHGs were insufficient for their needs. Many people were borrowing from MFIs with relatively high interest rate, even though they could get loans at 3 per cent through their SHGs. MFIs provided them easier access and client-focused service not otherwise available.

While many poor people did take loans from MFIs for the reasons cited above, others hesitated to take loans because of:

1   the rigidity in frequency of collections (most MFIs require weekly repayment – irrespective of the cash flows of the clients);
2   compulsory weekly meetings (which put pressure on the clients' time);
3   stricter collection practices;
4   higher interest rates.

Sectoral stakeholders have been advocating the need for product innovation and enhanced usage of technology to reduce the delivery costs. Most MFIs were happy rolling out vanilla group products with repayments at weekly frequency. All this has changed overnight after the ordinance issued by the Government of Andhra Pradesh.

Perspective of clients' in Andhra Pradesh on microfinance

After the Andhra Pradesh state government issued the microfinance ordinance in October 2010, matters have become worse for MFIs, banks and clients themselves. The general trend has been that clients have stopped repayment of loans to MFIs – due to pressure from elected representatives and active workers of various political parties, as well as other local leaders or because MFI staff are not coming to collect or due to peer pressure. There are three broad categories of client reactions to this, which are discussed in the following sections.

Those who are willing to pay despite the situation

Some clients are willing to pay as they feel that it is better to pay weekly instalments now, than to pay larger amounts later, when the issue is resolved. But these clients are unable to pay because MFI field staffs are unable to come for collections. Even amongst clients willing to repay, the general perception has been that the MFIs might collect repayments, but not sanction any further loans. In Rudrapur, clients are willing to repay as long as the MFIs promise them to give further loans. In the Rayapuram village, clients who recently completed repayment of their loans, and are waiting for new follow-on loans are not happy with the ordinance which stopped MFIs' disbursements. Hence, uncertainty is building up amongst clients and chances of repayments are reducing with every passing day.

Those who want a clarification from the government before making payments

Some MFI clients do not want to repay their loans unless the government makes a clear, formal announcement on repayment to MFIs through prominent TV channels. Local panchayat presidents, ward members and political representatives expect an official letter from the local mandal development officer or mandal revenue officer regarding repayment of MFI loans; otherwise, they do not want to allow MFI staff to enter villages/towns. MFI loan officers say that people do not attach any value to the registration certificate issued by DRDA (District Rural Development Agency), asserting that these documents have been produced by MFIs, rather than obtained officially through the DRDA.

In Gajulapalli, MFI clients say that many of the families have taken so many loans from MFIs that now it has become very difficult for them to pay all the instalments due. Some families have to make loan repayments every day of the week, other than on Sundays. These people are now expecting/hoping that the government will waive all MFI loans. In contrast, in Peddapalli village, MFI clients want the government to show them alternative sources of credit – otherwise they will have to go back to the informal moneylenders.

Those who are taking the opportunity to default on repayments

In some places there are dominant members, including the centre leaders, who are not allowing the members to repay, as they want to use this as an opportunity to default on or renegotiate their loans. The extensive discussions of MFI interest rates and other charges (e.g. processing fee, insurance and business development service fee) in various forums, especially in the electronic media, have increased the clients' awareness of the costs of borrowing from MFIs. In Kothapalli village, one of the MFI clients who had recently taken loan from a prominent MFI attended a meeting about the ordinance, and calculated the entire amount she was supposed to pay to the MFI in addition to the principal amount. After this calculation, she concluded that the MFI was charging exorbitant interest, and spread this information to the entire village. As a result, all the members decided not to repay their loans, demanding that the MFI reduce the interest rate to Re 1 per Rs 100 per month.

Non-clients' perspectives of MFIs

Non-clients' perspectives on, and prejudices about, MFIs have been strengthened. Many of the non-clients do not know how MFIs operate, as MFI staff members do not share their norms and terms of business with anyone other than their clients. Many of them believe that MFIs are charging higher interest rates than local moneylenders. The present crisis, publicised through media, has made the MFIs infamous – even amongst those who have never before heard of microfinance. Many such non-clients believe that poor people across the state have committed suicide because of pressure from MFIs and the use of coercive practices for repayments.

Speculation on the future of financial services for the poor in India

As Collins et al. note in 'Portfolios of the Poor', three needs drive much of the financial activity of poor households.

1 *Managing basics*: Cash-flow management to transform irregular income flows into a dependable resource to meet daily needs;
2 *Coping with risk*: Dealing with the emergencies that can derail families with little in reserve;
3 *Raising lump sums*: Seizing opportunities and paying for big-ticket expenses by accumulating usefully large sums of money (Figure 2.1).

To meet these needs, as a bare minimum, poor people need the following financial services delivered in a reliable, convenient, flexible and structured manner:

1 A current savings account into which they can deposit, and from which they can withdraw, conveniently
2 An emergency or general loan that can be taken and repaid quickly

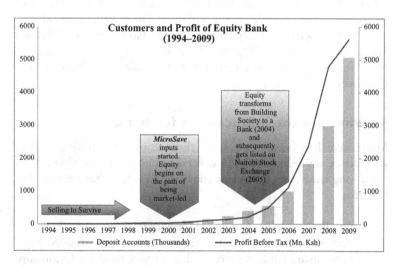

Figure 2.1 Customers and profit of Equity Bank, 1994–2009

3   Contractual savings products, similar to recurring deposit scheme
4   A loan that can be used for a wide variety of purposes

After a period of selling-focused struggle and limited growth, Equity Bank consulted its clients and refined its products in 2001. Since then, Equity Bank has delivered these services, and witnessed extraordinary growth as a consequence. This growth was built and maintained on a commitment to:

• listening to clients and responding to their needs;
• excellent customer service; and
• technology/delivery channels: IT/ATMs/POS/m-banking.

Similarly, Grameen Bank's under-recognised transformation in 2002 saw a massive increase in clients – including many who repaid loans that were long overdue in order to gain access to the new range of products offered by the bank. As Stuart Rutherford noted in 2006, 'Grameen took 27 years to reach 2.5 million members – and then doubled that in the full establishment of Grameen II.' Since then, the bank has added another three million members. As part of it fund-raising drive, Grameen offered fixed and recurring deposit products not just to its poor members, but also to the better-off people in the villages. These savings products were very generously priced, and now the bank has a significant, and growing (nearly USD500 million at the end of 2009), excess of savings over the amount of loans it is able to push out to its members.

So what are the implications for India?

MicroSave has been advocating the use of the banking correspondence models to offer a diverse range of financial services for a long time now. It is clear that e/m-banking channels can be used to:

1   offer clients a suite of financial services in response to their full spectrum of financial needs – credit, savings, remittances, payments, insurance and so on – thus deepening the relationship with clients;

2   deliver proximity so that the transaction point is in the villages/ slums where the clients reside – allowing them to transact easily and as often as they need;
3   focus on convenience (including the ability to make small trans- actions) so that products respond to clients' needs, and not just those of the institution;
4   Leverage technology to increase transaction efficiency and reduce costs.

Until recently, when the RBI sanctioned charging 'reasonable fees' for transactions, this was largely a pipe dream in India. But, in the current regulatory environment, and the banks' realisation that the RBI is absolutely committed to achieving real financial inclusion with active accounts, supported by the growing number of mobile network operators and dedicated agent network providers, the dream is set to become a reality. The *Aadhaar* project, linking each person's unique identification number with his or her bank account and mobile number, means that the potential for the rapid roll-out of effective agent networks is significant. With reasonable charges, the stage is set to move beyond the double break-even dilemma, under which it was more lucrative for agents to just to sign cus- tomers up and then let the account lapse into dormancy. Because paying for remittances, withdrawals and payments is an accepted norm in Africa, it is ahead of Asia in the roll-out of mobile money. Although the poor in India are indeed willing to pay, MicroSave's recent research in Uttar Pradesh suggests that transactions in rural bank branches are time-consuming (often 1–2 hours or more is required for a basic deposit or withdrawal) – resulting in cash losses and opportunity costs in the range of Rs 25–150. It is unsurprising, therefore, that the poor are willing to pay for a convenient service close to their homes.

In the long term, as multiple products are offered across the mobile money platforms, this will revolutionise financial inclusion, and the poor will have access to savings, remittances, payments, insurance, individual cash-flow-based loans and airtime top-up, plus a host of other services through agents based within a few yards of their houses. It is the deepening of this relationship that will allow the banks to better manage credit risk, and thus begin to make small advances to customers on the basis of their savings/ insurance histories. For larger loans, detailed appraisals of the cash flows of both the household and the business to be financed will be required – but MicroSave estimates that these are indeed feasible for loans in excess of Rs 25,000. The stage in India is set for very significant change.

References

Andhra Pradesh Microfinance Institutions (Regulation of Money Lending) Ordinance, (2010), Briefing Notes http://www.serp.ap.gov.in/SHG/index.jsp

Anjaneyulu, B., and L.B. Prakash, (Apr 2009), 'Delinquency in Self Help Groups', *MicroSave* India Focus Note #15.

Anjaneyulu, B., and TVS Ravi Kumar, (May 2010), *MicroSave* India Focus Note #44, 'Savings Mobilisation in SHGs: Opportunities and Challenges'.

Carolina, L., and B. H. Matthews (25 Sep 2009), Making Business Correspondence Work in India, *MicroSave* India Focus Note #24.

CGAP (Sep 2004), 'Interest Rate Ceilings and Microfinance: The Story So Far', CGAP Occasional Paper, No 9.

Christopher, M., Sharma, Manoj K., and Graham A. N. Wright, (Oct 2009), 'Dinosaurs and Rabbits – Indian Microfinance Market Evolution', *MicroSave* India Focus Note #25.

Collins et al. (Jun 2010), 'Portfolios of the Poor: How the World's Poor Live on $2 a Day: Understanding Priceal', PoP Briefing Note #8.

Denny, G., Venkata, N.A. and T. Mugwang'a (Jul 2010), 'Managing Individual Lending', *MicroSave* Briefing Note #85.

EDA Rural Systems, (2010), 'Competition and the Role of External Agents: The 2009 Delinquency Crisis in Microfinance in Southern Karnataka', EDA/CGAP.

Matthews, B.H., (Jan 2010), 'Making Business Correspondence Work – Crossing the Second 'Break-Even', *MicroSave* India Focus Note #32.

Matthews, B.H., and Devi G. Trivikrama, 'SHGs Should Balance or Break', *MicroSave* India Focus Note #19.

Natu, A.J., (Oct 2009), 'Market Strategy Development and 3rd Generation Microfinance in India', *MicroSave* India Focus Note #26.

Sinha, S. (2 Aug 2007), 'Benefits of Loan Portfolio Audit for MFIs', *MicroSave* Briefing Note #62.

Thacker, K., and T. Mugwang'a, (Jul 2010), 'Individual Lending for MFIs – Strategic Issues to Consider First', *MicroSave* Briefing Note #84.

Wright, Graham A.N., (May 2010), 'Microfinance in India: Built on Sales Targets or Loyal Clients?', *MicroSave* India Focus Note #42.

Wright, Graham A.N., Cracknell, D., Mutesasira, L. and R. Hudson (24 May 2004), 'Corporate Branding and Identity – Why They Are Important for MFIs', Briefing Note #27.

Wright, Graham A.N., and D. Cracknell (16 Aug 2007), 'The Market Led Revolution of Equity Bank', Briefing Note #63.

Wright, Graham A.N., and D. Cracknell with S. Rutherford, 'Lessons from the Grameen II Revolution', Briefing Notes on Grameen II #8.

Wright, Graham A.N., and Manoj K. Sharma, (May 2010), 'Commercialisation of Microfinance in India: Is It All Bad?', *MicroSave* India Focus Note #43.

Chapter 3

Strengthening governance in microfinance institutions

Some random thoughts[1]

Anand Sinha

Microfinance, involving extension of small loans and other financial services to low-income groups, is a very important economic conduit designed to facilitate financial inclusion and assist the poor to work their way out of poverty. It has the potential to fill the critical gap left by formal financial institutions in providing financial services to low-income groups. Mainstream institutions shied away from providing financial services to the poor, considering them unviable, owing to high costs involved in reaching out to the unbanked/under-banked areas where there is not enough scale of operations due to low numbers and low value of transactions. Other reasons cited for such exclusion are perceived high risk and inability of poor borrowers to provide physical collateral for raising loans.

Microfinance evolved to fill this critical gap. It became a leading and effective strategy for poverty alleviation with the potential for far-reaching impact in transforming the lives of poor people. It is argued that microfinance can facilitate the achievement of the Millennium Development Goals as well as national policies that target poverty reduction, empowerment of women, assisting vulnerable groups, and improving standards of living. As pointed out by the former UN secretary general Kofi Annan during the launch of the International Year of Microcredit (2005), 'sustainable access to microfinance helps alleviate poverty by generating income, creating jobs, allowing children to go to school, enabling families to obtain health care, and empowering people to make the choices that best serve their needs.'

Although microfinance cannot be seen as a panacea for poverty reduction, it can, when properly harnessed, make sustainable contribution through financial investment, leading to the empowerment of people, which in turn promotes confidence and self-esteem, particularly for women. More importantly, the global experience with microfinance has shown that even poor are creditworthy.

Studies have shown that microfinance plays three critical roles in development. First, it enables the very poor households to meet their most basic needs and protect/hedge against risks. Second, concomitantly it is associated with improvements in households' economic welfare. Third, by supporting women's economic participation, it helps to empower women and promote gender equity.

Microfinance and India

Inclusive growth always received special emphasis in the Indian policy making. The Government of India and the Reserve Bank of India (RBI) have taken several initiatives to expand access to financial systems to the poor. Some of the salient measures are nationalisation of banks, prescription of priority sector lending, differential interest rate schemes for the weaker sections and development of credit institutions such as regional rural banks.

Despite the policy efforts, a gap still remains in the availability of financial services in rural areas. The dependence of the rural poor on moneylenders continues, especially for meeting urgent requirements. Such dependence is more pronounced in the case of marginal farmers, agricultural labourers, petty traders and rural artisans belonging to socially and economically backward classes and tribes whose capacity to save is too small.

It is in this backdrop that microfinance emerged in India. The Self-Help Group (SHG)–Bank Linkage Program (SBLP) which was launched in 1992 on a pilot basis grew significantly in a short span of time. As per the latest estimates, SHGs enable more than 97 million poor households' access to sustainable financial services from the banking system and have an outstanding institutional credit exceeding Rs 42,927 crore as at the end March 2014. SBLP is considered to be the fastest growing microfinance initiative in the world. The other model of microfinance, that is, microfinance institution (MFI) model comprising of various entities, such as non-banking financial companies (NBFCs), non-governmental organisations (NGOs) and trusts, cooperatives, has also been growing significantly in the recent years.

Microfinance – both SBLP and the MFI sector – posted an impressive growth in the past few years with the combined client outreach increasing from about 4.8 crores[2] in 2006–07 to 8.6 crores in

2009–10. Loans outstanding to SHGs were Rs 42,927 crore while loans disbursed to MFIs by all agencies amounted to Rs 10,282 crore at the end March 2014.

MFI crisis

There had, however, been a sudden downturn in the prospects of the sector in the second half of 2010–11, owing to reported excesses of some MFI institutions and the consequent legislative response by the Andhra Pradesh state government. On account of these developments, the MFI segment took a severe beating with rising delinquency ratios and downgrades by rating agencies. Lenders turned wary, leading to drying up of funding channels seriously impinging on the business. It was reported that disbursements by MFIs in the then-united Andhra Pradesh plummeted significantly in the second half of 2010–11. The recovery rates that were 99 per cent reportedly fell to a meagre 10 per cent, leading to huge non-performing assets (NPAs) which caused significant stress on the functioning of MFIs. While the loans given to MFIs during 2010–11 declined to Rs 8,448.96 crore from Rs10,728.50 crore in 2009–10, the amount of outstanding loans reduced from Rs 13,955.75 crore in 2009–10 to Rs 13,730.62 crore in 2010–11.

Many analysts attribute the crisis to the irrational exuberance of some MFIs who entered the segment with the sole emphasis on business growth and bottom lines. They, perhaps, did not take due cognisance of the vulnerability of the borrowers and the potential socio-political ramifications their aggressive approach could possibly lead to. The competition among MFIs led to these institutions chasing the same set of borrowers by free riding on SHGs and loading them with loans that borrowers possibly could not afford. It was reported that as at the end of March 2010, the number of loan accounts per poor household in Andhra Pradesh was, on an average, more than ten. In their eagerness to improve business, the institutions had given a go by to the conventional wisdom and good practices such as due diligence in lending and ethical recovery practices. Over-indebtedness of the borrowers led to difficulties in repayments, and forced recoveries by some MFIs led to public uproar and subsequent intervention by the state government.

The legislation enacted by the Andhra Pradesh government brought the customer protection issues to the centre stage. The legislation stipulated mandatory registration of MFIs, disclosure of effective interest rate to the borrowers, ceiling on the interest rates and strict penalties for coercive recovery practices. One of the fallouts of these developments had been the severe dent in the MFI business due to dwindling resources. Against the backdrop of the crisis, the RBI constituted a committee (chairman: Shri Y H Malegam) to study issues and concerns in the MFI sector. The committee examined the issues and made recommendations to address the present concerns. Some of the significant recommendations were as follows:

i   creation of a separate category of NBFCs operating in the microfinance sector to be designated as NBFC–MFIs

ii   imposition of a margin cap and interest rate cap on individual loans

iii   requirement of transparency in interest charges

iv   lending by not more than two MFIs to individual borrowers

v   creation of one or more credit information bureaus

vi   establishment of a proper system of grievance redressal procedure by MFIs

vii   creation of one or more 'social capital funds'

viii   continuation of categorisation of bank loans to MFIs, complying with the regulations laid down for NBFC–MFIs, under the priority sector

Recent developments

The recommendations of the committee brought out clarity in regulation of MFIs and led to the containment of the crisis without domino effect. Based on the recommendations of the Malegam Committee, the RBI issued detailed guidelines permitting categorisation as priority sector advance, of bank credit to certain eligible MFIs. Such eligibility is linked to core features of microfinance, such as lending of small amounts to borrowers belonging to low-income groups, without collaterals, with flexible repayment schedules and with particular emphasis on measures to curb over-indebtedness. Margin caps and interest rate caps have also been stipulated to ensure protection of borrowers[3] (interest rate cap has been made dynamic in nature in that it is lower of the cost of funds plus margin or 2.75 times the average base rate of top five commercial banks). The RBI also created a separate category of NBFCs dealing in microfinance – NBFC–MFI – and issued comprehensive guidelines covering, inter alia, fair practices in lending such as transparency in interest rates, non-coercive methods of recovery, measures to contain multiple lending and over-indebtedness. Currently, the number of NBFC-MFIs registered with the RBI stands at fifty-eight.

The signs of recovery of MFIs are clearly visible with substantial increase in the number of MFIs availing loans from banks during the year 2013–14[4] (28 per cent increase over last year). The total loans to MFIs by banks also increased by over 31 per cent during the year 2013–14. This is despite the fact that loans to MFIs for agricultural purposes are classified as 'indirect agriculture' loans under the priority sector as stipulated by the RBI during the year 2013–14. As per the data published by Microfinance Institutions Network (MFIN)[5], as of 31 December 2014, MFIs provided microcredit to over 28.7 million clients with the aggregate gross loan portfolio (excluding non-performing portfolio) at Rs 31,450 crore.

The Government of India has come out with a press release dated 1 March 2015 proposing to set up a Micro Units Development and Refinance Agency (MUDRA) Bank through a statutory enactment. MUDRA Bank would be responsible for regulating and refinancing all MFIs which are in the business of lending to micro/small business entities engaged in manufacturing, trading and service activities. The bank would partner with state-level/regional-level coordinators to provide finance to the last-mile financer of small/micro business enterprises. It is envisaged that the initiative would not only help in increasing access to finance to the unbanked but also bring down the cost of finance from the last-mile financers to the micro/small enterprises, most of which are in the informal sector. However, the role of MUDRA Bank, if any, with regard to NBFC–MFIs is not clear at this stage.

Key lessons and the way forward

While a number of reasons have been attributed for the turmoil in the sector, such as unjustified high rates of interest, lack of transparency in interest rate and other charges, multiple lending and overborrowing and coercive methods of recovery, I would consider the governance deficit coupled with people risk, process risk and relationship risk as the more critical factors that have precipitated the turmoil and need to be addressed. MFIs need to seriously examine their governance systems and align their practices with the overall objective of microfinance which is to facilitate financial inclusion and empower poor.

Governance in MFIs

Governance, as we all know, is essentially about doing business and maximising shareholders' wealth legally, ethically and on a sustainable basis. Being fair and to be seen as being fair to all the stakeholders without discrimination or bias is the test for good governance. Governance system represents the value framework, the ethical framework, the moral framework and the legal framework under which business decisions are taken. Governance would encompass self-regulation both at the individual entity level and at industry level through the self-regulatory organisation (SRO) mechanism. These two would form the first line of defence with the regulatory framework providing the backstop. In the absence of effective self-regulation, the regulatory framework becomes more prescriptive which raises costs to regulators and supervisors in administering the regulatory framework and also increases compliance costs to the regulated entities. This clearly is a suboptimal solution. The considerable intellectual appeal of *principles-based* regulation which had committed proponents is a case in point. In the wake of the subprime crisis of 2008, it has yielded considerable ground to the proponents of *rules-based* regulation. Let me clarify that *principles-based* regulations and *rules-based* regulations are not binary choices. What distinguishes them is the less or more of prescriptive regulations.

Governance is based on the basic tenets of transparency and accountability. Transparency in decision making provides comfort to all stakeholders, and accountability which follows from transparency fixes responsibilities for actions taken or not taken. Together, they safeguard the interests of the stakeholders in the organisation.

There were serious deficiencies observed in the governance framework of some of the MFIs. The corporate governance issues in the MFI sector were exacerbated by some of the 'for-profit' MFIs, dominated and controlled by promoter shareholders, which led to inadequate internal checks and balances over executive decision making and conflict of interests at various levels. Other undesirable practices such as connected lending, excessively generous compensation practices for senior management and founders/directors and failure of internal controls leading to frauds precipitated the crisis.

Some of the MFIs chased high-growth trajectory at the expense of corporate best practices. The listing and trading of the shares of the 'for-profit' MFIs generated a set of incentives which attracted investors looking for high returns. On the other hand, the capital suited for catering to the needs of the poor has to be *patient capital* (long-term capital). This disconnect led to further worsening of the situation. What is more disturbing is that there were enough warning signals of trouble in making over an extended period of time but the MFIs, at least some of them, carried away by their immediate success, failed to pay heed. These events have been narrated by Dr Y. V. Reddy, former governor, RBI, in an article titled 'Microfinance Industry in India: Some Thoughts' in *Economic and Political Weekly* (8 October 2011). Relating the events in Andhra Pradesh, he has stated that the Government of Andhra Pradesh always had discomfort with the NBFC–MFIs and every effort was made by the RBI to introduce a voluntary code of conduct. Resolution in this regard was thought to have been achieved in 2007. In retrospect, Dr Reddy says that perhaps the trust that RBI placed in the commitment of MFIs was misplaced, and given the track record, the RBI should have insisted on enforceable regulation and not been content with an advisory role. Dr Reddy's observations lead to another very important tenet of corporate governance, that is, the need to pay attention to the feedback loops, particularly the negative feedback loops and to take mid-course corrective actions. Those who fail to do so end up paying a heavy price.

Inclusive finance versus regulations[6]

History is replete with examples that good intentions may not always lead to good outcomes. Intentions need to be adequately backed by sound framework of governance and regulation. This is demonstrated by the experience of subprime housing loans in the United States and microfinance in India. When private sector emerged in microfinance, regulation responded positively by providing a supportive enabling environment: (a) lending by banks to MFIs is deemed as lending to priority sector, enabling banks to meet statutory norms, (b) banks were advised to lend to MFIs without a cap on interest rates and (c) group guarantees were deemed as collateral for the purposes of asset classification and provisioning norms. MFIs were expected to be carrying forward the agenda of inclusion, and were fully aligned with the banking system. MFIs, however, enamoured by the fast growth and expanding balance sheets, shifted goals, strategies and practices. Dr Reddy has observed (Reddy, 2011) that the assumption that the people working in MFIs were committed to a value framework that aims at profit making but not profiteering or profit maximisation was not validated, going by the organisational structures and incentive frameworks as well as the lifestyles of senior managers.

The MFI episode in India has, at least, two close parallels with the subprime crisis of 2008. First, the origin of the subprime crisis was about extending loans well beyond the borrowers' capacity to pay, and second, compensation practices were a major contributing factor to the crisis as these practices were designed to enhance risk taking and create value for shareholders but not to protect other stakeholders. Corrective actions are being taken in the context of regulatory reforms for banks through Basel III guidelines and for MFIs through guidelines based on the Malegam Committee recommendations.

Learning from the crisis, we need to build a regulatory framework which ensures a balance between flexibility to MFIs in their operations and regulations that ensure customer protection and financial health of the MFIs. In the long run, MFIs also will be benefitted by such regulatory framework as it enables orderly growth and reduces uncertainty. The envisaged regulatory framework must put in place restrictions and safeguards with regard to minimum standards of governance, management and customer protection as well as the financial health of MFIs. Naturally, robust regulations coupled with thorough risk-based onsite and offsite supervision are needed to foster entrepreneurship while encouraging inclusive and sustainable economic growth, especially with reference to end users. This balance would be provided by the regulatory framework derived from the Malegam Committee report and the SRO framework. Two institutions, MFIN and Sa-Dhan, have been recognised by the RBI as SROs for the NBFC–MFIs registered with the RBI.

Balancing the dual objectives: social and financial

There is no denying the fact that self-sufficiency and financial sustainability are the objectives that MFI could pursue. However, in the race to earn profits, the social objective should not be lost sight of. Mission drift, where the institution deviates from its original mission in pursuit of a conflicting unannounced mission, is a major risk the MFIs face. The boards of MFIs will have to balance the objectives of various stakeholders, namely, the equity holders, the donors, the borrowers and the overall society. Strong corporate governance could play a critical role in balancing seemingly exclusive but potentially complementary objectives from a long-term perspective.

The question of balance between maximising profits and serving the financial services needs of the poor is certainly an issue for MFIs. It is often asked that if the MFIs moderate their pace of growth and shift their priorities more towards social objectives, would they be able to attract enough investors who provide capital enabling MFIs to take forward their activities designed to help the poor. Similar questions have arisen in the context of substantially enhanced regulatory framework for banks under Basel III, in particular the higher capital and liquidity requirements. There is an apprehension that with much larger capital and liquidity requirements under Basel III to support similar level of activities, the RoE would go down appreciably, and consequently, banks may not be able to attract investors to provide capital. This line of thinking disregards the risk–return trade-off and the fact that banks can raise their productivity and efficiency levels to protect their RoEs, at least partially. It is hoped that when investors see a much more stable and safer banking system, they would be willing to supply capital at lower returns. Similarly, MFIs, which align their business objectives with the requirements of the social segment they cater to, would be seen as stable and less risky and would certainly prove attractive to the investors than the ones that provide extraordinary but unstable returns. In this context, I would like to draw your attention to Malegam Committee's recommendation of 'creation of one or more domestic social capital funds'.

Customer protection and responsible finance

Responsible finance is the most important lesson from the current episode. Given the vulnerability of their customers, MFIs need to be more mindful of their needs and capabilities. Chasing customers and sometimes, as it is alleged, poaching them from other segments of microfinance and loading them with more debt would lead to issues such as wrong selection of borrowers, over-indebtedness and eventually delinquencies.

MFIs, therefore, need to revisit their business model and ensure more responsible financing. This would require them to adopt approaches to select their borrowers with diligence, ensure that their lending is not leading to over-indebtedness and be more human and ethical in their recovery methods.

Building enabling organisational climate

There is a strong need to build good practices within the institutions and encourage organisational culture which values customer protection and well-being. The frontline staff need to be educated about the organisational values and social mission so as not to get swayed by the short-term performance targets. Further, the organisational culture should nurture values like honesty, respect, transparency and so on.

Self-regulation

Events in the last few years have indicated that the 'for-profit' model of microfinance, where there is a heightened emphasis on rapid scale and high profitability, has not been very successful in meeting the social objectives nor has such a model been sustainable. While regulatory responses are evolving to address these issues, a degree of self-regulation is a must in building robust and efficient microfinance institutions going forward. Self-regulation would require putting in place a code of conduct that would allow for a reputation-building mechanism and adherence to best governance practices. Recognition of two SROs by the RBI is a step in this direction.

Transparency

With the customer base being largely from the low-income group whose financial knowledge and sophistication cannot be taken for granted, it is incumbent upon the MFIs to be transparent about the interest charged and the total cost to be borne by the customers. It was reported that some MFIs not only charged excessive interest, but had also loaded many other components to the overall cost. MFIs need to remind themselves that while dealing with vulnerable sections of the society, the argument of caveat emptor does not always hold good.

Credit information

Absence of comprehensive credit information has been a handicap in the development of the sector. The multiplicity of financing institutions acting independently increases the level of information asymmetry among them, which may lead to delays in sanction, double financing and so on. The building up, and sharing, of credit information will help in enhancing synergies among the various institutions and also ensure avoidance of multiple financing and consequent over-indebtedness. In this context, let me add that as per Credit Information Companies (Regulation) Act, 2005, NBFCs, as credit institutions, were required to be members of at least one credit information company (CIC) (currently there are four CICs). However, to overcome the problem of incomplete/inaccurate credit information, pros and cons of certain possible alternatives were discussed in the 'Report of the Committee to Recommend Data Format for Furnishing of Credit information to Credit Information Companies' (chairman: Shri Aditya Puri) constituted by the RBI. Based on the alternatives suggested RBI has now mandated all credit institutions including NBFCs to become members of all CICs. What is also of significance is that credit data regarding all the borrowers should be furnished to the CICs accurately and in time and full use should be made of the database of CICs while extending credit, to guard against adverse selection and over-indebtedness. There are indications that MFIs have been increasingly making use of CIC databases. The recently introduced mandatory membership of all CICs by all credit institutions and use of such database would lead to improvement in asset quality and reduced incidents of overlending.

Diversification

It was observed that MFIs found a few geographies more profitable than others and against conventional wisdom which advocates diversification ran in droves to the same geographies, with southern region showing significant concentration of SHGs and MFIs. Excessive proliferation of entities in a few regions has led to immense and, sometimes, unhealthy competition leading to perverse practices. Learning from the recent episode, the MFIs are reorganising themselves and are spreading into hitherto untapped regions. Diversification helps not only MFIs in withstanding any region-specific shocks but also help customers at large by spreading the microfinance across the country. It is comforting to learn[7] that due to concerted regulatory efforts backed by the industry initiatives, the MFI coverage is quite diversified across the country. MFIs now cover thirty-two states/union territories with following coverage (gross loan portfolio): south, 29 per cent; east, 29 per cent; north, 21 per cent; and west, 21 per cent.

Improvising the business model: reducing costs

Microfinance is a labour-intensive sector involving significant delivery costs. While the entities could build these costs into their services and charge the customer, which many in fact did, the more efficient way of protecting or increasing one's margins is reducing the operational costs by enhancing efficiency and leveraging technology. MFIs should not pass on their operational inefficiencies to clients in the form of prices that are far higher than they need to be. Considering the profile of the borrowers who are poor, to whom even a small increase in rates could make a lot of difference, MFIs should strive to build more cost-effective and efficient delivery models to serve their clientele better.

Credit rating of MFIs

The rating of MFIs assumes critical importance as MFIs are sourcing financing from banks and other institutions. There are several MFIs in the country and their rating helps the lenders to choose the right ones. Further, such positive discrimination helps the better managed MFIs in reducing their borrowing costs and also acts as a dis-incentivising factor for not so well managed ones.

Moving beyond finance

The poorest sections of the poor require considerable handholding in terms of input supply, training, technical support, market linkages and so on. The formation and nurturing of such groups require providing of not only financial services but also institutional development services, all of which would require a greater role for the MFIs. In order to achieve its full potential in empowering the poor, microfinance should become an integral part of the financial sector and MFIs need to play a larger developmental role.

Summing up

At a time when financial inclusion is at the centre stage of the regulatory landscape, the last-mile connectivity provided by the MFIs has to be leveraged upon, to include the hitherto financially excluded. There is a great opportunity of building long-term sustainable business around microfinance. Balancing the interests of the vulnerable borrowers as also the viability of microfinance institutions, through enabling and effective regulation and also higher degree of self-regulation coupled with alignment of business objectives with that of social objectives, could help the microfinance sector to survive, sustain, flourish and also help achieve inclusive growth. MFIs should identify their unique role in the financial system and should put in place robust governance standards to balance the dual objectives of social utility and financial sustainability

Notes

1 Updated and modified version of the keynote address by Mr. Anand Sinha, deputy governor, Reserve Bank of India, at FICCI's Workshop on 'Strengthening Microfinance Institutions (MFIs): Good Governance and Strategic People Practices' on 23 April 2012 at Mumbai.

   Inputs provided by Ms. Deepali Pant Joshi, Mr. C D Srinivasan, Mr. A K Misra, Ms. Tuli Roy and Mr. Jayakumar Yarasi are gratefully acknowledged.
2 1 crore = 10 millions.
3 RBI circular dated 7 February 2014.
4 Report on Status of microfinance in India 2013–14, NABARD.
5 Micrometer (Issue 12), MFIN.
6 BIS Paper No. 62, January 2012.
7 Micrometer (Issue 12), MFIN.

References

Bank for International Settlements, (2012), 'Financial Sector Regulation for Growth, Equity and Stability', BIS Papers No. 62.

CGAP-Consultative Group to Assist the Poor, (2004), 'Key Principles for Microfinance'.

Hulme, D., and Mosley, P., (1996), 'Finance against Poverty', volumes 1 and 2, London: Routledge.

Joshi, Deepali Pant, (2011), 'Microfinance for Macro Change', New Delhi: Gyan Books.

Littlefield, E., Hashemi, S. and Morduch, J., (2003), 'Is Microfinance an Effective Strategy to Reach the Millennium Development Goals?', Focus Note No. 24. Washington: CGAP-Consultative Group to Assist the Poor.

Moses, J.S., Rajesh, R., Prasad, G., Kumar, N. and Kumar, N., (2012), 'Microfinance in India – Progress and Problems'.

National Bank for Agriculture and Rural Development (NABRD), 'Status of Microfinance in India 2010–11 and 2013–14'.

Reddy, Y.V., (2011), 'Microfinance Industry in India: Some Thoughts', *Economic and Political Weekly* Vol. XLVI, No. 41.

Simanowitz, A., and Brody, A., (2004), 'Realising the Potential of Microfinance', *id21 Insights*, December, Issue 51.

Srinivasan, N., (2012), Microfinance India: State of the Sector Report 2011. New Delhi: Sage Publications.

United Nations, (2005), 'Building Inclusive Financial Sectors to Achieve the Millennium Development Goals', International Year of Microcredit 2005 Concept Paper, New York.

Chapter 4

Mobile technology in microfinance

Empowering the unreachable

Shubham Goswami

As one of the key transformative factors in a globalising world, the advances in information and communication technology (ICT) have transformed people's everyday life and how people interact and interconnect with each other, communities, states and markets. The so-called ICT-revolution, as noted and debated by scholars, politicians, and policy makers, has had an inordinate effect on economies and societies, leading to what has been termed a 'global shift'. This suggests fundamental alteration to the global political economy. There is a movement from an industry-based international economy to one that is information and knowledge-based.

Belief in the potential of mobile phones to help meet the financial service needs of the poor has been driven by rapid expansion of networks into previously unserved regions and communities of developing countries during the past decade. Unlike previous technologies, mobile technology is inducing changes that are not limited to people's relationships with the outside world, but also how people now view themselves. The major impact of the mobile is that it is making each individual addressable. The impact has been most noticeable in the least developed countries of sub-Saharan Africa and South Asia, where existing fixed-line infrastructure was particularly weak and underdeveloped. As mobile phones are becoming increasingly part of the everyday lives of the poor, it is argued that they have potential to become a low-cost accessible account or delivery channel for financial information, services and transactions, thus facilitating innovations including micropayments (m-payments), electronic money (e-money) and a mobile banking channel (m-banking).

In the year 2009, the Consultative Group to Assist the Poor (CGAP) teamed up with the Global System for Mobile

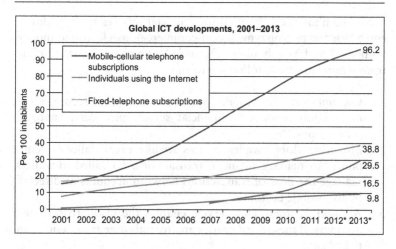

Figure 4.1 ICT Development Index, 2013

Communications (GSM) Association (GSMA) (a global trade association for the mobile communications industry) and McKinsey (a global management consulting firm) to measure the global market for financial services delivered via mobile phones (mobile money) in 147 developing countries. This is the first study of mobile money and the unbanked – those without access to formal financial services – estimated to be almost four billion worldwide. Based on the analysis, one billion people do not have a bank account but do have a mobile phone. According to a study by GSMA (2013), of the 2.5 billion people in the world who still lack access to the financial system, 1.7 billion already have a mobile phone. Seventy per cent of service providers are planning to increase investments in mobile money in 2014 (Figure 4.1).

Financial services over mobile

Mobile money refers to a suite of financial services offered through mobile phones and other handheld mobile devices. These services can include person-to-person transfer of funds such as domestic and international remittances, person-to-business payments for the purchase of a range of goods and services and mobile banking, through which customers can access their bank accounts, pay bills or deposit and withdraw funds.

Mobile phones can be used for financial services in three different ways: for micropayments (m-commerce), as electronic money (e-money) and as a banking channel. Value chain for the mobile transactions can be in following formats:

1   *Communication*: Mobile operator can offer secure communication services to financial service providers, enabling transactions.
2   *M-wallet*: Mobile wallet services are like a real wallet – a 'container' to manage financial transactions. So called m-wallets manage the flow of transactions between accounts as directed by the mobile customer.
3   *Account hosting*: This service enables the client to host the accounts of these third parties and to authorsze transactions on their behalf.
4   *Banking*: Beyond making and receiving payments, this service enables the end user to manage on-demand savings balances and potentially use a broader range of products that allow for safe storage of value, as well as credit and insurance (see Table 4.1).

Table 4.1 Value chain for mobile services (role of mobile operator in providing financial services)

Mobile operator in financial services	Telecom sector		Banking sector	
	Communication	M-wallet services	Account hosting	Account issuance
Strengths	Established wireless network, SIM security	User interface control	Real-time prepaid platform	Large customer base
Value to mobile operator	Driving additional data traffic	Customer churn reduction	Additional service revenues	Diversification
Risk to operator	Network security threat	Transaction security	Accounting error, breach in client data secrecy	Investment risks and application of regulations

Advantage for all

Service provider advantage

1   Better medium to reach remote and poor areas
2   24/7 availability on mobile network
3   Demographic changes – including a greater number of younger consumers coming into the market and greater mobility, at least within countries – will be favourable for the adoption of mobile-based services
4   Increase in customer reach and the added cash float available to the bank
5   The ability to advance funds into remote areas and have regular repayments that do not significantly inconvenience the user
6   Alternate medium for promoting schemes and educating for plans and services.

Operator advantage

1   New revenue from services offered; mobile operators can make big profits
2   Already has well-established network infrastructure
3   Mobile phone operators already know how to handle cash transactions for customers (airtime)
4   A significant increase in text messaging revenues and a large drop in customer churn
5   Promotion investments
6   Opportunity to diversify the services to customer.

User advantage

1   Increasing reach of mobile communication in rural areas
2   Poor are familiar with mobile phones
3   An opportunity to become engaged in the formal banking sector
4   Increases the efficiency of service delivery to the poor (e.g. weather information, market prices), or opens opportunities for new services (e.g. tracking of diseases)
5   Improving efficiency of markets, promoting investment, reducing risk from disasters and contributing to empowerment

6   Facilitate and reduce the costs of remittances; there is reduced
     cost on transport and access (no need to travel long distances
     for money transaction).

Some global initiatives

1   **M-PESA:** M-PESA programme in Kenya is one of the pre-
     mier examples of mobile facilitated money management.
     In March 2007, Kenya's largest mobile network operator,
     Safaricom (part of the Vodafone Group), launched M-PESA,
     an innovative payment service for the unbanked. 'Pesa' is
     the Swahili word for cash; the 'M' is for mobile. Since its
     commercial launch, M-PESA has achieved substantial scale
     along several key metrics. Nearly seven million customers
     have registered with the service. An average of 150 million
     Ksh (USD1.96 million) is transferred through M-PESA per
     day, mostly in small amounts averaging just over 1,500 Ksh
     (USD20) per transaction. So far, the system has handled over
     130 billion Ksh (USD1.7 billion). Services are distributed
     through 8,650 retail outlets countrywide (2,262 outlets in
     March 2008).

2   **WIZZIT:** In South Africa, customers of WIZZIT or MTN
     Banking use their phone as the primary way of accessing their
     bank account. MTN, a mobile network operator, is partnered
     with Standard Bank, and WIZZIT is partnered with the South
     African Bank of Athens. Customers load cash into their bank
     accounts at branches or automatic teller machines (ATMs), or
     through a direct deposit of salary, and can use their mobile
     phone to purchase airtime and make payments, transfers and
     balance inquiries.

3   **Celpay:** Celpay is one of the mobile banking companies that
     combine mobile payments solutions for consumers and cor-
     porates. Celpay was presented *Wall Street Journal*'s Europe
     innovation award in 2003. Celpay has operations in Zambia
     and the Democratic Republic of Congo and is soon to launch
     operations in Tanzania. Celpay's technology platform enables
     small, medium and corporate businesses alike easy mobile
     access to features such as account management, bill payments
     and mobile authentication.

4   **SMART Money:** 'SMART Money' service in Philippines by
     SMART communication which has teamed up with Banco de

Oro Unibank (country's largest local bank in terms of assets, loans and deposits) is a re-loadable payment card that may either be accessed through a smart mobile phone or a MasterCard powered card, similar to a debit/cash card. With SMART Money, a customer can make purchases, pay bills, buy airtime, transfer money, withdraw money, shop online and so on. SMART established mobile financial service platform linking local bank accounts to mobile handsets, providing significant convenience for banking consumers.

5 **G-CASH:** In the Philippines, Globe Telecom lets customers load cash (or G-cash) onto their mobile phones at partner merchants or Globe outlets. For one million customers, G-cash is real value that can be stored and withdrawn as hard cash, transferred to a friend across town or across the world or used to pay for products at restaurants and stores.

6 **True Money:** Thailand's True Money is a success story that merits closer attention. Launched in 2005, True Money is now used by six million customers, and the system processes over USD900 million in electronic payments and 120 million transactions per year. Marketed as a way to 'top up, pay, transfer and withdraw', today True Money consists of an e-wallet that can be loaded by cash card (like scratch card), bank account or credit card and a network of 8,000 bill payment agents known as True Money Express (TMX). Customers use the e-wallet and TMX agent network primarily to buy airtime, pay for True Group service, pay bills and, to a much lesser extent, transfer money.

7 **WU mobile money transfer:** In October 2007, Western Union (WU) announced plans to introduce mobile money transfer service with the GSM Association, a global trade association representing more than 700 mobile operators in 218 countries and covering 2.5 billion mobile subscribers. Its aim is to provide mobile financial services ranging from text notifications associated with WU cash delivery services to phone-based remittance options. WU's mobile money transfer service offering will connect its core money transfer platform to m-bank or m-wallet platforms provided by mobile operators and/or locally regulated financial institutions. Some of mobile operators to participate in this initiative are Globe Telecom (Philippines), Smart Communications (Philippines), Bharti Airtel (India) and Orascom Telecom (operators in six countries).

8   **WING:** In January 2009, Australia and New Zealand Banking Group Limited launched a mobile payments business in Cambodia, which targets unbanked customers known as WING. WING's unstructured supplementary service data (USSD)-based service will allow customers to save, make purchases, transfer money to both WING and non-WING users and perform a range of other financial services – all through mobile phones. Since WING account numbers do not have to be tied to a customer's mobile phone number, the service is also available to people who do not own phones.

9   **Zap:** In February 2009, international mobile telecom provider Zain has launched a new package of mobile banking services in direct competition with the M-PESA service operated by its main rival Safaricom. Zap, as the new service is called, allows customers to send and receive money through Zain outlets as well as to pay utilities bills, interact with their bank and perform other financial operations such as international money transfers. Launched in conjunction with Standard Chartered and Citigroup, Zain plans to bring mobile banking to over 100 million people in East Africa. In January 2010, Zain has announced the expansion of 'Zap', its mobile commerce service, to African nations of Niger and Sierra Leone and in the boundaries of a full commercial pilot in Malawi.

10 **Easypaisa:** It is the m-banking service in Pakistan by Telenor Group and Tameer Bank, which went live in October 2009. A total of 3,000 agents have been set up to handle both bill payments and remittances. Currently Easypaisa is starting with utility bill payments with many other products to be available soon. As of January 2010, 500,000 Easypaisa transactions had been processed in the previous four months.

11 **MMU Programme:** In February 2009, the GSMA, which represents the interests of the worldwide mobile communications industry, and the Bill & Melinda Gates Foundation announced an innovative programme called the Mobile Money for the Unbanked (MMU) which will expand the availability of financial services to millions of people in the developing world through mobile phones. Supported by a USD12.5 million grant from the foundation, the programme will work with mobile operators, banks, microfinance institutions, government and development organisations to encourage the expansion of reliable, affordable mobile financial services to the unbanked. It is estimated there will be three billion mobile subscribers in the world by

2010. The programme will support approximately twenty projects in developing countries, focusing on Africa, Asia and Latin America, with the goal of reaching twenty million previously unbanked people with mobile financial services by 2012.

Mobile in India

The wireless market in India has been growing at breakneck speed on year-to-year basis over the last few years. The Indian mobile market has continued to witness rapid increase in its subscriber base largely due to declining mobile tariffs (the pay-per-second plans with unlimited publicity done for them leave no stone unturned in tempting the end users) and availability of low-cost handsets in the country. The costs of mobile handsets begin at Rs 700 (around USD16). The telecom sector witnessed a decline in the number of subscribers during the year 2012–13. At the end of the financial year 2012–13, the overall telecom subscriber base was 898.02 million as compared to 951.34 million at the end of the financial year 2011–12 (TRAI, 2013 annual report). The total subscriber base of wireless services has grown from 33.69 million in March 2004 to 867.80 million in March 2013 (see Figure 4.2).

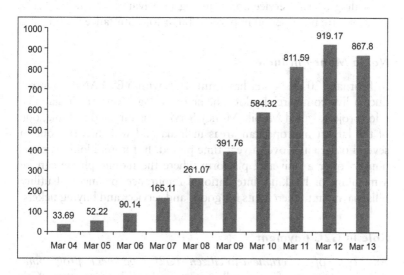

Figure 4.2 Wireless subscribers (in millions)

Source: Telecom Regulatory Authority of India (TRAI) report 2012–13.

Some Indian M-initiatives

Eko with State Bank of India

On 23 February 2009, Eko, a low-cost payment infrastructure to enable instant small value financial transactions over a mobile phone, with State Bank of India (SBI) launched the SBI Mini Savings Bank Account at Uttam Nagar, New Delhi (SBI has appointed Eko Aspire Foundation as its business correspondent). SBI Mini Savings Bank Account holders can do a host of financial transactions including deposit and withdrawal from their accounts through their mobile phones at various SBI Eko customer service points. The CGAP supports Eko in the creation of an agent network to deliver savings and remittance services to new customers for SBI. Agent locations are being set up in Delhi and rural locations in two states – Bihar and Uttar Pradesh. Delhi–Bihar and Delhi–Uttar Pradesh are part of major remittance corridors in India.

CGAP and Eko have completed the first phase of the project, which was primarily focused on developing a business model and making improvements on Eko user interface. In addition, since March 2009, Eko has opened 2,000 no-frills savings accounts and is serving these customers through an agent network of over 140 points in urban low-income slum areas of Delhi. CGAP and Eko are now working on scaling up the service and bringing in private investment. Agent locations are being set up in parts of Bihar for remittance from Delhi.

Nokia Money in India

In February 2010, Nokia has teamed up with YES BANK to introduce a live commercial pilot scheme of Nokia Money in India. The pilot project, called Mobile Money Services, is initiated in Pune, one of the largest metropolitan areas in India and will then roll out to several other cities over a year time period. In future, Nokia is planning to offer a universal platform where the mobile phone can be a medium for banking, international remittance, payment of utility bills, payment to merchants for goods and services and buying tickets.

Role in G2C payment

Any type of government-to-citizen (G2C) payment programme includes social transfers as well as wage and pension payments. With appropriate experimentation, these payments have the potential to become a vehicle for extending financial inclusion and improving the welfare of poor people. *G2C payment is an opportunity to increase access to financial services. Roughly 155 million poor people around the world receive regular payments from their governments, but less than 25 per cent receive them via a bank account through which they can save, withstand financial shocks and build assets.*

More than 45 million people received a payment under the National Rural Employment Guarantee Act (NREGA) in 2008.[1] Recipients can choose from four ways to receive payment: post office savings account, bank account, village officials and, in the state of Andhra Pradesh, electronic prepaid account accessed via smart cards issued by two technology firms – Financial Inclusion Network and Operations (FINO) and A Little World (ALW). Recipients using smart cards can withdraw NREGA payments at agents in 20 to 60 minutes, including travel and wait time. This is twice as fast as the time recipients take to make withdrawals from the post office and ten times faster than making a withdrawal from a bank branch. Some other players in the field include Suvidha Beam, Paymate, and mChek, who provide similar services. Following is the introduction to solution provided by ZMF and FINO in social transfer in Andhra Pradesh.

ZMF

ZERO Microfinance and Savings Support Foundation (ZMF) has been a pioneer in the field of financial inclusion space as a business correspondent to twenty-five banks in India including the SBI. ZMF helps banks increase their outreach in 'Rural Unbanked India' through its customer service points working as village branches using the branchless banking technology. ALW is the technology provider for all the banks who have engaged ZMF as a business correspondent. ALW provides the technology as a service to banks under its brand 'ZERO'. ZMF creates the last-mile operations network in villages, under pre-defined service agreements with banks and front-ends the delivery of full-featured transactional services on behalf of banks for financial inclusion on the ground.

As per a typical agreement between ZMF and a bank, ZMF's scope of services includes:

1   enrolment of customers for no-frills zero-balance savings accounts and other account types that may be specified by the bank;
2   enrolling, training and equipping of customer service points in villages to provide various kinds of transaction services including, but not limited to, cash deposit, cash withdrawal, transfer of money, payment of utility bills, disbursal of loans, collection of loan installments and cashless payments at local and remote merchant establishments;
3   engaging the customer service points to provide enrolment services for opening no-frills account;
4   third-party cash collection;
5   cashless payments at local and remote merchant establishments;
6   management of cash;
7   lending activities on behalf of the bank (as an MFI) and other services as may be advised by the bank in writing to ZMF, and which ZMF agrees to perform.

The ZERO platform is based on new-generation mobile phones and fingerprint authentication, which converts low-cost NFC (near field communication) mobile phones with large storage capacities, as a secure, self-sufficient bank branch, with biometrics-based customer identification (ID), for customer enrolments for no-frills accounts and all types of transactions in the village, with the local customer service point operator acting as a teller. Existing mobile communication networks are used for all transaction uploads, downloads and application updates. The platform employs biometrics-based ID, radio frequency identification smart cards, and NFC mobile phones as acceptance and enabling devices [with merchants and field forces of microfinance institutions (MFIs) and as cashless ATMs]. As evident from the platform's applications, ZMF also works closely with government departments so that benefits reach in time to the rightful beneficiaries for government programmes like NREGA, social security pensions (SSPs), scholarships, housing grants and so on.

To deliver NREGA wages and SSPs via smart cards in Andhra Pradesh, ZMF staff carries a single mobile phone along with a fingerprint reader capable of communicating with the phone via Bluetooth. ZMF staff record most client details through the use of paper-based forms, with only the beneficiary's fingerprints, photo and voice recording of the person's name being captured digitally. Bank accounts are opened for all such government beneficiaries by ZMF.

ZMF also helps government departments to automate processes such as attendance and job Demand for NREGA, using the beneficiary fingerprint authentication and by ascertaining the global positioning system coordinates of the work sites. ZERO platform has been built as a cost-effective method for banks to extend all their products and services such as savings, loans, recurring deposits and so on to customers. The platform is also built as an easy-to-use option for illiterate and semi-literate population in villages, with features like graphical user interface and voice guidance. About four million customers have been enrolled under the financial inclusion programme. Multiple state governments are disbursing their NREGA wages and SSPs using the ZERO system at the customer service points of ZMF.

FINO

FINO is an Indian technology multibank-promoted company, providing smart card–based multiapplication solutions to the 'unbanked' in banking, microfinance, insurance and government sectors, primarily located in rural and semi-urban areas of India. Gemalto (leading microfinance technology solution provider), along with FINO and multiple banks under FINO, has introduced smart card technology with biometric authentication on smart cards to accelerate the development of micro-banking in India since June 2007. FINO works on national priority projects (NREGA, Rashtriya Swastya Bima Yojana, SSP, etc.), similar to ZMF in Andhra Pradesh. Before processing payments, FINO collects fingerprint and other KYC (know your customer) data from each beneficiary. Payments are delivered on behalf of banks by local agents using a biometric-enabled transaction-processing device. FINO provides biometric smart cards to each beneficiary.

In August 2009, FINO-MITRA, a comprehensive package of mobile-enabled banking solutions to address the needs of microfinance sector or the huge unbanked population, was introduced. FINO-MITRA enables enrolment as well as banking transactions through the use of mobile technology, increasing capability at reduced costs. The company has tie-ups with fourteen banks, twenty MFIs and three insurance companies for providing smart cards to rural customers and to the unbanked population in urban areas. The financial institutions include Corporation Bank, Union Bank of India, Punjab National Bank, Sewa Bank, ICICI Bank, ICICI Lombard, ICICI Prudential, Axis Bank, ING Vysya Bank and Life Insurance Corporation of India. FINO enrolled more than six million people within three years. With the help of biometric smart cards and business correspondents, FINO enrolled 25 million customers.

Impact and empowerment

Observing the impact on poor people using mobile financial services, especially an impact study by CGAP in November 2008 of M-PESA in Kenya, reveals some facts related to these services in developing countries. There are two types of users for mobile financial services: urban senders, who are mostly men, and rural recipients, who are mostly women. M-PESA services are used as a storage mechanism by both the banked and the unbanked. The product concept is very simple: an M-PESA customer can use his or her mobile phone to move money quickly, securely and across great distances directly to another mobile phone user. The customer does not need to have a bank account, but registers with Safaricom for an M-PESA account. Customers turn cash into e-money at Safaricom dealers, and then follow simple instructions on their phones to make payments through their M-PESA accounts; the system provides money transfers as banks do in the developed world.

Some other facts for the impact study are that the income of rural recipients increased by up to 30 per cent since they started using M-PESA. Such an increase is the result of money being sent more frequently. By breaking up their transfers, urban migrants end up remitting more money back home. Also, rural recipients save money when retrieving cash. They no longer need to pay for transport costs to urban centres, where most of the money transfer services are located. Instead, they make the withdrawal directly from Bukura, a place in Kenya. Such an increase is vitally important for the rural recipients, who depend heavily on remittances for their livelihoods. M-PESA empowers rural women by making it easier for them to solicit funds from their husbands and other contacts in the city. This has increased the financial autonomy of the women and has made them less dependent on their husbands for their livelihoods.

Rapid adoption and frequent use of m-services engendered a variety of positive outcomes, as well as unintended consequences. This service releases money flows in developing countries and allows such flows to penetrate rural areas where cash is difficult to access. Also, as these services reached a critical mass of users, network effects began to develop. Each new m-service user has the potential to tap into an extensive network of potential remitters and lenders. Many of the rural residents are realising this potential and using this network to increase their income.

Challenges and recommendations

A major hurdle in scaling up of the operations is to find the right business model for commercial viability of all stakeholders in the ecosystem, for example, customer service point operators, banks and mobile financial service provider. Some other issues are like mobile banking applications are not yet interoperable: In most countries, it is not yet possible to send money between any two mobile phones easily and at low cost. Mobile phone payments may not conform to international security standards. Mobile phone banking may not be easy to use for illiterate and older users because most mobile banking interfaces and processes require literacy. The regulatory environment is also unclear. Kenyan banks are threatened by the low cost of the M-PESA service, and are arguing that the service should be frozen until there are rules to address money laundering and the compensation of clients in the event of losses. Further adaptation and training will be required for all customers, particularly illiterate and older customers, to adopt this system. Some of the usage barriers for urban users include failed transactions and inability to get help from service providers. For rural users, barriers include cash float shortages and public trust in the system. Some recommendations to improve the performance in this sector are as follows:

1   **Work with partners:** Service providers have to constantly work with all the partner institutions to arrive at the right commercial models in all specific geographies. Training and awareness

programme can be conducted by implementer; road shows, plays, camps and so on will enhance the grass-roots intermediatories and people to participate.

2   **Treat pilot as real:** Each project has to be tested, even in the pilot level, on dimensions like outreach, technology reliability and project replicability to other regions. Always provide real data/condition to pilot project because many projects, successful at pilot level, are not able to sustain in real implementation.

3   **Track profitability:** Strong business model for sustainability of operator and service provider is required. We also need to track the profitability for banks. Governments and donors that are linking social protection and banking should build a rigorous analysis from the start, not just on impact for the poor, but also on whether the business works for banks.

4   **Diversification of usage:** So far, most mobile banking services offer only a limited range of products. Until customers pay for a range of financial services through their phone, the channel is unlikely to make money. So customers should be encouraged to diversify the usage of mobile phone to a large range of services.

5   **Role of mobile operators:** Mobile operators have some core strengths; they have an established network of physical retail outlets, compared to banks, which can support cash-in and cash-out services, as well as perform KYC procedures. In emerging markets, mobile network operators have strong brands backed by mass marketing capacity that has reached lower-income people in ways that banks often have not. Despite their advantages, mobile operators also have some capacity gaps when it comes to offering a mobile payment service. For example, maintaining the integrity of a payment system demands strong internal controls at the customer front-end. But mobile operators have a comparative advantage in the creation of a mobile payments service. Their existing customer base includes a large number of unbanked people, and hence they can convert users among their existing base rather than needing to acquire new customers. A bank, on the other hand, would have to reach beyond established customer segments to offer mobile banking, justifying it on incremental revenues.

6   **Impact studies/research work:** It is also evident that research linking technical solutions to the requirements of unbanked users in developing countries is largely absent. In particular, little research was identified arising from within developing

countries related to the development of appropriate user interfaces and user environments. A high level of practitioner involvement and a high level of positive interaction between the research community and the mobile phone industry are needed.

7 **User interfaces:** Easy user interfaces should be designed with local language support for the end user. Voice-based system/ multimedia can be used for initial training for the system.

8 **Sustainable connectivity and power alternatives:** Alternate sources of energy, like wind and solar energy, should be used to ensure sustainable connectivity.

9 **Network management:** Proper management of the service delivery agent is key for the success of any project. Identification and hiring of agents and installation of technical infrastructure are needed for agent operations. Further, training agent staff that will operate correspondent systems at stores, which includes both technical (systems functionalities) and business training (characteristics of financial products and services) is necessary. Proper support like help-desk and remote assistance to retail stores through private branch exchange to solve problems related to systems operation, technical support and on-site repair and replacement of malfunctioning equipment are some of important issues to be closely considered by the service provider.

Conclusions and avenues for future work

The mobile communication–based platform can be easily deployed for the services like biometric identity, cash deposit, cash withdrawals, money transfer, NREGA/pensions, microcredit, micro-insurance, cashless payment, utility payments and self-help group utilities like disbursals, repayment and record of attendance. Much more remains to be done to realise the potential of mobile financial services and mobile payments in developing countries. Current success stories involve money transfers as opposed to financial services with long-term benefits, such as savings. Initial experiences with branchless banking channels point at three areas for further attention. First, policy makers should think broadly about ways to balance improved access with appropriate regulation and oversight. Second, further study is needed to understand what key design features will render technology channels comfortable, convenient and trustworthy to poor customers, and thereby generate the transaction volumes required to make them profitable for banks. Finally, MFIs must evaluate the challenges and opportunities created by technology channels.

To successfully apply technology solutions to improve financial access on a large scale, a number of things need to happen: there must be multiple physical retail access points, low-cost and tailored services, simple and clear product disclosures and sound providers. All these can emerge only with changes in institutional cultures, consumer behaviors and a common set of regulatory approaches. Solving these problems requires having a deep understanding of poor customers' options and preferences, providing risk-taking incentives for commercial players, sensitising central bank authorities to new regulatory approaches and finding creative ways for everyone in the system to benefit from these services. While security concerns about cash crime will continue to drive the adoption of electronic transaction channels, the rise of electronic crime will affect consumer confidence and test the risk management of financial providers. Internet browsing via mobile phones will reduce costs of financial transactions and enable new players to offer financial services. New business models will emerge in partnerships with a wide range of stakeholders, from grass-roots organisations to local businesses, to telecommunications companies and to governments.

Note

1 Ministry of Rural Development Report 2009.

References

'2013 State of the Industry', GSMA (Global System for Mobile Communications) (February 2014), Mobile World Congress.

'Advancing Financial Access for the World's Poor', CGAP (Consultative Group to Assist the Poor), Annual Report 2009.

'Annual Report 2012–13', Telecom Regulatory Authority of India (TRAI).

Datta, K. (16 February, 2010), 'Nokia Launches Mobile Money Transfer Platform', *Economic Times*.

Duncombe, Richard and Richard Boateng, (2009), 'Mobile Phones and Financial Services in Developing Countries: A Review of Concepts, Methods, Issues, Evidence and Future Research Directions', *Third World Quarterly*, Vol. 30, No. 7, pp. 1237–1258.

Eko Aspire Foundation, 'SBI Mini Saving Account – Pilot Project', Available at: http://www.eko.co.in/pilot.html. Accessed 20 February 2010.

'GSMA and Gates Foundation Partner to Expand Availability of Financial Services through Mobile Phones', Bill & Melinda Gates Foundation (17 February 2009), Press Release.

Ivatury, Gautam and Mark Pickens, (2006), 'Mobile Phones for Microfinance', *CGAP Brief*.

Lokanath, Panda, (2009), 'ZERO MASS Foundation-Development Initiatives', *i4D-Innovation for Development*, pp. 32–33.

Morawczynski, Olga and Mark Pickens, (2009), 'Poor People Using Mobile Financial Services: Observations on Customer Usage and Impact from M-PESA', *CGAP Brief*.

Pickens, Mark, (2009), 'Window on the Unbanked: Mobile Money in the Philippines', *CGAP Brief*.

SMART-Money, Available at: http://smart.com.ph/money/. Accessed 22 February 2010.

WING, Available at: http://www.wingmoney.com/. Accessed 25 February 2010.

Zero Mass Foundation, Available at: http://www.zero-mass.org/. Accessed 20 February 2010.

Chapter 5

ICT in microfinance

A case study of microfinance banks in Pakistan

Umar Rafi

Background

Pakistan is a highly populated country, with a large poor population, a well-developed and regulated banking sector, a broad pool of professionally qualified workforce and a decent enough telecommunications infrastructure with the ninth largest mobile phone user base in the world (larger than all European countries, other than Germany and Russia). Pakistan's microfinance sector is amongst the fastest growing globally, expanding 47 per cent in 2007. Pakistan is thus simultaneously encouragingly hi-tech and discouragingly poor. It has been argued, anecdotally, that more Pakistanis have cell phones than toothbrushes. These reasons make Pakistan a test case for how information and communicatin technology (ICT) can be used in microfinance. Appendix A5.1 shows the total population of Pakistan to be around 160 million. Out of these, according to the Pakistan Microfinance Network, 27 million people – a population nearly equal to that of Canada – is the target market for microfinance banks (MFBs) in the country.

This chapter will address the impact of ICT in microfinance, using Pakistan's MFB sector as an example. In doing so, it will also provide the readers an introduction to the microfinance sector of Pakistan. The suggestions in this chapter can be used as a set of best practices for MFBs anywhere in the world that may be making ICT decisions in the future. This chapter is divided into the following parts:

1   *Pakistan's microfinance sector*: a brief history of Pakistan's microfinance sector, as well as its current state
2   *Conventional ICT landscape*: how ICT is used by conventional banks

Financial dynamics of microfinance

Before going into the details of Pakistan's financial services industry (FSI) and microfinance sectors, it will be useful to understand the current status of microfinance across the world: statistically speaking, 40 per cent – 2.6 billion out of the total population of 6.5 billion – of the world lives on less than USD2/day,[1] which is the price of a cup of coffee in many wealthy countries. The poor of the world normally do not have reliable 9-to-5 jobs. They rely on inconsistent, labour-intensive jobs to earn a living. They work in the informal economy, for example, selling cheese and milk in the market (in Mexico, a country wealthier than many countries in Africa and Asia, this is over 60 per cent of the total economy[2]). Thus, the vulnerability related to living on less than USD2/day lies not only in the smallness of the amount, but also in the fact the USD2 is not available on a regular basis. This leaves the poor with limited options for gaining reliable and periodic access to funds and loans from banks. Due to this, they are forced to rely on moneylenders, offering extremely high interest rates, for daily survival. These moneylenders work in the form of a cartel, and charge interest rates of 10 per cent or more a day (known as 10 plus 1), that is, someone borrows ten units of currency in the morning and has to pay back eleven units at the end of the day. The cumulative annual interest rates, in such situations, can range between 300 per cent and 3,000 per cent.[3]

Obstacles to the growth of MFBs

Figure 5.1 indicates that in 1997, around 13 million people had access to microcredit worldwide. By 2000, the number had doubled to approximately 26 million, and by 2006, it had grown ten-fold to around 130 million. As of 2009, more than 150 million people in

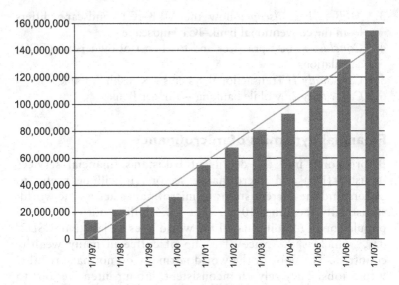

Figure 5.1 Growth of worldwide microfinance customer base

Source: Innovative Solutions to Global Poverty, available at www.unitus.com. Accessed 12 January 2010.

the world have access to microfinance. While this may seem like a very large amount, it is only 6 per cent of the total of the 2.6 billion poor, living on less than USD2/day.

According to Unitus[4] – a global microfinance *accelerator* – the total market for microfinance in the world is estimated to be USD50 billion. The worldwide rate of payment of microfinance loans is 97.5 per cent. The above statistics indicate that, by all standards of market growth and market opportunity, microfinance is a potential high growth market and a high opportunity market.

However, as of 2006, after 25–30 years of successful implementation of microfinance, out of the 3,000 active microfinance providers [MFPs – a blanket term used in this chapter to refer to MFBs/ microfinance institutions (MFIs)/non-governmental organisations (NGOs)/rural support programmes (RSPs)] in the world, 70 per cent were serving 2,500 clients or less, and only 2 per cent serve 100,000 people or more. According to Mike Murrey – former chairman of Unitus – the above indicates an interesting anomaly in how MFPs function. The fact that 2 per cent of the MFPs have grown to 100,000 clients or more indicates there is a strong possibility of growth. The fact that 98 per cent have not grown indicates that those possibilities are not being realised, that is, there is an artificial impediment hindering the growth of MFPs, which only 2 per cent of the MFPs have been able to counter successfully.

Unitus feels there are two obstacles in the growth of MFPs. The first is the lack of availability of funds via capital investments and a large asset base. The other major obstacle is the lack of internal capacity for the MFPs to grow. This includes lack of middle-management skills and lack of know-how and utilisation of ICT systems. The use of ICT for MFPs, thus, needs to be understood keeping in mind the above facts and figures.

Microfinance banks are the most sophisticated form of an MFP. MFIs, NGOs and RSPs are subject to the commercial laws of the country but not to formal banking regulations. Such institutions cannot offer full banking facilities; for example, they cannot take deposits. MFBs are full-fledged banks, and can take on deposits; hence they fall under the national banking regulatory rules.

Pakistan's microfinance sector

The Pakistan banking industry took a major turnaround twenty years ago. Until then, the banking sector was dominated by five state-owned banks – National Bank of Pakistan (NBP), Habib Bank Limited, United Bank Limited, Muslim Commercial Bank and Allied Bank Limited. Other than NBP, the rest had, originally, at their formation, been privately held banks; however, they were nationalised in the 1970s. Within the past twenty years, all of the above, other than NBP, have been (re)privatised leading to the current situation where less than 10 per cent of the Pakistani banks are government owned – controlling only 20 per cent of the national financial asset base.

During the first half of the decade of 2000, Pakistan experienced strong economic growth, resulting in a sizeable increase of the financial sector and in a proliferation of privately held banks. Since then, the central bank – State Bank of Pakistan (SBP) – issued a moratorium on the issuing of new licenses, and raised the minimum paid-up capital requirements to PKR6 billion (approximately USD100 million, at that day's exchange rate). The only exception to this rule was for Islamic banks and MFBs, which can still receive new licenses.

As Pakistan's FSI sector was being privatised, the distribution of financial services started becoming more urban-centric. At the moment, only 33 per cent of the branches of Pakistan's banking sector are in rural areas, while the remaining branches are in urban areas. This is exactly the opposite to the population distribution, where 67 per cent of the population lives in the rural areas.[5]

The above has created a need for the Government of Pakistan (GoP) to explicitly take initiatives to expand penetration of financial services into the lower-income sector of the Pakistani society – specifically in rural areas. The Government of Pakistan, under the UN Millennium Declaration, set the target of halving Pakistan's poverty levels by 2015. SBP defined certain policies to support this, which include an annual branch licensing policy, requiring all commercial banks with over 100 branches opening at least 20 per cent of their branches outside big cities. All banks have to introduce a basic banking account, which carries automatic teller machine (ATM) facilities, no fee and no minimum balance requirement. This account can be opened with a minimum deposit of PKR1,000. Most of all, SBP defined a detailed microfinance strategy, accompanied by a comprehensive set of prudential regulations for the microfinance sector.

The current microfinance landscape in Pakistan is as follows: eight MFBs have come into existence – Karakuram Bank, Kashf Foundation, Khushaali Bank, Network Microfinance Bank, Rozgar Microfinance Bank, Tameer Microfinance Bank, Pak Oman Microfinance Bank and the First Microfinance Bank. There are six major MFIs – Asasah, Kashf, Sindh Agricultural and Forestry Workers Coordinating Organization, Akuwat, Buksh and Orangi Pilot Project. There are four large RSPs/NGOs in Pakistan working in the finance domain – National Rural Support Programme, Provincial Rural Support Programme, Development Action for Mobilization and Emancipation, and CSC. Two commercial financial institutions – Bank of Khyber and Orix Investment – have also taken some interest in the microfinance sector.

As of the first half of 2008, the last year for which formal figures are available, 73 million people are a part of Pakistan's labour force out of which 72 per cent are male, and an unemployment rate of 7.2 per cent. Pakistan's microfinance sector had approximately 1.6 million borrowers and 1.7 million active savers, with a gross loan portfolio of PKR16.5 billion and savings of PKR4.2 billion. There were 1.4 million holders of life and health insurance in this sector.

To reach the target of three million microfinance account holders, by 2010, it is estimated, an incremental USD600–700 million is required in debt, deposit and equity.[6]

Conventional banking–ICT landscape

To map correctly the usage of ICT for MFBs, one has to first understand how ICT is used by conventional banks. From the view of a conventional banking domain, the FSI sector is divided into various types of financial institutions – commercial banks, investment banks, retail banks, corporate banks, small and medium enterprise banking, asset management companies, credit card companies and so on. From an organisational point of view, the above will involve systems that cover the front office, middle office and back office of the banks. The front office refers to the customer-related functions – marketing, sales, and service departments. Middle office refers to the departments that carry out the oversight duty on the transactions generated from the front office, for example, position-keeping tasks and ensuring the transactions are capturing all the information correctly. Back office refers to the transactional processing systems of the bank, which carry out the administrative functions and the heavy lifting processing that are non-customer facing. From a functional point of view, FSI–ICT systems can be divided into four categories:

1   **Transactional systems:** These systems handle the day-to-day online transactional processing (OLTP) – customer relationship systems, core banking and administration systems.
2   **Analytical systems:** These systems handle the online analytical processing for the bank. They work, primarily, on the consolidated data, after they have been collected by the OLTP systems. These include data warehouses, reporting systems, business intelligence systems, risk management systems and compliance systems.
3   **Infrastructure systems:** These systems form the software infrastructure of the banks. These include database servers, application servers and web servers. In many cases, they are embedded into the transactional and analytical systems.
4   **Channels and interfaces:** These systems constitute the communications part of ICT. Channels are the end-user access points. Interfaces are mechanisms for integrating with other systems; both inside the bank's firewall and with IT systems outside the bank.

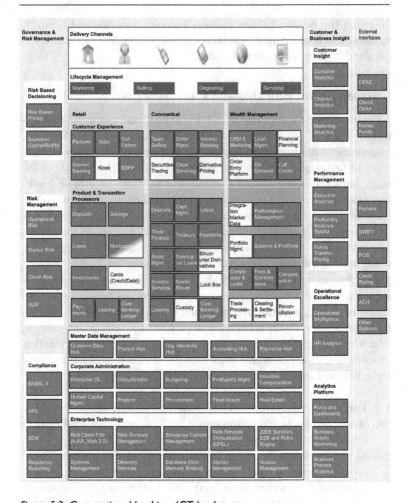

Figure 5.2 Conventional banking–ICT landscape

Source: Oracle Financial Services Software (2008). Financial Services Footprint.

Figure 5.2 describes the possible layout of ICT systems for a large conventional bank.[7] Based on the systems described above, it is necessary to understand each section of the diagram, and then, one by one, remove the sections which will not be applicable to MFBs. The ultimate aim is to develop a similar landscape, which will map directly to the business requirements of an MFB.

The section titled 'Delivery Channels' constitutes the channels through which customers/users interact with the transactional systems. Traditionally, the standard channels for a bank are branches, Internet, interactive voice response (IVR), mobile banking, ATM/point of sales (POS), short message service (SMS) banking, and call centres. These are, generally, external third-party systems which are integrated to the banks' internal transactional systems.

The sections in the middle of the diagram – Lifecycle Management, Retail, Commerical, and Wealth Management – constitute the main transactional systems of the ICT landscape. Lifecycle Management systems and Customer Experience fall in the category of front office systems and will consist, primarily, of customer relationship management (CRM). Retail, Corporate and Wealth Management fall into the category of middle office and back office systems, and will consist of core banking services.

The section in the centre titled Master Data Management constitutes the data integration infrastructure technologies, which are used to maintain the overall data of the bank in a consistent state, so that the data can be accessed efficiently. The software systems that cover these areas include various data hubs.

Under the Master Data Management is the Corporate Administration, which falls into the category of back office systems. They consist of Accounting systems, Human Resource (HR) systems, Budget and Planning systems, Procurement systems, etc. Much of this space is covered by Enterprise Resource Planning (ERP) systems.

The section below the Corporate Administration, titled Enterprise Technology, consists of the software infrastructure systems on which all the transactional and analytical systems are constructed.

The section at the far right of the diagram, titled External Interfaces, consists of third-party systems within a bank's firewall, and business networks outside the firewall – SWIFT and other clearing houses – with which the bank's systems may need to integrate. These are different from channels, in the sense they are not directed towards the end users or towards the customers of the bank.

The second section from the right, titled Customer & Business Insight, consists primarily of analytical systems. The main purpose of these systems is to analyse the accumulated transactional data to achieve greater efficiencies via Customer Insight, Performance Management, etc. These will consist of financial analytics systems and performance management systems, plus the dashboards, reporting systems and the portals to present the information.

The section to the far left titled Governance & Risk Management consists of analytics systems which primarily cater to meeting the regulatory requirements under which the bank needs to operate, for example, risk management systems and anti–money laundering (AML) systems etc.

MFB–ICT landscape

Microfinance banking is one of the newest additions to the FSI space. While it is a subset of this space and faces many of the same challenges faced by conventional banks, and thus requires many of the same ICT systems, it has its unique features as well. Due to this, one cannot simply take the existing conventional ICT landscape and map it *as-is* to MFBs. Prior to picking and choosing the sections, subsections and functional modules required by an MFB, it is important to first understand the unique requirements and constraints of MFBs. This will dictate the ICT systems, which will be purchased by the MFB.

A major obstacle, which relates directly to ICT costs, is the high *cost per transaction* for MFBs, which is significantly higher in comparison to conventional banks. This requires further explaining: banks incur large costs for managing the complete lifecycle of their interactions with a client. This includes loan-origination processes, accounting processes, recovery processes, regulatory processes, risk management processes around the bank's exposures and so on. Most of these processes apply to all customers regardless of the asset/liability portfolio of the customer. This has a direct impact on the ICT systems selected by a bank. This is why commercial banks have a break-even point, below which it becomes too costly for them to handle loans and deposits.

The cumulative cost of these transactions needs to be balanced out against the possible profit of the bank, vis-à-vis, the portfolio of each customer. A bank carrying out 50 transactions, involving a deposit PKR1,000 each will end up with roughly the same asset base as if it were to process one transaction of PKR50,000. However, in the former case, the bank may use up roughly 50 times the ICT-processing power (as well as manpower), as the later single transaction. This will include filling out systems, filing reports to the tegulator and so on.

In addition, while an MFB with x number of customers (e.g., >200,000) will have a portfolio, which will be a fraction of a conventional bank (with the same number of customers), it will still need to maintain certain standard information and manage it in an

Table 5.1 Total cost of administrating a loan

	Big Lenders (i.e. Banks)	Microfinance Institutions
Cost of Capital	10%	10%
Loan Loss	1%	1%
Total Cost of Capital	11%	11%
Total Amount of Loans Disbursed	$1,000,000	$1,000,000
Loan Size	$1,000,000	$100
Number of Loans	1	10,000
Yearly Transactions	4–12	120,000–520,000
Cost of Administering Loan	3%	20%
Total Cost to Institution	14% (11% + 3%)	31% (11% + 20%)

Source: Unitus – Innovative Solutions to Global Poverty, available at www.unitus.com. Accessed 12 January 2010.

efficient manner – customer information, general ledger (GL) information, portfolio information, management information system (MIS)–related information for management reporting, transaction history and so on. Thus, much like a commercial bank, it will, after it reaches a certain customer/account base, need to rely on the ICT systems including back-up systems, disaster recovery systems and so on, albeit at a much higher *cost per byte of storage*.

Thus, the total cost for ICT systems will actually be much higher for an MFB in comparison to a conventional bank, as its cost per transaction and cost per unit storage will be much higher. Due to this, the operating costs per financial transaction for an MFB are significantly higher than those for a conventional bank. This is why MFBs charge interest rates that are generally around +/–25 per cent, more than twice that of conventional banks. Table 5.1 breaks down these operation costs, explaining them in more detail. The series of steps that need to be taken to map the conventional ICT landscape to an MFB–ICT landscape are as follows:

1   From the conventional banking ICT landscape in Appendix A5.1, we need to pick out the key business areas corresponding to transaction systems that will be needed by an MFB.
2   After the transactional systems have been decided, the same needs to be done for analytics systems.

3   After that, we need to pick out the channels which MFBs may need to reach its consumers.
4   Finally, we need to decide the interfaces an MFB will need to implement.

MFB–ICT transactional systems

The first set of transactional systems, which need to be looked at, are the CRM systems. CRM systems are designed to allow the bank to streamline its sales and marketing processes, up-sell and cross-sell, provide customer analytics and so on. Due to the nature of the clientele and the high cost per transaction, as well as the manual interaction required with its customers, an MFB will probably not require automated systems to carry out marketing, selling, originating and servicing, and enhancing the customer experience. Hence, we can take CRM systems out of the conventional ICT diagram.

Next, we move to the core banking systems. The lower income segments of a society will not be involved in private banking/wealth management; two areas targeted exclusively to high net-worth individuals. Hence this section can be taken out of the diagram. MFBs will also not target the corporate sector (if any of the potential clientele of the MFBs grows to a level where it can carry out corporate deals, it will have moved out of the microfinance sector). However, more and more MFBs are building out a treasury department to invest the deposits they collect. Hence, from the corporate side, only a treasury system/module may be needed; and that too, only by some of the more advanced and larger MFBs.

MFBs will also not target investment banking as none of its clientele will have excessive cash to invest in capital markets. Consumer leasing is, however, an area which MFBs may want to target. This is currently untouched by Pakistani MFBs; however, future plans may require the need for leasing systems.

The third set of transactional systems is the back office systems covering corporate administration. These cannot be considered mission critical from the get-go, specifically in the case of smaller MFBs. At the same time, as an MFB grows towards hundreds of thousands of customers, at the very least it will require modules to cater for general ledger, fixed assets and human resources. As it grows further, it may need to bring on systems to manage budgeting and procurement, as well as to manage its profitability. These modules do not need to be (purchased and) brought online, simultaneously. They can be brought online in stages as the customer and account base of the bank increases.

Before proceeding further, it is important to understand the business architecture of core banking systems, since in many cases core banking systems can carry out, at a basic level, many of the transactional tasks, which fall functionally outside core banking. Core banking systems have built-in low-end CRM facilities and also some low-end back office administration facilities – general ledger and others. They may offer basic loan-origination features. To some extent, they also include rudimentary analytical capabilities (risk management, AML, etc.), as well as relatively well-developed reporting capabilities. The basic point being that core banking systems do not assume that other transactional systems will be available to the banks, and provide such facilities, at a basic level, themselves. These facilities can be leveraged by MFBs.

Thus, many of the smaller conventional banks do not purchase domain-specific transactional systems (CRM, accounting, etc.) and rely on their core banking systems to handle such tasks. It is only when conventional banks get to the mid- to large range that they migrate out such tasks from core banking systems into subject-specific transactional systems, and then integrate those systems with core banking systems in batch mode. MFBs can do the same, and would perhaps wait even longer – bringing in subject-specific transactional systems, only when their sizes become larger than a comparative conventional banks – thereby justifying the costs.

MFB analytics systems

Analytics systems are not mission-critical systems, that is, they are not needed to keep the bank functioning on a day-to-day basis. The main motivation of analytics systems is two-fold: compliance related to satisfying regulatory requirements and improved competitive performance of the bank via analytics.

The clear line to draw here is that any functional task related to regulatory requirements needs to be handled preferably by an automated system. While those systems related to performance improvement are *good to have* systems that can improve the efficiency of the bank, they are not mission critical. Such *good to have* systems are usually purchased by mid- to large sized conventional banks, which can justify the costs of the systems in relation to the earned benefits. In addition, using such systems efficiently requires a large amount of transactional data to be available in a clean format. Collection, massaging and cleansing of such a large amount of data is a challenging task, even for conventional banks, and may be beyond the scope of most MFBs.

The business and customer insight systems provide the bank with information on the amount of business various channels and market and customer segments are generating. Performance management and operational excellence are for improving performance and relating it to other factors like risk. The information calculated by analytical systems is presented through various dashboards and portals. These will be a luxury for MFBs, and have been taken out.

Once an MFI becomes an MFB, it is bound to comply with a large number of regulations, applicable to the banking sector of the country. All banks have to make capital investments into governance risk and compliance (GRC) systems to comply with such regulations. This may be a cost the MFBs will have to absorb, since many of the regulatory requirements will require sophisticated ICT systems, for example, compliance with capital adequacy regulations like Basel II as well as international AML regulations. Much like the cost per transaction issue, explained in an earlier sections, the *cost of analytics* will also be high for MFBs. However, initially, until the MFB grows very large, the GRC task can probably be managed manually, relying on the data and reporting capabilities available in a robust core banking system.

MFB channels

Out of the six standard channels utilised by a conventional bank, we need to decide the ones needed by a MFB. A branch network will obviously be required. This is where most of the transactions are currently being carried out. In many cases, these will not be full-fledged branches, but will be service centres. If the customers are given debit cards, then ATMs will also be needed. The third channel which is expected to be a major growth area is mobile banking. POS terminals are a channel which is being utilised in different manners by different countries. In its traditional form, the MFB clientele may not have much usage for POS transactions. However, certain countries, like Brazil, are using POS as the backbone of a flourishing microfinance correspondent banking industry.[8] This leaves out IVR, Internet and call centres as three channels which are put in place by conventional banks, but may be beyond the reach of the microfinance clients. Hence, the channels cater to include branch, ATM, SMS/mobile banking (with POS, IVR, call entre and Internet being considered at a later stage, or as needed).

It needs to be highlighted here that an area that may revolutionise microfinance banking (in fact, banking in general) is mobile banking. This may become the main channel for accessing banking facilities. This has been discussed in subsequent sections of this chapter; perhaps it requires a separate chapter of its own.

MFB interfaces

There is no way to avoid integration-related tasks and costs. The bank's internal systems will need to integrate with each other to transfer data, in a real time and/or batch manner, e.g., treasury system integrating with the GL. The bank will need to put in place interfaces to external systems for domestic funds transfer. If the bank handles international remittances, it will need to connect to the SWIFT network. Some MFBs may even require market feeds for their treasury transactions.

Interfacing with other systems usually does not require a separate purchase of software systems. Banking systems generally have built-in mechanisms for interfacing. Interfacing can be done as a systems integration exercise. Such an exercise is services-intensive. However, if analysed and done correctly, it will result in a good return on investment (ROI) for the bank. In Pakistan, none of the MFBs is currently linked in with international networks like SWIFT, and there are very limited facilities made available by MFBs for domestic inter-bank transactions.

Table 5.1 shows a possible ICT landscape for MFBs. The sections of Retail, Corporate Administration and Regulatory Reporting are *must have* systems. MFBs may already be using certain ICT systems to handle such tasks. Assuming availability of funds and scalability demands, this chapter provides a road map to upgrade such legacy systems to state-of-the-art platforms. Other sections indicate *good to have* systems, which can be brought online as needed.

Table 5.1, basically, shows an MFB being a retail bank (plus some treasury-related requirements). Practically speaking, an MFB is a subset even of a retail bank. In its simplest form, MFBs give out loans based on a few simple loan products and receive periodic loan payments. The MFB banking system(s) aggregates this information and updates the transactional entries in its back office ledger system. The banking system(s) also stores basic customer and account information related to the loans.

MFBs tend to grow along similar paths: starting from basic loan products, they move up by offering current and Savings Account (CASA) facilities to their clients, as well as term deposit products. Once the customer is allowed deposit accounts, debit cards and mobile banking facilities may be needed. The bank may start offering mortgage products to its customers, after which an MFB may start offering consumer leasing facilities. This could be followed by insurance-related products and remittance processing. In addition, some of the more sophisticated MFBs may set up a treasury department to invest their deposits. All of the above can be handled by a good core banking system (other than, perhaps, insurance products).

Total cost of ownership

It should be clear that an MFB–ICT implementation is significantly simpler than that for conventional banks, since the former requires far fewer modules, channels, analytics and so on. This is a fact borne out by the author's personal experience. However, MFBs have limited budgets. Can they afford high-priced state-of-the-art ICT systems? Do they even require them? These are the million-rupee questions.

Each MFB will have to tackle these questions independently based on their budgets, growth plans, availability of funds and so on. However, the management of MFBs needs to, at the very least, understand two points: the impact (or lack thereof) ICT has in assisting an MFB to scale and the costs and possible architectures involved in fully automating its processes via ICT. Even if a bank's management decides against such ICT purchases, it should be making an educated decision. Hopefully, this chapter will help banks in understanding the ICT landscape, thereby reducing any possible financial and architectural blunders in their purchases.

The systems described in this chapter are business centric, not software or vendor centric. An MFB can map the functional landscape, presented in Table 5.1, to low-priced local ICT systems, or it can go for state-of-the-art tier-1 systems. It can also develop some modules in-house. As long as the management is clear on which systems are needed, and how they are functionally modularised and integrated, it will make the correct decision.

Top-line ICT systems are generally sold in modules. Each set of module falls within a certain category and has a common supporting software infrastructure. Core banking systems consist of one set of modules, ERP systems covering corporate administration would be another set and so on. Each one of the modules, within a category, can be purchased separately and brought online as needed.

It is important to understand the concept of TCO of ICT systems. Using core banking as an example, a TCO will include the following costs (a similar set of costs will apply to accounting systems, HR systems, GRC systems, etc.; some of these costs may overlap and can be shared between systems): hardware and technology (hardware servers, desktops, storage, disaster recovery set-up, etc.), software infrastructure licenses (databases, integration servers, reporting tools, etc.), software product licenses (core banking software licenses), network and wide area network communication costs (routers, switches, access to satellite/mobile/ATM links to remote areas, etc.) and implementation costs (for the services company doing the implementation). These costs will be divided into capital expenditures and operating expenditures. In addition, all costs will include a certain percentage paid to the vendors, every year, for annual maintenance and support.

Figure 5.3 shows a possible TCO for a top-of-the-line core banking system for an MFB planning to grow to a million customers in five years. It takes into account the replacement of existing systems and addition of new capacity. The aim is to show the percentage of costs for the various components of the TCO, and not the actual USD amounts, as the USD amounts will vary depending on the country and the sophistication of systems purchased. The main variable in the cost is the software infrastructure and software systems licenses (as well as the corresponding annual maintenance fees). These can reduce drastically, thereby changing the overall percentage costs of other components, if the MFB moves

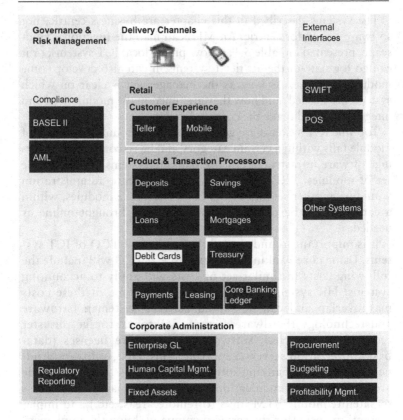

Figure 5.3 Percentage of TCO for core banking components

towards tier-2 and tier-3 systems, or relies on in-house development. However, such savings could be counterproductive for MFBs with long-term growth plans.

It is nearly impossible to put an exact dollar figure around the TCO, due to the differences in costs, demographics, regulations, infrastructure, implementation skill sets, discount ranges and so on for MFBs operating in different countries. Each category of modules can be priced, by the vendors, on the basis of number of active accounts and/or active customers, and/or active branches and/or active central processing units. At discounted regional prices, and even with the very limited number of modules required by MFBs, the cost of a top-of-the-line core banking software system can be around USD1/account (accounting systems, HR systems, and analytics systems, are, generally, quite a bit less expensive, as are tier-2 and tier-3 core banking systems).

As a ballpark figure, with discounts included, for an MFB wanting to fully automate all its transaction systems in a manner where they can be integrated with channels and outside interfaces, with some level of minimal automated GRC capabilities, growing to 500,000 accounts over five years can be in the range of USD2.5–3.5 million (spread out over five years). This would include state-of-the-art core banking, accounting and HR systems used by large conventional banks, plus the other costs mentioned in the TCO (networking, implementation, hardware, disaster recovery systems, etc.). For an MFB planning to grow to one million accounts over five years, the costs could grow to USD4–6 million (spread out over five years).

The above-mentioned costs may seem mind blowing for the management teams of many MFBs, which are used to operating on a shoestring budget. However, the author has worked with MFBs that are considering the deployment of such systems. This is a clear indication that many MFBs are seriously looking to upgrade their ICT systems to match those of conventional banks. Obviously, they see a good ROI. They seem to have concluded it is impossible for their MFB to scale profitably beyond a certain client base without sophisticated ICT systems.

Some food for thought

Research indicates that access to periodic loans from MFBs assist the poor in streamlining their day-to-day lives, perhaps, because it can bring down their interest rates from the 300–3,000 per cent range to a range of 20–30 per cent. However, there still is no definitive research available on whether MFBs actually bring the poor out of poverty, on a large scale. On its own, accessibility to a loan cannot turn a poor person (or even a rich person, for that matter) into a budding entrepreneur. Entrepreneurship requires management skills, business acumen, innovation and so on. According to the Consultative Group to Assist the Poor, spending money on one year of girls' education does more to remove poverty than spending money on one year of microcredit. However, MFBs have a strength that makes them unique: education for the poor is based, perpetually, on grants and subsidies; however, well-managed MFBs can become self-sustainable profitable entities, which will not require continuous grants and subsidies to survive.[9]

A large majority of the assets in microfinance, worldwide, are managed by non-banking MFPs (e.g., over 80 per cent in India[10]), not by MFBs. Less than 10 per cent of the MFIs use commercially developed MIS. Specifically within Pakistan, barely any, if any, MFP is making a profit. Most are not breaking even and are dependent on grants for survival. This is perhaps the trend around the world. A key component of becoming self-sustainable, in any business, is scalability, thereby lowering the cost per transaction. The best way to do this is via efficient use of ICT. The author would like to present a possible model that may be considered *food for thought* by donors and government agencies, involved in supporting microcredit.

Based on personal experience and discussions with various MFB executives, as well as research, it seems more and more clear that the only channel that can be used by MFBs to scale in a cost-effective manner is mobile banking. Some branches will be needed for administrative purposes; however, it is difficult to fit a branch-centric set-up, with ATMs and the pre-requisite supporting infrastructure/networking to far-flung areas, into a scalable and cost-effective business model for MFBs. Setting up an ICT infrastructure to access banking systems, via mobile phones, is not rocket science; nor are the infrastructure costs too high. Since sophisticated financial products are not involved, nor is customer service a priority, mobile phones need to be pushed as the main channel.

On the host side, governments and donors may want to look at centralising around the hosted model, that is, the transactional and analytical systems infrastructure is hosted at a common data centre with logical slices used by each MFB (or MFP). The MFBs pay for the services on a 'per transaction' basis. The MFBs will save the very large capital expenditures of setting up their own data centres and they will not have to hire a highly skilled IT department. They will only pay the operating costs to the entity running the data centre. This is becoming known, in microfinance lingo, as the Financial Inclulsion Network and Operations (FINO) model.

FINO is an entity in India, which provides complete transaction banking and administration facilities in a hosted model, to MFPs. As of now, FINO is hosting fourteen banks, twenty MFIs, three insurance companies and seven government entities on its systems, serving over 26,000 locations with over ten million enrolments.

The jury is still out on whether the FINO model can be implemented profitably by private sector entities (or by governments) in most countries. Based on the author's personal experience in the data centre market, it is challenging enough to implement a banking system for one bank; setting up an environment that will host multiple banks increases the complexity (and cost) manifold. It will thus be difficult, though not impossible, for a private entity in most countries to set up a similar model successfully. FINO is unique because India has a very well-developed ICT services sector, which operates at a low cost and is sophisticated enough to manage such large projects. In addition, India has a much larger potential MFB client base than other countries.

However, the government sector in Pakistan (and in other countries) could carry out such an initiative. Instead of offering grants to MFBs/MFIs for ICT, it could spend the money on setting up a hosted ICT environment that could be used by the MFBs/MFIs on a service-based formula. Once certain economies of scales are reached, the government may end up making a profit on its investment. At the very least, it will allow the MFBs/MFIs to scale, without resorting to very high capital expenditures. Such a hosted set-up, accessed by a nationally centralised mobile banking data hub (available to all MFBs/MFIs), may go a long way in reducing per-transaction costs.

The next two sections highlight the efforts of two Pakistani MFBs in upgrading their ICT systems – the first bank is in the process of bringing in top-of-the-line transactional systems; the second has a mixed home-grown and third-party transactional systems environment, and has put in place the country's largest mobile banking infrastructure for accessing these systems.

Case study 1: transactional systems – Kushhali Bank

Khushhali is an Urdu word meaning *prosperity*. Khushhali Bank[11] – KB – is the largest MFB in Pakistan in terms of coverage. Its operations span across all the four provinces of the country and the federally administered tribal areas. It is also the first MFB in Pakistan, established in 2000 and is regulated by the SBP. KB has over 2,000 employees and over 100 branches/service centres. It is jointly owned by fourteen national/multinational private sector banks and one public sector bank in Pakistan. Over the past ten years, KB has disbursed over two million loans worth PKR22 billion (approximately USD300 million). At the moment, KB has approximately 320,000 active borrowers. It had after-tax profits, in 2008, of approximately PKR100 million, with an asset base of approximately PKR7 billion.

For the past few years, KB has been modernising its ICT systems to cater to the expected growth in customers covering the next five years. Moving forward, the bank will require all customers opening a loan account to open a CASA account as well. After five years, KB expects to have a total of one million active loan plus CASA accounts, which will be catered to by its 100 branches/service centres spread around the country.

KB currently runs a combination of home-grown and off-the-shelf applications to support the transactional needs of banking operations (with limited branch-based processing capabilities) to process its loan products and basic savings products. In case of loan processing, the current business process involves customer information being collected manually at the various branches/service centres. This information is passed onto the central loan-processing facility where the operations department enters it into the current loan management system. This is a time-consuming process, which has large bottlenecks due to manual processing in the workflow and cannot scale to meet KB's expected plans, both in terms of new accounts and in terms of new product offerings.

KB started its transactional system overhaul by successfully putting into place a state-of-the-art HR management system to handle payroll, recruitments, employee benefits and so on. As its next step, the KB team has initiated a complete overhaul of its banking operations-related systems. They will bring in a state-of-the-art core banking system to centralise its banking transactions, provide real-time branch-based banking, ATM access, mobile banking, CASA facilities, signature verification and automated funds transfer facilities.

In addition, KB is also planning to bring in a state-of-the-art accounting system, in the near future, to handle its enterprise GL, fixed assets and so on. With a sophisticated HR, accounting and core banking system in place, KB will be up to date on the transactional side with sophisticated conventional retail banks. After this, there will be a requirement to integrate these systems to further increase their utility.

KB's channel overhaul will start by bringing its branches/service centres online in a real-time fashion. KB plans to allow its customers to open loan and CASA accounts directly, via its 100+ branches/service centres, with complete failover and recovery available at the branches in case of network discontinuity. KB will automate all branches in a phased approach. In the first year, ten branches/service centres will be brought online, moving to the complete 100 in next two to three years.

In addition, KB is planning to diversify its channels via ATM and mobile banking. Currently, KB does not offer ATM facilities. However, it will progressively bring ATMs online with an aim of having 100 ATMs on its network by five years. Besides this, KB plans to, like most MFBs in the country, utilise mobile phones as a channel as well.

The KB.s current and planned technology landscape can act as a good case study of other MFBs interested in incorporating state-of-the-art systems, in a profitable manner, to achieve high-growth targets. All the KB systems are architected in an approach that is compatible to conventional banks – consisting of disaster recovery, high availability, high-speed network connections and failover capabilities.

While, in terms of banking products and business verticals, KB, like all MFBs, will have a very limited portfolio in comparison to conventional banks, in a time frame of five years, with one million open accounts, KB will have moved into the same category as that of mid-sized conventional banks. This will go a long way in establishing microfinance as a profitable mode of banking in the country.

Case study 2: mobile banking – Tameer Bank

Tameer is an Urdu word meaning *to build*. Tameer Bank[12] is a private sector commercial MFB, created under the microfinance ordinance of 2001, catering primarily to the urban poor of Pakistan. Tameer, based out of Karachi, distinguishes itself from other MFBs by being one of the first nation-wide, private sector, non-NGO transformed, commercially sustainable microfinance institutions in Pakistan. The aim of Tameer Bank is to commercialise microfinance on a sustainable basis, moving it out of the domain of international aid. In an attempt to break away from traditional MFI practices,

70 per cent of Tameer's loans are to individuals and are not group-based. Despite this, it has been able to keep its loan delinquency to less than 1.5 per cent. It offers products and services in the micro-lending, micro-savings, micro-leasing, micro-insurance, micro-transacting and micro-franchising areas.

Tameer, currently, has 122,000 active clients, out of which over 75,000 are active borrowers. It has total deposits of PKR1.25 billion, and has disbursed loans of over PKR2 billion. It services its customers from over 80 branches/service centres. It has over 1,000 employees.

Tameer works more like a conventional retail bank than most other MFBs. It offers cheque facilities, interbank transfer facilities, pay order facilities and utility bill payments, allowing its depositors to open an account with only PKR100 (approximately USD1.50). It offers ATM and debit card facilities from more than 3,000 ATM clients. In addition, it also offers point of sales services.

In November 2008, Tameer Bank was purchased by Norwegian owned Telenor in a foreign direct investment of PKR1 billion (approximately USD13 million). Telenor is Pakistan's second largest telecommunication company. It has over 18 million mobile subscribers in Pakistan, controlling 23 per cent of the local market. On 15 October 2009, Telenor and Tameer Bank launched Easypaisa – a convenient way of managing bank accounts, via mobile phones.[13]

The penetration of mobile phones amongst the world's population is larger than the penetration of bank accounts. In certain countries, like Pakistan, the gap is huge. Currently in Pakistan, only 12 per cent of the adult population has access to banking facilities, while penetration of cell phones is at the international average of 60 per cent. While mobile banking offers large opportunities for increasing accessibility to financial services in all countries, the above-mentioned gap indicates that Pakistan has better opportunities in this area.

In agriculture-based economies like Pakistan, poor people live in sparsely populated rural areas, and rarely have documented credit histories. Due to this, banks have found these potential clients of little interest and too costly. To reach such markets, it is necessary to focus on inexpensive delivery channels and to develop low-cost means of handling transactions. Visiting bank branches during working hours can carry a significant expenditure. Bank employees visiting the low-income groups personally and offering doorstep collection of small deposits on a regular basis could be a solution. However, this escalates the *cost per transaction*.[14]

Based on available technologies, the most efficient manner for solving this problem is via mobile phones. In Philippines, a transaction that costs USD2.50 through a bank branch when automated using a mobile phone gets reduced to USD0.50. Figure 5.4 shows the channel-based per transaction cost distribution for the United States of America. In Kenya, mobile payment services via M-PESA – the mobile money scheme launched by Safaricom – has seven million users; this is 18 per cent of the total population of Kenya.[15]

Tameer, via Easypaisa, has ventured into this market to reach the unbanked sectors of the Pakistani economy. Tameer also plans to use its Easypaisa platform to offer mobile banking services to the affluent population. This will include paying utility bills, sending/receiving money within Pakistan, receiving money from abroad and so on. This service will be available to non-Telenor and non-Tameer bank customers as well. Easypaisa services can be availed from over 4,000 agent locations. This will be a first, where an MFB in Pakistan will be pioneering a technology infrastructure, which will also be used by the conventional banks.

Tameer's transactional landscape is based on a state-of-the-art bank end accounting system, which is used to manage the bank's enterprise GL, fixed assets and so on. Tameer built an in-house software system, which provides core banking facilities, as well

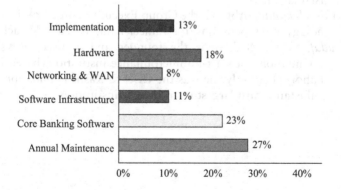

Figure 5.4 Unit transaction costs from M-Com18
Source: Fiserve (2009).

as customer relationship facilities. This home-grown system is integrated real time with the enterprise GL, thereby allowing all transactions to update the enterprise GL in real-time, rather than a batch roll-up.

This transactional set-up is accessible via the bank's current channels – branch and ATM/POS. Mobile banking is the next addition to this list of channels. Transactions can, now, originate from a mobile phone and travel to a hub, from which they can hit the systems of organisations outside the bank, as well as travel to the bank's own core systems, in real time. This real-time linking of mobile phones to the bank's transactional systems is an infrastructure that very few conventional banks have been able to put into place.

Acknowledgements

The author would like to thank the following individuals in India, UAE and Pakistan for reviewing the chapter, and for offering valuable feedback:

Vijay Sharma: Vijay is the SVP Consulting – Oracle Financial Services Software, based in Bangalore.

Samina Rizwan: Samina is the Senior Director – Industry Business Unit, for Oracle Corporation, based in Dubai. Formerly she was a board member of Khushhali Bank.

Nasir Naqvi: Nasir is the CIO of Khushhali Bank, based in Islamabad.

Abbas Sikander: Abbas is the Group Executive Director – Technology and Operations, for Tameer Bank, based in Karachi.

Sadaffe Abid: Sadaffe is the founder and CEO of Buksh Foundation – a start-up microfinance institution, based in Lahore. Formerly she was the CEO of Kashf Foundation – Pakistan's third largest microfinance institution.

Appendix

Table A5.1 Pakistan's macroeconomic indicators of poverty

Poverty profile of Pakistan[16]

Poverty band	Percentage of population	Head count (millions)	Adult population (millions)
Extremely poor (<50% of poverty line)	0.5	0.81	0.4
Ultra poor (>50% and <75% of poverty line)	5.4	8.69	3.8
Poor (>75% and <100% of poverty line)	16.4	26.39	12.3
Vulnerable (>100% and <125% of poverty line)	20.5	32.99	16.9
Quasi non-poor (>125% and <200% of poverty line)	36.3	58.41	33.1
Non-poor (>200% of poverty line)	20.9	33.63	21.9
Total population	100	160.9	88.4

Key macroeconomic indicators for Pakistan[17]

	FY04	FY05	FY06	FY07	FY08
Real GDP growth rate (%)	7.5	9.0	5.8	6.8	5.8
Per capita income (USD)	669	733	836	926	1,085
Inflation rate (%)	4.6	9.3	7.9	7.8	10.3
Current account balance (% of GDP)	1.9	−1.4	−3.9	−4.9	−6.9
Fiscal deficit (as % of GDP)	2.4	3.3	4.3	4.3	6.5
Foreign direct investment (USD million)	949	1,524	3,521	5,140	3,482
Average exchange rate (Rs/ USD)	57.6	59.4	59.9	60.6	61.6
Unemployment rate (%)	7.69	–	6.20	5.32	–

(Continued)

Table A5.1   (Continued)
Social development indicators: regional comparisons[18]

	Pakistan	India	Sri Lanka	Bangladesh	China
Human development index rank	136	128	99	140	81
Adult illiteracy rate (%)	50.1	39.0	9.3	52.5	9.1
Infant mortality rate (per 1,000 births)	79	56	12	54	23
Life expectancy at birth (years)	64	63	71	62	72
Gender-related development index	125	113	89	121	73

GDP: gross domestic product.

Notes

1 Innovative Solutions to Global Poverty, Available at www.unitus.com. Accessed 12 January 2010.
2 Ibid.
3 Ibid.
4 Ibid.
5 Pakistan Microfinance Network (2008): Microfinance Industry Assessment: A Report on Pakistan. Citi Network Strengthening Program.
6 Ibid.
7 Software infrastructure systems will not be discussed, since they fall into the technical side and not the functional side. In addition, in most cases, they are embedded into the functional systems.
8 HEC Montreal (2008). The Role of ICT in Improving Microcredit: The Case of Correspondent Banking in Brazil.
9 CGAP (2009). Does Microfinance Really Help Poor People.
10 LKY School of Public Policy (2009). Regulating India's Microfinance Sector: A Suggested Framework.
11 www.khushhalibank.com.pk. Accessed 2 January 2010.
12 www.tameerbank.com. Accessed 5 January 2010.
13 www.easypaisa.com.pk
14 HEC Montreal (2008). The Role of ICT in Improving Microcredit: The Case of Correspondent Banking in Brazil.
15 LKY School of Public Policy (2009). Regulating India's Microfinance Sector: A Suggested Framework.
16 Ibid.
17 Ibid.
18 Ibid.

References

CGAP. (2009). *Financial Crisis Snapshot – South Asia.*
GC Capital Ideas. Available at www.gccapitalideas.com
International Banking System. (2009). *Case Study: Women's World Bank.*

Chapter 6

Empowerment through self-employment in rural areas

The role of ICT and SHGs

Lavneet Singh, Jaspal Singh and Rajeev Sharma

Usually, a self-help group (SHG) is defined as 'A small economically homogeneous and affinity group of rural poor, voluntarily formed to share and mutually agree to contribute to a common fund provided to its members as per group decision'. The members are linked by a common bond like caste, subcaste, blood, community, place of origin or activity in these 'natural groups'. The SHGs provide the benefits of economies in certain areas of production process by undertaking common action programmes like promoting democratic culture, fostering an entrepreneurial culture providing a firm base for dialogue and cooperation in programme with other institutions and processing credibility and power to ensure participation and individual members' management capacity.

The SHG movement in India constitutes one of the largest microfinance networks in the world. However, SHGs' decentralised nature and theoretical independence from any one promoting agency prelude the ability to aggregate, analyse and monitor their data at state, regional or national level. Current methods of evaluating SHG credit are ad hoc, consisting only of cursory reviews of ledgers and transaction statements. Controls on internal member accounts are non-existing in many cases. Further, performance monitoring of products and services on economic and social impact parameters is at most tertiary, hence disallowing critical input in improving services and products for better impacts. The main problem in rural financial services is the non-availability of accurate, timely and needed information for decision making at higher levels. In microfinance sector, due to the lack of information, the SHG members cannot ascertain the financial position (profitability) of their group and provide the documents required to apply for loans and repayment to portray their strengths.

The focus of this chapter is on Uttar Pradesh Sodic Land Reclamation Project (UPSLRP) launched by Uttar Pradesh Bhoomi Sudhar Nigam, which is involved in all-round development activities in the area, wherever they have emerged. The project personnel encourage the formation of SHGs and to start different economic activities by its members for increasing employment and income of the SHG, which is essential for the development of weaker sections. The members can get loan to start any economic activity in agricultural and non-agricultural fields to raise their employment and income.

Adequate savings helps them to get away from the clutches of the moneylender. Savings can also be ploughed back into the business. The savings are actually carried out through SHGs and the animator of the group collects the money and deposits it in the banks, in the name of the group. The savings can also be given weekly or fortnightly, in the meeting itself, to enable them to save the meagre amount, in the Rs 25–50 savings group. Microcredit providers themselves identify the beneficiaries independently or through non-governmental organisations (NGOs)/SHGs. The repayment period is generally very short. The amount is increased, based on the borrower's repayment history. In microcredit, the National Bank for Agricultural and Rural Development's (NABARD) role has been two-fold, namely, promotional and financial. Promotional efforts assume the formation of the SHG–Bank Linkage programme and facilitating training. Financial involvement is in terms of providing refinance, revolving fund assistance, and providing grants.

NABARD's efforts towards increasing the access of the rural poor to formal banking services through promotional efforts, credit linkage of SHGs of the rural poor and other microfinance initiatives have gathered momentum during the last two years. As on 31 March 2009, a total number of 4,224,338 SHGs had an outstanding bank loan of Rs 22,679.85 crore as against 3,625,941 SHGs with bank loans of Rs 16,999.90 crore as on 31 March 2008, with a growth rate of 16.5 per cent (number of SHGs) and 33.4 per cent (bank loan outstanding with SHGs). The linkage programme has managed to involve participation of diverse stakeholders, consisting of all 48 commercial banks, all 196 regional rural banks and almost all 316 cooperative banks. It partners with over 3,000 NGOs from different parts of India. The cumulative progress made in linking SHGs to bank loan in India, up to March 2009, is given in Table 6.1.

Table 6.1 Progress in SHG Linkage Programme in India (Rs in crore)

Year	No. of SHGs linked with bank	Bank loan	Re-finance assistance
1992–93	255	0.29	0.27
1993–94	620	0.65	0.46
1994–95	2,122	2.44	2.30
1995–96	4,757	6.06	5.66
1996–97	8,598	11.84	10.65
1997–98	14,317	23.76	21.39
1998–99	32,995	57.07	52.06
1999–2000	94,645	192.98	150.13
2000–2001	263,825	480.88	401.00
2006–07	1,105,749	6,570.39	6,480.21
2007–08	1,227,770	8,849.26	8,825.11
2008–09	1,609,586	12,253.51	12,237.38

Source: NABARD.

The objective of this chapter is to estimate contribution of SHGs in capital assets formation of beneficiaries and its effect on their income and employment.

The present study is confined to Etah District of western Uttar Pradesh (U.P.). Out of fifteen blocks in Etah District, Sakeet block was selected as it has the maximum number of SHGs. Ten villages, from Sakeet block, where SHGs existed, were selected randomly. There were forty-seven SHGs functioning in these villages. About one-third (15) SHGs were selected, by random sampling, for the study. All the 182 members in 15 selected SHGs were categorised on the basis of enterprise for which they obtained loan, that is, beneficiaries of agricultural loan and beneficiaries of non-agricultural loan. Further, a sample 120 cases (60 beneficiaries of agricultural loan and 60 beneficiaries of non-agricultural loan) were drawn randomly in proportion to their number in each enterprise. The study was based on primary as well as secondary data. The secondary data (benchmark data, 1991–92, before the formation of SHG) were collected from records of the office of UPSLRP, while the primary data related to year 2007–08 were collected, by survey method, through interviewing the members of SHGs personally. Thus, the study shows the changes that have taken over a ten-year period.

Results and discussion

Value of assets

For working out the value of assets per farm, durable assets like value of livestock, value of implements and machinery, value of farm building and value of irrigation structure were taken into consideration. Land is mostly inherited and inclusion of land would have made the comparison less sensitive with respect to other assets, but in the present study, it is essential to estimate the value of land because there is a huge difference in the value of land before and after the reclamation by the UPSLRP. This project is equally responsible for motivating people and formation of SHGs for financing agricultural and non-agricultural enterprises.

Table 6.2 clearly shows that the overall value of assets has increased about four times in all the categories of beneficiaries of agricultural and non-agricultural loan, which was mainly due to the many-fold change in the value of land (Appendix A6.1). The multiple increases in the value of land were only due to the improvement in the quality of land after reclamation. Within the various categories of beneficiaries of agricultural and non-agricultural

Table 6.2 Annual percentage change in the value of assets on different categories of respondents before and after joining the SHG at current prices, 2007–08

Categories	Land	Livestock	Buildings	Implements & machinery	Deposits in bank	Total
Beneficiaries of agricultural loan						
Agriculture	43.77	1.96	0.99	8.08	134.32	40.23
Allied	43.26	4.62	0.40	0.96	41.76	34.94
Ag+allied	42.55	9.85	1.44	1.39	67.78	38.81
Overall	43.48	4.11	0.75	5.14	78.54	37.91
Beneficiaries of non-agricultural loan						
Glass bead	70.56	2.55	3.04	32.39	17.98	45.49
Bulb	57.19	4.80	3.52	20.83	15.19	36.09
Carpet	68.33	7.08	0.42	15.13	15.30	35.47
Tailoring	65.00	9.18	3.29	–	18.54	45.45
Overall	72.32	5.28	3.36	20.37	17.20	43.78

loan, maximum annual change in the value of land was observed in case of agricultural beneficiaries among beneficiaries of agricultural loan and glass beads beneficiaries among the beneficiaries of non-agricultural loan.

Total income of households from various sources

Table 6.3 shows that total income from all the sources was maximum in case of beneficiaries of agricultural loan involved in allied and agriculture, followed by those having only agriculture as main occupation. In case of beneficiaries of non-agricultural loan, maximum income was observed in case of bulb manufacturers. Beneficiaries of non-agricultural loan, besides earning from their main occupation for which they obtained loan from SHG, got additional income from agriculture. The additional income from agriculture to these enterprises, that is, glass beads, bulbs, carpet manufacturing and tailoring, came to about 21, 7, 9 and 23 per cent of their total income, respectively.

Thus, it can be concluded from the table that the beneficiaries of non-agricultural loan who are also involved in agriculture earn more as compared to those who obtained loan for agricultural purposes only.

Family labour employment in different occupations

Table 6.4 reveals that the overall per household total availability of employment in agriculture and other allied enterprises came to about 180, 161 and 58 man-days for male, female and children, respectively. Within all these categories, maximum per household labour availability was observed in case of the beneficiaries of agricultural loan taken for agriculture enterprise. As the holding size of the respondents was not sufficiently large, respondents involved in agriculture also hired out labour for meeting their immediate cash requirements.

In case of beneficiaries of non-agricultural loan, average per household employment availability was 463 days for males, 432 days for females and 70 days for children, per annum. The table further reveals that maximum employment was available in bulb manufacturing followed by carpet enterprise. It is very interesting to note that children were employed in carpet enterprise only.

Table 6.3 Total income of households through various sources (in Rs)

Categories	Agriculture	Wages	Animal rearing	Other allied	Glass beads	Bulb	Carpet	Tailoring	Total
Beneficiaries of agricultural loan									
Agriculture	37,498.16 (56.73)	15,665.00 (23.70)	12,935.00 (19.57)						66,098.16 (100.00)
Allied	23,032.33 (35.64)	3,250.00 (5.03)	37,050.00 (57.32)	1,300.00 (2.01)					64,632.33 (100.00)
Allied+ Ag	29,123.41 (38.29)		13,780.00 (18.12)	33,150.00 (43.59)					76,053.41 (100.00)
Beneficiaries of non-agricultural loan									
Glass beads	11,880.91 (21.19)				44,187.00 (78.81)				56,067.91 (100.00)
Bulbs	10,005.83 (7.26)					127,725.00 (92.74)			137,730.83 (100.00)
Carpet	9,783.77 (9.22)						96,304.00 (90.78)		106,087.77 (100.00)
Tailoring	10,416.00 (23.02)							34,840.00 (76.98)	45,256.00 (100.00)

Note: Figures in parentheses indicate percentage.

Table 6.4 Per household's family labour utilisation in different occupations in case of agricultural and non-agricultural loan beneficiaries during 2007–08

(A) Beneficiaries of agricultural loan (in man-days)

Categories	Crop production			Labour hired out			Animal husbandry			Total		
	M	F	C	M	F	C	M	F	C	M	F	C
Agriculture	71	31	12	170	130		−15	45	40	256	206	52
Allied	47	20	8	30	20		−35	85	60	112	125	68
Allied+ Ag	55	24	11	–	–		−12	48	36	67	72	47
Overall	59.67	25.83	10.25	97.50	73.33		−23.08	61.92	48.00	180.25	161.08	58.25

(B) Beneficiaries of non-agricultural loan

Categories	Crop production			Non-Agri. occupation			Total		
	M	F	C	M	F	C	M	F	C
Glass beads	28	12		336	300		364	312	–
Bulbs	20	9		690	560		710	569	–
Carpet	20	8		297	464	280	317	472	280
Tailoring	20	9		294	242		314	251	–
Overall	22.67	9.75		440.75	422.83	70.00	463.42	432.58	70.00

Therefore, in a nutshell, we can say that these SHGs have generated more income as well as employment in the enterprises related with agriculture.

The CAM model as ICT for SHGs framework

The 'CAM – Mobile Enabled SHG Microfinance Management System' is an innovative development made for the collection of rural SHGs' financial information and portrays them on online server to enable the stakeholders to access and retrieve the required financial information – anytime, anywhere. This enables the rural women to utilise various services like financial services, banking services and so on at their doorstep. Computer-aided manufacturing (CAM)-enabled mobile service framework for microfinance is a three-tier document-based architecture for providing remote rural information services for SHGs in microfinance. The user tier consists of a set of paper forms that people use to record information, ask queries and conduct transactions. It uses standard web application server, which can reside locally, in a nearby town or virtually in the Internet. The middleware resides on the mobile phone, which plays the role of scanner, user interface, network, cache and pre-processor in the system. The system creates a decentralised management information system, increases efficiency of fund management and reduces credit journey cycle. Since the data are captured using a mobile phone and sent to the online server, the field staff monitoring the SHGs would supply the computer-printed reports to the SHGs, which help them to overcome all types of difficulties in terms of reports, bookkeeping and portfolio management. This also enables the other stakeholders like SHG federations, banks, non-governmental organisations (NGOs), self-help promoting institutions (SHPIs), and microfinance institutions (MFIs) to track their loan repayment online and arrive at decisions on time.

ICT in SHG–Bank Linkage

Since the programme is continuously expanding its outreach, challenges are also to be met in phases. One such task is the bookkeeping of the SHGs. Bookkeeping in SHG–Bank Linkage Programme includes maintaining of all primary books of accounts such as cash book, ledgers, members' passbooks, individual members' ledger, receipt book and vouchers in the SHGs. A balance sheet is also a part of the requirements. It is also important that the record keeping is done accurately. The records should clearly state each member's savings, loans outstanding, interest and principal paid and other relevant information. Furthermore, it is also essential that the accounts are kept up to date. Summarising, SHG bookkeeping means completeness, accuracy, up-to-date information and transparency. A good bookkeeping is a major challenge for SHGs and their members, especially when illiteracy or low levels of education are still a reality in many backward areas of the country. Some NGOs have originated a concept and a system where a so-called Munshi handles the accounts of a large number of groups. These Munshis reside in the village and maintain the accounts of the SHGs for which they are trained by the NGO. NABARD, through one of the well-known NGO, PRADAN, went even further and developed a system which computerises the accounts that these Munshis maintain. The Munshis are trained only in the use of this software and are referred to as computer Munshis. This is an innovation, which deserves attention, and could become a learning case for many other SHG-promoting institutions and MFIs. The computerised accounting system in PRADAN is a community-based system in which the computer Munshi acts as a service provider, equipped with a computer and financial software for SHGs. The financial transactions of every SHG meeting are recorded and channeled from about 100 SHGs via a collection system using drop boxes and messengers. After putting the handwritten data into the computerised system, the computer Munshi prepares financial statements for the following SHG meeting. The records are in the local language so that group members can understand and use them. The computer Munshi acts as service provider and is paid by the SHG members. The software being used by the computer Munshi is also capable of generating statements and information for monitoring by the SHPI and the bank. The more the users for the information, the better it is from the sustainability point of view. In March 2005, about 6,000 SHGs, promoted by PRADAN, were served by forty-eight computer Munshis. Currently, the average workload for a computer Munshi is about 100 to 125 SHGs. It is estimated that a viable scale of economical operations would be reached at a level of 150 to 200 SHGs, expandable up to 300 SHGs. The computer Munshi would collect his/her monthly fee, which amounts to about Rs 2,500 per month. This should attract him/her to run it as a viable business in the longer run. Each computer Munshi has a computer that is loaded with standardised software and a printer. The computer is placed in a developed locality with electricity supply for about five to six hours a day, which includes normal supply as well as backup battery. For an effective functioning of this system, certain criteria need to be followed:

1   Records must be in local language;
2   A functioning and reliable collection/distribution system for the records should be in place;
3   Computer Munshis should be trained and have a functional working place;
4   Supportive role must be provided by the promoting agency;
5   Understanding and awareness of the SHG members about the necessity of accounting and payment to the service providers should be encouraged.

Design

The SHG accounting system, designed by PRADAN, is comprehensive. The software links bookkeeping and management information requirements of SHGs, while a trial balance is prepared every month. The formats are simple, easy to understand and transparent. The software generates trial balance and other information, required by the promoting institution.

Consistency

In all the 6,000 SHGs, the same system of bookkeeping can be used. The computer Munshi system is based on viability over a period of time. SHGs are responsible for the payment to the service provider.

Replicability

The concept of the computer Munshi has a good potential for replicability. SHGs promoted by PRADAN are perceived as high-quality groups. There are some efforts by other organisations in other parts of India to replicate this practice.

Better information from such a system

This system can offer information to various stakeholders. Individual SHG members can get information on their cumulative savings, outstanding loan and the overall financial position of their group. The bank manager can assess performance of the SHGs with respect to loan repayment from the accounting records. The promoting institution can observe regularity in terms of attendance of members and savings in each meeting. A trial balance of a SHG for three to four consecutive years would indicate the direction of the growth of the group and this is also an indication of the accumulation of the group capital. The computer Munshi could eventually act as a service provider, not just to SHGs under one promoter, but also for other SHGs with different promoters in the same region, including the banks.

Conclusions

Thus, the observations and findings reflects that these SHGs have created the atmosphere of economic assistance, which is a direct help to create more assets in rural areas, and the SHGs finally have attracted rural youth to engage themselves in self-employment in the rural area itself. SHGs have certainly increased income and employment in rural area on one hand, and have kept a check over rural migration to cities on the other.

To be able to ensure that the challenges of banking the unbanked are met effectively and converted into growing and sustainable business for banks, there is no alternative but adoption of information and communicatin technology (ICT) solutions on a very large scale and range. ICT solutions are required to capture customer details, facilitate unique identification, ensure reliable and uninterrupted connectivity to remote areas and across multiple channels of delivery, offer multiple financial products (banking, insurance, capital market) through same delivery channel while ensuring consumer protection, develop comprehensive and reliable credit information system so essential for efficient credit delivery and credit pricing, develop appropriate products tailored to local needs and segments, provide customer education and counseling and enable use of multimedia and multi-language for dissemination of information and advice.

The regulations relating to information technology (IT) solutions for banking services in general and financial inclusion in particular relate to ensuring integrity of banking system and ensuring customer protection. These cover customer identification/authentication, customer confidentiality/privacy, know your customers)/ anti-money laundering issues, outsourcing, bank's responsibility for their agents, ensuring inter-operability and open standards, imaging standards and adherence to payments system regulations.

On the way forward, the challenges are going to be banks using multiple channels for delivery of variety of financial services, developing synergies with MFIs and SHGs by introducing seamless ICT-based models linked to such intermediaries, availability of skilled manpower to facilitate the adoption of IT on such large scale, use of IT for credit information and efficient credit delivery and risk management in a much bigger way, moving away from the use of cash and emergence of enough leaders in the banking system especially in the public sector banks/regional rural banks and cooperative banks to recognise the opportunities and take advantage of their specific strengths including location.

References

Dayachari, P., Subrahmanyam, P. and G.R. Reddy, (2000), Additionally feasibility, convergence of income and substitution effects of microcredit: Findings of an empirical study in Andhra Pradesh, *Journal of Rural Development*, 10(2):1–17.

Ojha, R.K., (2001), Self-help groups and rural employment, *Yojana*, 45:20–23.

Puhazhendhi, V., and K.J.S. Satyasai, (2002), Empowerment of rural women through self help groups – An Indian experience, *National Bank News Review*, Mumbai, 18(2):39–47.

Qazi, M., (1996), Self help groups – A novel approach to rural development, *State Bank of India, Monthly Review*, 36(9):460–465.

Samanta, R.K., (1998), Empowering women: Key to third world development, *Yojana*, 45:16–18.

Seleth, R.M., (1988), Occupational diversifications among rural groups – A case study of rural transformation in Tamil Nadu, *Economic and Political Weekly*, 42(3):32–30.

Appendix

Table A6.1 Value of assets on different categories of respondent before and after joining the SHG at current prices, 2007–08

Categories	Size of groups	Holding size	Before joining the SHG						After joining the SHG					
			Value of land	Livestock	Buildings	Implements and machinery	Deposits in bank	Total	Value of land	Livestock	Building	Implements and machinery	Deposits in bank	Total
Beneficiaries of agricultural loan														
Agriculture	30	1.14	68,900.00 (88.44)	3,978.00 (5.11)	2,631.85 (3.38)	1,693.90 (2.17)	698.10 (0.90)	7,7901.85 (100.00)	370,500.00 (94.69)	4,758.00 (1.22)	2,891.85 (0.74)	3,062.36 (0.78)	10,075.00 (2.57)	391,287.208 (100.00)
Allied	25	0.98	59,800.00 (77.55)	11,577.80 (15.01)	3,296.28 (4.27)	1,214.20 (1.57)	1,222.72 (1.59)	77,111.00 (100.00)	318,500.00 (91.92)	16,922.35 (4.88)	3,426.35 (0.99)	1,331.20 (0.38)	6,328.40 (1.83)	346,50E.292 (100.00)
Allied+ Ag	5	1.03	63,700.00 (87.97)	3,874.00 (5.35)	2,795.00 (3.86)	1,222.00 (1.69)	819.00 (1.13)	72,410.00 (100.00)	334,750.00 (94.72)	7,689.60 (2.18)	3,198.39 (0.91)	1,391.78 (0.39)	6,370.00 (1.80)	353,399.774 (100.00)
Overall	60	1.06	64,675.00 (83.87)	7,135.92 (9.25)	2,922.30 (3.79)	1,454.70 (1.89)	926.77 (1.20)	77,114.67 (100.00)	345,854.21 (93.61)	10,070.78 (2.73)	3,140.10 (0.85)	2,201.82 (0.60)	8,205.17 (2.22)	369,472.038 (100.00)
Beneficiaries of non-agricultural loan														
Glass beads	20	0.58	23,400.00 (61.15)	3,315.00 (8.66)	9,165.00 (23.95)	743.60 (1.94)	1,644.50 (4.30)	38,268.10 (100.00)	188,500.00 (88.76)	4,160.00 (1.96)	11,952.20 (5.63)	3,152.24 (1.48)	4,602.00 (2.17)	212,366.44 (100.00)
Bulbs	20	0.43	20,800.00 (57.82)	1,651.00 (4.59)	9,321.00 (25.91)	728.52 (2.03)	3,471.00 (9.65)	35,971.52 (100.00)	139,750.00 (84.30)	2,444.00 (1.47)	12,599.99 (7.60)	2,246.14 (1.35)	8,742.50 (5.27)	165,782.63 (100.00)
Carpet	15	0.47	19,500.00 (37.78)	2,223.00 (6.46)	12,774.67 (37.12)	4,095.00 (11.90)	2,321.35 (6.75)	40,914.02 (100.00)	152,750.00 (82.11)	3,796.00 (2.04)	13,313.25 (7.16)	10,292.53 (5.53)	5,872.53 (3.16)	186,024.306 (100.00)
Tailoring	5	0.51	22,100.00 (57.46)	1,423.50 (5.24)	8,866.00 (32.66)	-	1,261.00 (4.64)	33,650.50 (100.00)	165,750.00 (88.84)	2,730.00 (1.46)	11,781.25 (6.31)	2,714.40 (1.45)	3,598.40 (1.93)	143,518.50 (100.00)
Overall	60	0.50	19,608.33 (53.92)	2,211.08 (6.63)	9,355.67 (28.05)	1,514.46 (4.54)	2,285.50 (6.85)	34,975.04 (100.00)	161,416.71 (85.81)	3,377.83 (1.80)	12,494.14 (6.64)	4,598.79 (2.44)	6,216.17 (3.30)	188,103.504 (100.00)

Note: Figures in parentheses indicate percentage to total.

Chapter 7

The role of ICT in economic growth
The case of Andhra Pradesh

D.H. Malini

The twenty-first century is the age of information explosion, due to advance of information and communication technology (ICT) affecting various phases of human life. ICT is transforming rural lives in the information era. ICT is designated as a facilitator tool to fight against poverty and its negative outcomes. It is a tool to provide developing nations with an unprecedented opportunity to meet vital development goals such as poverty reduction, basic health care and education, more effectively than ever before. ICT will increase agricultural production in rural areas. It is giving scope for the rural poor to enhance the sources of income for their upliftment and social security. The introduction of ICT has brought revolutionary change in the economic and socio-structure of rural poor. It is providing opportunities for applying the new ICT techniques in bringing the change in rural India.

Major initiatives were taken up by the Government of Andhra Pradesh to improve the standard of living in rural areas and remote villages. Agriculture activities may be prominent in this case whereas economic activities would relate to the primary sector, production of food grains and raw materials. Rural development actions mostly aim at the social and economic development of the rural areas. Rural development is a process, in which typically a large number of players in many different sectors of society are involved: farmers, administrators, representatives of tourist boards, business managers of the food industry, local politicians, to mention just a few. Moreover, the process is affected by a broad spectrum of underlying driving forces – from the ongoing demographic changes and emerging trends in technology and from changes in consumer preferences and lifestyles to new legislations and subsidy policies.

Rural development in India

Seventy-two per cent of India's population resides in rural areas and about 50 per cent of the villages have poor resources and lack of infrastructure. Since the independence, the government is concerted to improve the living standards of the rural masses. These are stream effects of poverty, unemployment, poor and inadequate infrastructure in rural areas or urban centres by way of mushrooming slums, and consequential social and economic tensions, which manifest themselves in economic deprivation and urban poverty.

India's economy from rural sector contributes to about 29 per cent of its gross domestic product. Rural development is concerned with economic growth and social justice, improvement in the living standards of the rural people, becomes essential.

The ICT basically focuses on the rural development and poverty alleviation, better livelihood opportunities and provision of basic amenities and infrastructure through innovative programmes of wage and self-employment. Since the last decade, the concept of rural development has changed. The major thrust area in rural areas is quality and not quantity, development and empowerment have replaced charity, and welfare has been overthrown by self-help. However, it was realised that for a sustainable development, rural development has to be more holistic which includes not only agriculture development but also the economic betterment of the people, a better and higher quality of life and social transformation.

Andhra Pradesh at a glance

Andhra Pradesh, located in the southern part of India, is spread over 2.78 lakh sq. km., and has 23 districts, 1,100 mandals and 25,000 villages. It is the fifth largest and fifth populous state in India and has abundant natural resources and large mineral base. The state, with a population of over 7.55 crores, has literacy rate of over 61 per cent. It is termed the 'Rice Bowl' of India with 65 per cent of the employed working in agricultural sector. It has over 2.3 million enterprises, employing over 6.4 million labourers, across the state.[1] The service sector in the state accounts for nearly 43 per cent of gross state domestic product and employs 20 per cent of the workforce. Table 7.1 summarises the demographics of Andhra Pradesh. Table 7.2 provides the income dimension of human development.

Table 7.1 Demographics of Andhra Pradesh (in millions)

	Population	Literacy	Employed	Cultivators	Agri. labour	Indl. worker	Other worker
Male	38.53	23.45	21.66	5.20	6.45	6.45	9.30
Female	37.68	16.49	13.23	2.66	7.38	7.38	2.26
Total	76.21	39.94	34.89	7.86	13.83	13.83	11.56

Source: 2001 Census.

Table 7.2 Income dimension of human development: per capita district domestic product in constant (1993–94) prices across districts of Andhra Pradesh

Sl. no.	District	Per capita GDDP	
		1993–94	2004–05
1	Srikakulam	4,975	8,845
2	Vizianagaram	5,664	8,316
3	Visakhapatnam	8,265	17,504
4	East Godavari	7,840	12,883
5	West Godavari	8,161	12,975
6	Krishna	8,395	12,249
7	Guntur	8,501	12,137
8	Prakasam	7,554	11,175
9	Nellore	8,511	11,588
10	Chittoor	7,778	10,774
11	Kadapa	7,488	9,642
12	Anantapur	7,601	9,578
13	Kurnool	7,346	9,877
14	Mahabubnagar	4,766	8,996
15	Rangareddy	9,360	14,948
16	Hyderabad	7,686	15,743
17	Medak	8,838	14,366
18	Nizamabad	6,193	10,082
19	Adilabad	7,179	10,067
20	Karimnagar	7,126	11,426
21	Warangal	5,452	9,598
22	Khammam	7,766	13,653
23	Nalgonda	6,260	9,301
24	Andhra Pradesh	7,416	11,756
25	CV	17.9	22.6
26	Min	5,382	9,037
27	Max	11,095	20,260
28	Range	5,712	11,223

Note: GDDP – gross district domestic product; CV – coefficient of variation.
Source: DES, Hyderabad.

ICT as a tool for e-governance

ICT broadly means the tools and activities that facilitate electronic means of processing, transmitting and displaying of information. ICTs are often spoken of in a particular context, such as ICTs in industry, education, health care, governance and libraries. Economic growth is the increasing ability of the state to produce more goods and services. The higher level of ICT capital stock per capita allows a typical economy to achieve a higher growth rate for given levels in labour and capital inputs. ICT is being increasingly used by both the developed and the developing countries, world over, to achieve higher economic growth. Let us look at ICT and significant results achieved though its application.

Advantages

1 It provides access to information, reduces the need to travel and provides a means to undertake many activities that previously needed physical transport. The introduction of applications like e-mail, online banking and e-commerce have significantly reduced the physical transportation costs of mailing, banking and purchase of goods.
2 It opens opportunities for entrepreneurship through information technology (IT), even from a distance. Individuals can transact business online and access markets and customers globally.
3 Virtual collaboration is possible through the means of instant communication and exchange of information.
4 The use of technology and applications to the areas of manufacturing and services will enhance the productivity of the individuals and workers.
5 Automation of processes and procedures reduces the time to deliver, enhancing the productivity and reduces the waiting time.
6 Applications in the areas of e-governance enable easy access to forms, applications, rules, regulations, information, guidelines and so on. ICT helps to also reduce the government cost in delivering these services to the citizens.
7 It enables applications like distance learning, tele-medicine, audio/video conferencing and web conferencing.
8 Quality and reliable infrastructure to deliver ICT brings investment and job opportunities.

9   To manage the ICT infrastructure, applications and their distribution across the state, new jobs are created.

10 It increases private sector participation and investments due to increasing market for telecom services, education, health care and so on.

11 It provides timely and accurate information to agriculture sector on weather, markets, demand for products, pricing, latest trends and so on.

12 It enables rapid growth of small- and medium-scale enterprises (SME) and small office – home office segments of business to address the growing demand, increased purchasing power and entrepreneurship.

13 It helps in bridging the gender gap and increasing the opportunities for the women child and adult through access to information and opportunities.

14 Online availability and accessibility of information brings in transparency, accountability and ownership.

15 It brings about E-justice systems set-up for fair, accessible, timely and efficient delivery of justice to common man.

16 Access to information and sharing of knowledge brings in learning and innovation.

Core objectives of the Andhra Pradesh's e-governance initiatives

It is recognised across the globe that the ICT is the tool to achieve higher growth and to bridge the gap between the digital divide. Australia, Canada, Finland, Germany, Italy, Japan, the United Kingdom and the States of America have achieved remarkable growth through ICT. In the past five years, AP government has undertaken many initiatives in the areas of e-governance, to improve the efficiency, transparency and accountability in provision of public services, citizen services at their doorstep and enhancing internal efficiencies of the departments.

ICT outcomes in Andhra Pradesh

The following are some of the initiatives taken by the Centre for Good Governance to design e-tools for good governance in Andhra Pradesh. Many of the tools are being used and can be replicated in other states.

1 AP Metadata Framework, Standards & Operational Specifications has been prepared by the Centre for Good Governance to provide the framework, standards and operational specifications for structuring and managing metadata.

2 E-data dictionary comprising data standard definitions for all the data elements comprising the multipurpose household survey of Andhra Pradesh enables the developers of e-governance applications to hold fast to the set of data standards, thus making communication between the systems clear.

3 Andhra Pradesh Transmission Corporation (AP Transco) introduced Online Energy Audit System, a web-based tool, to demonstrate the use of information technology to track the extent of commercial losses at the 11KV (Kilo Volt) feeder level. It records the gap between the energy supplied to the feeder and the energy billed to the consumers.

4 Introducing online legal cases management system, a web-enabled software, enables the government to track the status of cases from the time of filing to disposal/judgment/appeal.

5 The Government of Andhra Pradesh, to allow citizens to query information about government services or for redressal of grievances, introduced a call centre system titled 'Parishkaram'. Parishkaram means resolving complaints and problems through management information systems.

6 Stores Automation and Information System has been developed for automating the system of stores management in AP Transco and the distribution companies. It automatically processes the stores accounting data, which reduces the manual processes.

7 The Online Letter of Credit System through IT to automate the entire process funds release and allocations of projects can be undertaken online. The system ensures transparency and accountability and enables the department functionaries and the secretaries to monitor the budget, releases and expenditure on a day-to-day basis.

8 Instantaneous Access to Information Station provides information about concerned department functionaries by various means of communication such as e-mail, Fax or short message service. Instructions can also be instantaneously transmitted from various levels.

9 Online Petition Monitoring System facilitates officials in the Chief Minister's Office to register the petitions into the system, including details pertaining to the petitioner and the nature of

grievance, and those can be routed automatically through the system to the district collectors and the heads of department for prompt action and redressal.

10 Performance Management System, based on performance indicators, has been introduced to track, measure, and review and improve the performance of government departments.

11 E-Seva Service Centre provides the convenience of paying utility bills, registration and renewal of licenses, passport applications, birth and death registrations and so on.

12 The portal www.APonline.com provides information on various government departments.

13 In August 2004, the government launched Rajiv Internet Village Programme with the aim to improve the quality of life of rural people, to provide IT-enabled education, health care and better governance. As part of this programme, 6,000 kiosks are being set up in the rural areas, under the management of SHGs, for providing electronic citizen services, computer literacy to at least one person in each family in rural areas and broadband connectivity to villages by June 2006. These kiosks will deliver government-to-citizen (G2C), government-to-business (G2B), business-to-business (B2B), business-to-citizen (B2C) and citizen-to-citizen (C2C) services.

14 In terms of infrastructure initiatives, the state has also recognised the need for skilled technical manpower to cater to the needs of global IT companies choosing Hyderabad as their destination. The government encouraged private sector in technical education, by increasing the number of private engineering colleges to 164 with annual intake of 45,654 students, and colleges offering master's in computer application to 212 with annual intake of 8,555 students. On its part, the government is strengthening the educational infrastructure in the rural areas by building new schools and hostels and through midday meal schemes encourages more and more children to get educated and also reduce the percentage of dropouts.

15 Self Help Groups of Womens' Programme (thrift groups) has mobilised and organised 4.8 million poor women in the rural areas into 370,000 groups. These women groups have built up a corpus fund of Rs 7.50 billion, consisting of their savings, borrowings from banks and Development of Women and Children in Rural Areas (DWCRA) and revolving fund from government. The empowerment process has enabled the

members of DWCRA and thrift groups in addressing poverty in all its dimensions. DWCRA movement has contributed to the augmentation of incomes, improvement of nutrition and better childcare and enhanced the status of women in rural households. A total of 33,000 Chief Minister's Empowerment of Youth groups are assisted to access self-employment opportunities since 1996 with an investment of Rs 34.2 billion.

16 Another area where technology has improved governance is the Chief Minister's Information System (CMIS). ICT for decision making in government, in the form of CMIS, which is already working in Andhra Pradesh, enables the chief minister and other top-level officials to monitor implementation of development projects, VIP references and public grievances on real-time basis.

17 The Vijayawada Online Information Centre in Andhra Pradesh is a project delivering municipal services online.

Challenges ahead

E-government and e-governance are key challenges for governments today, as they involve multiple stakeholders and multiple processes and demand considerable coordination and collaboration as well as managerial and financial resources.

Complexities of e-government

Knowledge Management

1 Programme Management
2 Expectation Management
3 Technology Management
4 Procurement Management
5 Resource Management
6 Process Reform Management
7 Resource Management

Source: Dr P. K. Mohanty, e-tools for good governance.

Promoting Andhra Pradesh as a role model in e-governance

The Government of Andhra Pradesh is a front runner in providing e-governance services aimed to benefit the common man, touching the cross sections of the society and to the last mile of the state.

The e-governance projects of the state government, such as e-seva, e-procurement, computer-aided registration of documents and citizen friendly services of transport are widely known across the globe and are well acknowledged. However, the government is not complacent on what it has achieved in the area of e-governance in the state. As such, keeping the past experiences in view, in order to rejuvenate and sustain the e-government services more effectively, efficiently and transparently, it has been decided that the following action plan is implemented in further extending e-governance services:

1) APSWAN

AP State Wide Area Network (APSWAN) is under implementation connecting state headquarters with 23 district headquarters and district headquarters to respective 1,088 mandal (revenue unit) headquarters and is the backbone for all government applications of voice, data and video services. A total of 5,690 government offices spread across the state of Andhra Pradesh are connected to APSWAN. (b) Connect all village Panchayats through PPP model, (c) To enable broad band penetration to rural areas of the State by using Universal Service Obligation (USO) funding (DOT).

2) Common Service Centres

The Government of India has formulated a national e-governance plan with the vision of providing all government services in an integrated manner at the doorstep of the citizen, at an affordable cost. The project Common Service Centres provides delivery of 'Web-enabled Anytime, Anywhere access' to services in rural India. A total of 4,687 ICT-enabled centres in the rural areas covering all the districts will be created. The target fixed for the year 2015 is 10,000 common service centres.

3) AP State Data Centre

(i) This is a communication network–based initiative useful for all government departments to have secure data storage through a state-of-the-art data centre. It provides 50 TB storage space expandable to 500 TB where all government departments' data, application servers, web servers and mail servers can be resided.

4) Sofware in Telugu

The government encourages developing software in Telugu so that citizen services can be offered in Telugu.

The following are specific incentives for implementation of e-governance initiatives:

1   Seed money for pilot project implementation: Maximum of Rs 1.00 crore (for software development only) up to five departments in a year.
2   Assistance in preparation of IT road map detailed project report: To assist departments who come forward to implement e-governance initiatives, towards consultancy, preparation of IT road map detailed project report, an incentive limited up to 10 lakhs up to ten departments in a year is made available.
3   Online workflow management: Providing the online workflow management software developed by Andhra Pradesh Technology Services (APTS) to departments to encourage online file management system, with budget not exceeding 50.00 lakhs per annum.
4   Audit for security and functionality: Providing third-party audit for security and functionality for ten user departments to ensure security with budget not exceeding Rs 1.00 crore per annum for all departments.
5   Allocation of budget for IT projects by the departments: In line with the Government of India guidelines to keep the e-governance as one of the priority sectors for the 10th Five Year Plan, the Government of Andhra Pradesh also issued GO Ms no. 14 dated 23 June 2003. Guidelines are issued to all departments to implement the prioritised e-governance to earmark 2 per cent budget other than salaries. The respective departments are directed to meet all the expenditure of e-governance initiatives out of the earmarked budget provided under separate head created for this purpose.

Role of women in the growth of ICT industry

The government wants to impress upon the ICT industry to adhere to and enforce certain key measures scrupulously to promote the participation of women in the knowledge economy. Women need to be promoted into key roles as decision makers and entrepreneurs and in other senior positions. All efforts are to ensure that the confidence of women is to be held up at all levels in the organisation. Women participation must be encouraged in all public and internal activities of the company. In effect, the following policies will be impressed upon the industry to meticulously adhere to as part of their HR policies.

(i)   Introduce an affirmative action initiative to increase the participation of women at various levels in the organisation – board of directors, vice presidents, executives, senior managers, and leaf-level employees.

(ii)   Follow fair practices with respect to recruitments, promotions, career opportunities, project allocations, and training opportunities.

(iii)   Provide congenial conditions for smooth working of the women employees.

(iv)   Provide requisite safety and security for women employees at their workplace.

(v)   Provide necessary escort services for women to enable them reach their residences safely after work.

(vi)   Implement in letter and spirit the statutory provisions pertaining to women employees with regard to their various types of leave entitlement such as medical, maternity, earned and privilege leave.

(vii)   Provide professional counseling arrangements to the needy women employees for handling adverse situations related to gender.

(viii) Provide a forum wherein the women employees can represent their issues and mutually interact for bettering their working conditions.

(ix)   Provide periodic training to women at all levels for better performance.

With the above initiatives, ICT sector in the Andhra Pradesh state is slated to grow and penetrate rapidly to the last mile of the state not only for providing gainful employment for rural educated youth but also for overall balanced socio-economic development of entire state.

Conclusions

Andhra Pradesh has taken up many initiatives to transform rural India into IT knowledge–based economy. The high literacy rate, growing manufacturing and service sector, availability of skilled manpower, private sector investments, good telecom, power and road infrastructure and the like have enabled the state government to formulate ICT policies and initiatives to speed up growth and bridge the digital divide. The present ICT model and approach is the replica of South Korea. The Government of Andhra Pradesh is not only making efforts to meet the needs but also concentrating on bringing in policies that would create opportunities for employment and encourage the entrepreneurial spirit that exists among the women and youth of the state.

Note

1   Director of Economics & Statistics, 1999.

References

Asian Development Bank, (May 2000), 'Rural Asia: Beyond the Green Revolution', Asian Development Bank, Manila, Philippines.

Badshah, A., S. Khan and M. Garrido (ed), (2003), 'Connected for Development: Information Kiosks and Sustainability', Series 4. United Nations Department of Economic and Social Affairs, Information and Communication Technologies Task Force, New York.

Bagga, R. K., Kenneth Keniston and Rohit Rai Mathur (eds), (2005), 'The State, IT and Development', Sage Publications, New Delhi.

Bhatnagar, S., and R. Schware (eds), (2000). 'Information and Communication Technology in Rural Development', Sage Publications, Thousand Oaks.

Dreze, J., and A. K. Sen, (2003), 'India: Development and Participation', Oxford University Press, New Delhi.

Guelph, O. N., 'Multi-Stakeholder Engagement for Rural Telecommunications: Engaging Communities in Telecommunications Planning', Canada.

Gupta, D., (1998), 'A Question of Quota', Seminar No. 471, November, pp. 57–62, New Delhi.

Haqqani, A. B. (ed), (2003), 'The Role of Information and Communication Technologies in Global Development: Analysis and Policy Recommendations', Series 3. United Nations Information and Communication Technologies Task Force, New York.

Heeks, R., (2001) 'Understanding e-Governance for Development', Working Paper No. 11, Manchester University, Manchester, UK.

http://www.afdb.org
http://www.developmentgateway.org
http://www.dfid.gov.uk
http://www.idrc.ca
http://www.iicd.org

http://www.nic.in

http://www.undp.org

http://www.unesco.org

http://www.worldbank.org/poverty/strategies/chapters/rural/rural.htm

IDRC, (1999), 'Success Stories of Rural ICTs in a Developing Country', Ottawa, Canada.

IFAD, (2001), 'Rural Poverty Report 2001: The Challenge of Ending Rural Poverty', Oxford University Press for IFAD, Oxford.

Industry Monitor – Andhra Pradesh, Confederation of Indian Industry.

Keniston, K., and D. Kumar (eds), (2004), 'IT Experience in India: Bridging the Digital Divide', Sage Publications, New Delhi.

Parikh, S., (1997), 'The Politics of Preference: Democratic Institutions and Affirmative Action in the United States and India', University of Michigan Press, Ann Arbor, MI, pp. 172–5.

Richardson, D., (1996), 'The Internet and Rural Development: Recommendations for Strategy and Activity', FAO, Rome.

Sachinanandan, S., (1999), 'Rural Development: Theories and Experiences', Allied Publishers, New Delhi.

Satyanarayana, J., (2002), 'Vision of e-Government in Andhra Pradesh', *ASCI Journal of Management* 31(1, 2), pp. 127–34.

Shore, K., (1999), 'The Internet Comes to Rural India', IDRC, Telecomm Development Group (N.D.).

Singh, H., (1995), 'Administration of Rural Development in India', Sterling Publishers Private Limited, New Delhi.

United Nations Development Programme, Accenture and the Markel Foundation, (July 2001), 'Creating a Development Dynamic: Final Report of the Digital Opportunity Initiative', New York.

Chapter 8

Impact of federations on the functioning of SHGs

An empirical study

Sunil Kumar

The Self-Help Group (SHG)–Bank Linkage Programme is nearing two decades of existence. While the growth has been phenomenal in terms of number of groups, there are several concerns that are emerging on the sustainability of the programme. The premises on which the programme has been built are that the groups will manage on their own after the initial capacity is built; the self-help promoting institutions (SHPIs) will build the capacity of the groups, link them to the banks and scale down their involvement. If banks are the SHPIs, the relationship continues more as a lender than as the capacity builder. Further, once the groups are linked to the banks, they will not need external assistance, and the banks will continue the banking relationship seeing it as a business opportunity. However, field-level experiences of the last two decades show that these two premises are not holding good. The moot question is 'Can groups manage on their own?'

The tremendous success of the SHG movement relied, and continues to rely, heavily on promoting institutions, to mobilize, train and support groups. As groups strengthened and the number of groups increased, there arose a need to bring together SHGs to deal with issues beyond the reach of these small groups. The networks of SHGs, referred to as federations, have come together in various forms.

Networking of SHGs was inspired by the felt need of the SHGs that are not able to deal with issues that are beyond their reach. SHGs having a membership of 10–20 women are too small and informal to deal with larger issues to realise the needs and aspirations of women members. Inter-group lending, ability to negotiate with higher-level structures and greater bargaining power were the reasons for which informal SHG networking was initiated by non-governmental organisations (NGOs). SHG federations have been promoted by the NGOs and the government to address the issues of ensuring quality while up-scaling, ensure that costs of promotion are low and create sustainable institutions to facilitate withdrawal of the promoting organisation, from some of its functions and roles.

The role of SHG federations has been a keenly debated subject at policy as well as grass-roots level. The present chapter is an attempt to study whether there has been a positive influence of SHG federations in imparting sustainability to constituent SHGs by comparing groups belonging to federations with those groups that are not part of any federation.

Objective of the study

The objectives of the study are as follows:

1   To identify the services provided by the federation and analyse their benefits to SHGs;
2   To study financial parameters of federations to evolve benchmarks for their sustainability;
3   To assess the influence of existence of federations on SHGs, by comparing the differences between SHGs under the umbrella of federations and other SHGs that are not part of federation, in terms of governance, systems-related variables and financial management–related variables.

Data and methodology

Study sample

As per a study conducted by Andhra Pradesh Mahila Samatha Society in 2007, there are around 69,000 SHG federations in the country. Of these, 66,310 are primary federations, 2,571 are secondary federations and 22 are apex federations. Of the total federations, 88.94 per cent are in the southern region of the country and the rest are in the remaining five regions. In the southern region, Andhra Pradesh (AP) is ahead with 42.48 per cent followed by Kerala (22.39 per cent) and Tamil Nadu (21.23 per cent). In the northern region, Orissa (5.8 per cent) and West Bengal (2.22 per cent) have a higher number of federations compared to other states.

Table 8.1 Selection of sample states

S. No.	Region	State	No. of SHG federations*	Remark (Why the particular state was selected as a sample state?)
1	Northern India	Rajasthan	147	Other states in North India (Punjab, Haryana, Himachal Pradesh and Jammu and Kashmir) do not have any SHG federations.
2	Southern India	AP	29,273	AP has highest number of SHG federations in South India.
3	Western India	Maharashtra	600	Goa does not have any SHG federation and Gujarat has only 64 federations.
4	Eastern India	Orissa	4,000	Orissa has the highest number of SHG federations in the region.
5	Central India	Uttar Pradesh (UP)	161	UP is a large and backward state, and SHG–Bank Linkage Programme has had a late start in the state. So, to get a flavour of issues in respect of a late-starting state, UP has been included in the sample.

*Source: APMAS (2007).

Keeping in view the uneven regional distribution and differing maturity levels of SHG federations, the study attempted to capture a pan-India picture by focusing on five sample states described in Table 8.1.

In each of the states, two SHG federations from two different districts were selected for detailed study. A multistage sample design was adopted for selecting the sample SHG federations. The classification of the districts into 'developed' and 'less developed' was made with respect to data on development indices (such as literacy rate, poverty level and infant mortality rate), number of SHGs and the extent of bank branch network in rural area in the district. Thus total number of sample SHG federations which have been studied in five states is ten.

For each sample federation, ten SHGs under the federation and ten SHGs outside the federation (control group) have been studied to identify their differences in terms of the quality of SHGs based on critical rating index (CRI) developed by the National Bank for Agriculture and Rural Development (NABARD). Non-federation groups were selected on a random basis in the same/adjoining village so that the socio-economic and political milieu was similar for federation and non-federation groups. The CRI has been used as proxy to measure financial and organisational sustainability of SHGs with or without federation. Thus, the total number of sample SHGs which have been studied in five states is 10 × 10 × 2 = 200.

Using the above framework, federations indicated in Table 8.2 were selected for detailed study.

Research tools

Two different sets of detailed interview schedule were developed and administered to collect data from ten sample SHG federations and 200 sample SHGs. The interview schedule used for data collection from federation was designed to elicit qualitative responses from promoters and office-bearers of SHG federations. The interview schedule used to collect response from federation SHGs as well as control group SHGs was based on NABARD's CRI and this was supplemented by member-wise loan sheets and external loan details. The CRI basically consists of two sets of variables, namely, governance- and systems-related variables and financial variables. Governance-related parameters are periodicity of meetings, attendance in the meetings, decision-making process in the meeting, observation of norms, saving and loan installment collection methods, lending procedure, rotation of leadership, bookkeeping and so on. Financial parameters include periodicity and regularity of saving, use of savings for internal lending, lending rates, lending norms, regularity in loan repayment and so on.

The interview schedule was prepared with a lot of discussions and review. It was field-tested in Raebareli District before it was finalised. This was supplemented with focus group discussions with federation leaders, federation office-bearers and federation-promoting

Table 8.2 Sample federations selected for study

S. No.	Name of the federation	District/state	Promoted by
1	Mahila Sangharsh Manch (MSM)	Alwar/Rajasthan	Ibdata, Alwar
2	Saheli Samiti (SS)	Dausa/Rajasthan	PRADAN
3	Gramin Mahila Swayamsiddha Sangh (GMSS)	Pune/Maharashtra	Chaitanya, Pune
4	Savitribhai Phule Sawadhan Kendra Karanja (SPSKK)	Wardha/Maharashtra	Nagesheara Charitable Trust, Nagpur
5	Mahbubnagar Zila Mahila Samakhya (MZMS)	Mahbubnagar/AP	World Bank's Project – SERP (Society for Elimination of Rural Poverty)
6	Samsthan Narayanpur Kalanjia Sangamitra (SNAKS)	Nalgonda/AP	Dhan Foundation
7	Maneswar Matrushakti Block Level Federation (MMBF)	Sambalpur/Orissa	Women & Child Development Department of Government of Orissa
8	Janani Mahila Vikash Parisada (JMVP)	Bharatpur, Khurda/ Orissa	Swayamshree Micro Credit Services
9	Shakti Block Mahila Sangathan (SBMS)	Raebareli/UP	Rajiv Gandhi Mahila Vikas Pariyojna, Raebareli
10	Annapurna Sewa Sansthan (ASS)	Sant Kabir Das Nagar/UP	Grameen Development Services, Lucknow

organisations to assess the impact of SHG federations on working of SHGs.

Data collection

A three-member team, comprising the author and two more faculty members of Bankers Institute of Rural Development, conducted field visits in ten districts of five identified states for collecting data from SHG federations and SHG members. The data collection was done during the period February–April 2010.

SHG federation: a theoretical discussion

The concept of federation emerged from the felt need of the SHGs that have been functioning well and were keen to come together for sharing and learning. The federation was to serve the purpose of undertaking those roles that cannot be performed well by individual SHGs on their own. Some of these roles are as follows:

1   **Expansion of SHGs:** As the number of groups grows with continuous addition of new groups, the promoter's degree of involvement and even direct contact with the groups start diminishing. At this stage, the promoter begins to think of setting up an apex-level body (federation) that is able to take on many of the promoter's tasks, thus enabling it to leverage its limited resources in the most judicious manner possible.

2   **Imparting sustainability:** The promoting organisation cannot continue working in the same area for an indefinite period of time. To provide sustainability to SHG activity initiated and developed by the promoter, it is necessary to build people's institutions that can eventually and independently carry forward the social and economic empowerment agenda.

3   **Community actions:** In a few cases, groups may have come together informally either on a particular issue/crises or for exchanging information and experiences through joint meetings. In such cases, the initiative for a collective organisation comes from the SHGs themselves but the setting up of a formal structure is usually promoted and guided by the promoting agency. Usually, these groups have been formed to take up community action programmes and mobilise and lead collective action on wider social issues like child labour, female infanticide, illicit liquor, representation of women in panchayats and violence against women.

4   **Collective bargaining power:** When dealing with local bodies and institutions, individual groups do not carry much weight, but as a collective representing a large number of people, they gain both visibility and impact. As a collective, it is possible to establish linkages with banks and other financial institutions to access greater funds and influence rules of the game in their market segment.

Although the merits of having federations, as described above, are numerous, there are also several competing arguments highlighting disadvantages or dangers associated with the promotion of federations. The following are the major limitations of SHG federations:

1 Majority of the well-functioning SHGs have bank linkage. SHG federation is not required to play the financial intermediary role as SHG–Bank Linkage is a sustainable relationship.
2 India has a good network of bank branches enabling rural poor an accessible place at which to make deposits or take loans. Therefore, federations may not be required to provide the same services.

Review of earlier studies on SHG federations

Malcolm Harper[1] in his paper *Do We Really Need SHG Federations? (Ten Commandments)* has strongly argued against formation of SHG federation. According to him, it is not justified to add any new layer of middlemen to any transaction, unless it can be clearly shown that the new intermediary adds value. The burden of proof is on anyone who proposes a new intermediary; he must show that it serves a purpose whose value outweighs its cost. He has given following arguments against having SHG federations.

1 SHG federations were a necessary but temporary measure when very few branch banks were willing to deal with SHGs and it was necessary to mobilise more pressure than a single group could muster. That is no longer necessary, except in a small and rapidly decreasing number of locations.
2 The initial savings deposit of an SHG, perhaps Rs 2,000, and the initial loan of possibly Rs 8,000–10,000 are reasonable first transaction amounts for a bank branch, similar to what they can expect with their usual customers. After a year or so, SHG deposits of Rs 10,000 and SHG loans of Rs 50,000 are not uncommon. The SHG itself achieves the necessary bulking-up function for the individual members, but as these are profitable accounts, there is no need for a federation to bulk them up further.
3 India has the largest network of bank branches in the world, and most villages are within quite easy distance of a branch of some sort; there is no need to have a federation in order to provide a more accessible place at which to make deposits or take loans.

4   Some federations are themselves federating and aim to create quite new financial institutions. India already has commercial banks, regional rural banks, primary agricultural credit societies (PACS) and district central cooperative bank branches; some are not functioning properly, but the way to improve matters is to reform them, not to create yet another set of institutions.

5   The existing financial institutions are not properly regulated, or supervised, and there are frequent failures and frauds. There is no way by which the authorities can take on yet another type of institution; SHG federations will need supervision but will not receive it.

6   Loans and other benefits of SHG membership already flow away from the poorest to the most powerful and least needy of the members, as happens in all institutions. This process of marginalisation will also happen within federations, so that whole groups will be marginalised, not just individual members within groups.

7   The process of promoting an SHG is not easy but bankers and new SHG members themselves are increasingly taking over the task, thus reducing the need for dependence on NGOs and subsidies. Promoting a federation is much more difficult and a federation requires much longer 'hand-holding'. This may suit NGOs that need a reason to exist, but it perpetuates dependence on external assistance.

8   A single SHG does not contain enough voters to be worth 'hijacking' by political interests but a federation is a very attractive target.

9   The day-to-day operations of a federation cost money. This may come in the form of contributions or interest spreads paid by member SHGs or from individual members' voluntary work. SHG members already complain, rightly, about the amount of time that their membership demands and about the interest rates they have to pay. Federations will make these burdens worse.

10 One of the most 'empowering' aspects of SHG membership is the way it allows members to pick and choose between financial service providers. At last, banks, PACS and microfinance institutions (MFIs) are obliged to compete for SHG members' business. Federations can demand 'loyalty', which is essentially a loss of freedom.

However, there are a number of other studies which have found lot of merits in promoting SHG federations. Nair[2] examined the potential of SHG federations in providing sustainability to SHGs through financial and organisational support. Specifically, the study examined issues like (i) variety of services provided by the federations and their benefits to SHGs, (ii) financial variability of SHGs and SHG federations and the cost of promoting them, (iii) identification of constraints of promoting SHG federations and (iv) policy recommendations to strengthen SHG federations. In terms of services provided by SHG federations and thrift cooperation to SHGs, the study found that the most common service is savings and loan facilities. Savings include general savings and particular savings for education, housing, marriages and festivals. Loans include both small and large loans at costs lower than those available in the market. Besides these services, the SHG federations helped SHGs to internalise all operational costs and reduce the cost of promoting new SHGs. Further, SHG federations provide all essential services to SHGs with minimum costs. These services were often provided by the promoting agencies in the initial stage of SHG development. They include auditing, capacity building (e.g., training the SHG members, leaders and accountants), and forming a common forum for reviewing the performance of SHGs. The federations also help in resolving conflicts among SHG members, between SHGs and between SHGs and banks. Another important aspect is that they assist in reducing the transaction costs of SHG–Bank Linkage Pprogramme by grouping 10–20 accounts into one single SHG account. The federations help in reduction of loan default – both within SHGs and from SHGs to banks. They provide micro-insurance services and social services such as education, health and livestock support. The federations employ their own resources in promoting new SHGs while minimising the promotional costs as compared to other agencies like banks and NGOs. They also help in empowering the SHG members.

Mysore Resettlement and Development Agency (MYRADA),[3] Sa-dhan,[4] CS Reddy[5] and Shashi Rajagopalan[6] are the other prominent SHG federation-related studies that have been conducted in India. These studies broadly bring out the rationale behind the promotion of a federation in following terms:

1 It helps in strengthening existing SHGs.
2 It facilitates formation of new SHGs of the poor.

3   It enables SHG members to access myriad services which individual SHGs could not have managed to access.
4   It helps in developing a sense of solidarity among members of different SHGs in an area.
5   It enhances sustainability of SHGs.
6   It facilitates SHG–Bank Linkage.
7   Federations play an important part in SHG capacity building and conflict resolution – both internally and externally.

As per these studies, the concept of federation emerged from the felt need of the SHGs that have been functioning well and were keen to come together for sharing and learning. Each promoter has different reason(s) for federating SHGs at different levels. The reasons include (i) scaling up, (ii) withdrawal strategy, (iii) issues, (iv) collective bargaining power and (v) principle of subsidiary.

A few studies have been conducted eliciting opinions of federation promoters on the need of federations. MYRADA[7] points out that federations should not be built for external reasons (such as taking over the NGO's role after withdrawal from a project) but that they should grow in response to a push or need from the primary groups. The primary condition for sustainability of a cluster-level federation is that it should have evolved based on a felt need of its members. Artificially propped-up structures will not last.[8] The Development of Humane Action Foundation's annual report cites the breaking up of rigid caste barriers as an example of social development. It mentions that Kalanjiam clusters are coming together to celebrate festivals. However, this appears to be more of a social outcome of the SHG process rather than a direct social intervention on part of the cluster.[9]

A specific study on women empowerment[10]found that a high share of women SHG members reported significant development of their self-confidence and work efficiency. The study also reported that most of the women experience pressure, challenges and stress due to extra work and more responsibilities.

Findings of the study

The structure of federations visited by the study team is shown in Figure 8.1.

The federations generally have three-tier structures. There is a SHG at village/hamlet level that comprises of 10–20 members.

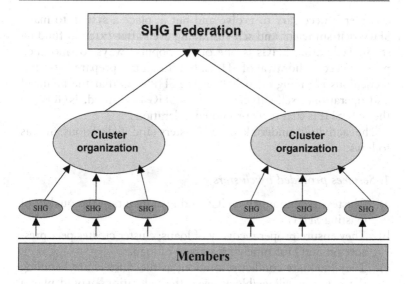

Figure 8.1 Structure of federations

Each SHG has three office-bearers. Of these three, two represent the group at the cluster level. A cluster typically comprises of 8–12 SHGs. The cluster has four office-bearers. All the clusters in one block/district form the federation. Two representatives from each cluster represent in the federation. The meetings of SHGs are organised fortnightly/monthly. The meetings of clusters and federations are held every month.

Services provided by the federations

SHGs in India have come out of their first phase of formation. A majority of SHPIs are also now in their consolidation stage, where they are exploring the idea of promoting second and third tier structures of SHGs (i.e., SHG clusters and federations) to make their SHG programme self-sustaining.

These higher-level groups are being promoted by SHPIs primarily as an exit strategy, that is, to gradually withdraw their support to SHGs, while also ensuring their sustainability. Further, many SHPIs have promoted SHGs with funding support under some specific projects. After completion of the project, most SHPIs find it difficult to continue supporting the SHGs because of lack of funds. So, they consider it necessary to evolve and put in place a system to make SHGs self-sufficient and self-sustaining even after external funding stops. Federating SHGs is one of the popular ways to smoothen post-project withdrawal of SHPIs, but it requires preparedness and meticulous planning on behalf of the SHPIs, so that the financial and operational self-sufficiency of its SHG is ensured. NGOs are the only SHPIs that have promoted federations.

The activities undertaken by clusters and federations are as follows:

1. Services provided by clusters

a)   Clusters promote new SHGs and also maintain the quality of existing SHGs.
b)   They ensure proper recovery of loans; cluster creates peer pressure on SHG for timely repayment of loan.
c)   They facilitate conflict resolution; as the clusters are handling the issues at village/block level, the federations would play a role at higher level.

2. Services provided by federations

a)   Federations make SHGs self-sustainable in all aspects, that is, financial, operational, governance and so on.
b)   Federation will act as a peer pressure for the loan repayments.
c)   Some issues (such as livelihoods, availing government facilities, etc.), are common in all the clusters and hence have to be addressed from a single platform for better results. This necessitates promotion of federations.
d)   They iversify the activities of groups/clusters, that is, to provide other services like livelihoods, health, insurance, education and so on.
e)   They ensure proper follow-up of the processes like bank loan application, bank linkage and preparation of accounts.
f)   They act as a forum which can take initiative by proper discussion for decisions relating to penalty for defaulters, identifying beneficiaries for any activities and so on.
g)   Federations act as host organisations for SHGs in terms of some outsourced grants/loans. Federations channelise the outsourced money as loan to the groups, which will meet the demand of larger loans. They will also maintain the quality of groups according to the governance, operation and finance.

h) Federations will do the planning, budgeting and monitoring of clusters and the SHGs.

i) Sometimes, issues have to be taken up at district level with district magistrate/government department heads, controlling offices of banks and others. Federations have a better chance of getting heard at these levels as compared to SHGs/cluster of SHGs.

SHG federations provide a valuable set of services to the SHGs and individual members, and support the SHPI's strategy in terms of providing economies of scale and an exit strategy. While the benefits associated with building federations are immense, the challenges related to their inception also need to be addressed. The services offered by ten federations studied by us are summarised in Table 8.3. From the table, it is evident that most federations are offering services like group formation and its development, facilitating credit linkage, providing livelihood support to group members and providing various types of non-financial services.

Table 8.3 Summary of services provided by SHG federations

Services provided	MSM	SS	GMSS	SPSKK	MZMS	SNAKS	MMBF	JMVP	SBMS	ASS
Group formation	√	√	√	√	√	√		√	√	
Group development	√	√	√	√	√	√	√	√	√	√
Credit linkage	√	√			√	√	√	√	√	
Financial services	√	√	√		√					√
Livelihood	√	√	√		√	√		√		√
Health								√		
Education								√		
Social security (insurance)		√	√							
Social education/ mobilisation	√	√	√	√			√	√	√	√
Linking with govt. programmes						√	√		√	√

Financial sustainability of federations

Following are found to be the main sources of revenue for federations visited during the study.

1   **Membership fee and service fee:** Federation collects a service fee on each service it provides to its subsidiaries and members. These services include training, bookkeeping, marketing and bank linkage. Higher share of this source of funds, in total funds, indicates that federation is more accountable to its constituents and members. On the other hand, the federations can also get service fee from government and others for implementation of their programmes or handling their service delivery. In that case, the accountability to its members would be relatively less.
2   **Interest income on its corpus:** Federations get interest on their corpus which includes savings from their constituents, grants they receive and bulk loans they take from financial institutions and others for lending to member SHGs.
3   **Personal support and recurring grants:** These are obtained from promoters.

Normally each federation gets funds/resources from all three sources in different proportion. Dominance of each source in total resources of a federation determines its evolution. To illustrate the case of SS in Dausa, the following services were offered by the federation and service charges were collected for the same:

1   **Providing Management Information Systems (MIS) Services:** It is one of important service extended by SS. Raw data around financial transaction from SHG regular meetings are entered in the software. Groups receive trial balance, membership balance, balance sheets and other reports as output reports for the purpose of matching thei financial transactions at group level, developing peer pressure for repayments from group members and sharing data with banks for getting external credits. Groups are charged for the MIS services received.
2   **Loans** (life cycle needs and livelihood activities): A service charge of 1.5 per cent is deducted from any loan given to group from external sources (including banks).
3   **Emergency loans:** These loans are for specific purposes like health, education and marriage, and are provided by federations at an interest rate of 18 per cent per annum.

4   **Insurance:** Various insurance products offered are life insurance, cattle insurance, goat insurance, etc.
5   **Veterinary services:** These services are provided by a veterinary doctor and a para-vet employed by the federation; service charges are collected from SHG members for providing services like animal health check-ups at regular intervals, de-worming, vaccination, animal treatment, responding to emergency calls, castrations and dehorning.
6   **Artificial insemination (AI):** AI services are provided with a view to induct quality-breed milch animals (especially crossbred cows) to SHG members. Service charge is collected for providing AI and repeat AI services.

Expenditures of SHG federation

The managerial staff at the federation office comprises a coordinator, an accountant and Munshis or field representatives. The experience of staff in NGOs ranges from one to twenty-five years. Many of the staff working in the federation have three to four years of federation experience.

The role of the coordinator is to ensure the smooth execution of the operations and implementation of the decisions made by the executive committee, maintenance of MIS, conducting committee meetings and helping members in agenda preparations. The salaries of coordinators and accountants are paid by federations. Munshis, generally, are women members who have gained considerable experience in managing the affairs of SHGs. They act as local resource persons on behalf of federations to strengthen other SHGs. SHGs pay an agreed amount to the federation towards services provided by Munshis. The amount paid by each SHG depends on the age of SHGs, average savings and so on and may range from Rs 50 to Rs 150 per month. A Munshi looks after 10–15 SHGs.

The field representatives/Munshis are responsible for:

1   formation of new SHGs
2   opening of SHG bank account
3   attendance in SHG and cluster meetings
4   maintaining records at SHG and cluster levels
5   documentation for bank loan application
6   supporting projects implemented by the federations
7   maintenance and regular update of accounts of the SHGs

Table 8.4 Items of expenditure of SS

S. No.	Particulars	Rate	Annual expenditure (Rs)
1	Rent – office	Rs 2,000 p.m.	24,000
2	Telephone, electricity, stationery, etc.	Rs 2,000 p.m. (average)	24,000
3	Salary – coordinator	Rs 15,000 p.m.	180,000
4	Salary – accountant	Rs 5,000 p.m.	60,000
5	Salary – field coordinators (4 in number)	Rs 4,000 p.m. × 4	192,000
6	Conveyance expenses	Rs 3,000 p.m. (average)	36,000
7	Miscellaneous/others		5,000
	Total		521,000

Table 8.5 Level of financial sustainability of federations

S. No.	Level of financial sustainability	Names of federations
1	**Low** (revenues meeting 0–50% of expenditure)	• Savitribhai Phule Sawadhan Kendra Karanja, Wardha • Mahbubnagar Zilla Mahila Samakhya • Maneswar Matrushakti Block Level Federation, Sambalpur • Janani Mahila Vikash Parisada, Khurda, Orissa • Shakti Block Mahila Sangathan, Raebareli
2	**Moderate** (revenues meeting 50–75% of expenditure)	• Mahila Sangharsh Manch, Alwar • Annapurna Sewa Sansthan, Sant Kabir Das Nagar, UP
3	**High** (revenues meeting 75–100% of expenditure)	• Saheli Samiti, Dauasa • Gramin Mahila Swayamsiddha Sangh, Pune • Samsthan Narayanpur Kalanjia Sangamitra, Nalgonda

The major items of expenditure (overheads) of SS in Dausa at the time of field visit (April 2010) are given in Table 8.4.

It was observed that the level of financial sustainability of federations varied between 0 and 100 per cent. Table 8.5 summarises the level of financial sustainability of federations studied.

It is observed that 50 per cent of the sample federations were having very poor level of financial sustainability, 20 per cent of the sample federations had moderate level of financial sustainability and 30 per cent of the sample federations had high level of financial sustainability.

Qualitative impact of federations on SHGs

During our field visits, we got an overwhelming feedback that SHG federations are promoted for strengthening existing SHGs, promoting new SHGs of the poor and helping member SHGs to access various services from government and banking sectors. We also observed that federations play an important part in SHG capacity building. Based on this, we can safely proceed with a hypothesis that SHGs belonging to federations have the benefit of constant oversight by higher tier, and their quality should be better as compared to other SHGs. To validate this, data were collected on various parameters to compare the quality of SHGs belonging to federations and other SHGs that do not belong to any federation. In this chapter an attempt has been made to compare the differences in quality of SHGs between SHGs under the umbrella of federations and other SHGs that are not part of federation. For this purpose, 100 SHGs belonging to ten federations and 100 SHGs working in similar socio-economic, cultural and geographical milieu but not parts of a federation have been studied and compared.

Quality is the major challenge that the SHG movement is confronted with at this point of time in the country. To assess the quality of SHGs, NABARD developed a rating tool known as CRI and advised all banks to assess the quality of groups using the CRI before every credit linkage. The CRI basically consists of two sets of variables, namely, *governance- and systems-related variables* and *financial variables*. Governance-related parameters are periodicity of meetings, attendance in the meetings, decision-making process in the meeting, observation of norms, saving and loan installment collection methods, lending procedure, rotation of leadership, book-keeping and so on. Financial parameters include periodicity and regularity of saving, use of savings for internal lending, lending rates, lending norms and regularity in loan repayment.

Various quality parameters of SHGs under the umbrella of federations and other SHGs have been collected based on CRI discussed above.

Characteristics of SHGs studied

Main characteristics of sample SHGs are given in Table 8.6.

From Table 8.6, it is evident that two sample groups (federation SHGs and non-federation SHGs) are more or less similar in terms of their membership size and age.

Composition of SHGs

SHGs are expected to primarily help poor people. The composition of SHGs in terms of people's BPL (below poverty line) membership has been summarised in the Table 8.7.

In terms of representation of BPL population in groups, it is observed that two sample groups (federation SHGs and non-federation SHGs) are almost identical. However, it is encouraging to note that BPL forms a sizeable chunk of membership of SHGs, both under federation category and under non-federation category.

Table 8.6 SHG sample description

Particulars	Federation SHGs	Non-federation SHGs (control group)
Number of sample SHGs	100	100
SHG – only women members	100	99
SHG – only men members	0	1
SHG – mixed	0	0
Average number of members per SHG	**13.4**	**13.8**

Age of SHGs

Particulars	Federation SHGs	Non-federation SHGs (control group)
0–2 years	22	24
2–4 years	34	38
>4 years	44	38
Average number of years of existence	**4.6**	**4.3**

Source: Compiled.

Table 8.7 Composition of SHGs

Particulars	Federation SHGs	Non-federation SHGs (control group)
Having only BPL members	18	15
Having >5 BPL members	42	41
Having 1–5 BPL members	40	44
Average number of BPL members per group	5.3	5.8
BPL members as a percentage of total members of SHG	39.5%	42%

Table 8.8 Frequency of meetings and savings of SHGs

Particulars	Federation SHGs	Non-federation SHGs (control group)
Once in a month	84	88
Fortnightly	0	0
Weekly	16	12

Source: Compiled.

Note: Figures in percentage of SHGs.

Frequency of meetings and savings of SHGs

Table 8.8 summarises the frequency of group meetings and the frequency at which savings are collected by the groups.

It is observed that meeting and saving on a monthly basis seem most popular as more than four-fifth of the SHGs seem to have preferred monthly meeting and savings to other kinds of periodicity, both under federation and under non-federation categories. Nearly 14 per cent of SHGs save weekly. We did not come across any SHG resorting to saving fortnightly or once in two months.

Level of awareness of SHG members

The SHG members' awareness and understanding about the purpose of the group and the reason behind the formation of SHG are considered to be the core sustaining factors for SHGs. Our field assessments have shown that members of SHGs (of both categories), by and large, have good awareness about the activities taking place in the group, individual savings, loan details bank procedures and so on. In some of the non-federation SHGs, especially in Dausa District of Rajasthan, Raebareli District of UP and Pune District of Maharashtra, it was observed that some of the processes followed by SHG members were not as per recommended practices. Some of the examples are given below:

1   Quality of bookkeeping was poor; there were delays in updation and absence of signature of members attending the meetings.
2   Group members did not remember when the group was set up.
3   Bank loan received by the group was distributed equally among the members.
4   One group, which was more than a year old, had saving of Rs 13,000 but it had not started internal lending nor had applied for bank linkage.
5   Savings amount was distributed among members after five years.

The SHG members of both categories were observed to actively participate in the group activities and the decision-making process. Further, it was also observed that about 90 per cent of SHGs belonging to both categories had written rules and regulations and the same was available to any SHG member when required.

Attendance in meetings of SHGs

The level of attendance in SHG meetings in both categories of SHGs has been summarised in Table 8.9.

It is observed that the level of attendance in group meeting in federation SHG is higher than that of non-federation SHGs. Based on our field observations, this can easily be attributed to that fact that federations monitor SHG meetings closely and by and large there is always some representative/community worker who is present during the meeting.

Average monthly savings of SHG members

The data relating to average monthly savings of SHG groups in both categories of SHGs have been shown in the Table 8.10.

Table 8.9 Attendance in meetings of SHGs

Particulars	Federation SHGs	Non-federation SHGs (control group)
0–2 years	94	89
2–4 years	95	87
>4 years	91	83
Combined average	**94**	**86**

Source: Compiled.

Note: Figures in percentage of SHG members.

Table 8.10 Average monthly savings of SHG members (%)

Amount (in Rs)	Federation SHGs	Non-federation SHGs (control group)
0–20	6	22
20–50	43	42
50–100	51	35
>100	0	1
Combined average	**Rs 72**	**Rs 62**

Source: *Compiled*

Based on the financial strength of the members, each SHG fixes a certain amount as mandatory savings. In our sample, the average saving per member amounted to Rs 67 per month. It is observed that members save more in case of federation SHGs as compared to non-federation SHGs. In case of federation SHGs, majority of them save more than Rs 50 per month, while only 36 per cent of non-federation SHGs save more than Rs 50 per month. Federation SHGs save higher amount as compared to non-federation SHGs because of better understanding of benefits emanating from cumulative effect of higher amount of regular savings.

Annual savings per member in terms of age of SHGs

The data relating to annual average savings of SHG groups in both categories of SHGs have been shown in the Table 8.11.

As observed earlier, members save more in case of federation SHGs as compared to non-federation SHGs.

Table 8.11 Annual savings per member in terms of age of SHGs (in Rs)

Age of SHG	Federation SHGs	Non-federation SHGs (control group)
0–2 years	576	480
2–4 years	828	696
>4 years	912	768
Combined average	**864**	**744**

Source: Compiled.

Table 8.12 Cumulative savings of SHGs in 2010 (in Rs)

Age of SHG	Federation SHGs	Non-federation SHGs (control group)
0–2 years	7,718	6,293
2–4 years	33,286	23,814
>4 years	61,104	41,992
Combined average	**49,860**	**33,660**

Source: Compiled.

Cumulative savings of group

The data relating to annual cumulative savings of SHG groups since the time of group formation (on the date of data collection) in both categories of SHGs have been summarised in Table 8.12.

It was observed that the average amount of funds available with SHG (including savings, interest earned, fines and other miscellaneous incomes) stood at Rs 49,860 for federation groups and Rs 33,660 for non-federation groups. One of the reasons for such a high difference in groups' funds was that in case of federation groups, two groups had distributed savings after five years whereas in case of non-federation group this was done in respect of eighteen groups. From this it is evident that non-federation groups did not clearly recognise the importance of growing kitty of group savings in terms of leveraging external credit, and in terms of high interest earning for each member, when the fund is used for internal lending.

Utilisation of SHGs' savings for internal lending

The data relating to utilisation of savings of SHG groups for internal lending (on the date of data collection) in both categories of SHGs have been given in the Table 8.13.

Table 8.13 Utilisation of SHGs' savings for internal lending

Age of SHG	Federation SHGs	Non-federation SHGs (control group)
0–2 years	54	32
2–4 years	64	44
>4 years	59	43
Combined average	61	41

Source: Compiled.
Note: Figures in percentage of SHGs' savings.

Table 8.14 Interest rate charged on lending by SHGs

Rate of interest	Federation SHGs	Non-federation SHGs (control group)
Depending on purpose	3	1
Less than 18%	9	8
18–30%	80	91
>30%	8	0

Source: Compiled.
Note: Figures in percentage of SHGs.

As on the date of data collection (during February–April 2010), it was observed that 51 per cent of groups' savings (along with interest and other receipts like fine), for the entire sample SHGs taken together, was deployed for internal lending to members. Rest of the amount was kept either in the savings bank account or in the form of cash with the group. The extent of deployment of groups' savings for internal lending was higher in case of federation SHGs as compared to non-federation SHGs. This is another indicator reflecting better financial management practice in federation SHGs as compared to non-federation SHGs.

Interest rate charged on lending by SHGs

Table 8.14 gives the details regarding interest rate charged on lending by SHGs.

Groups were found to charge same interest rate on internal lending as well as lending of funds received from external sources. It was observed that almost 80 per cent of groups were charging interest rate of 24 per cent per annum on internal lending as well as lending of funds received from external sources. Groups belonging to GMSS, SNAKS, and JMVP were charging around 30 per cent per annum from their members on loans taken by them.

Group members benefitting from internal lending

The data relating to extent of SHG members benefitting from internal lending (on the date of data collection), in both categories of SHGs, have been given in Table 8.15.

It is observed that the percentage of SHG members benefitting from internal lending in respect of federation SHGs was higher as compared to non-federation groups. This can be interpreted in terms of more inclusive beneficial impact of internal lending in case of federation SHGs as compared to the control group.

Percentage of SHGs credit linked

The data relating to extent of bank linkage of SHGs, of both categories have been given in Table 8.16.

Table 8.15 SHG members benefitting from internal lending

Age of SHG	Federation SHGs	Non-federation SHGs (control group)
0–2 years	24	16
2–4 years	66	46
>4 years	76	58
Combined average	**70**	**52**

Source: Compiled.

Note: Figures in percentage of SHG members.

Table 8.16 Percentage of SHGs credit linked

Age of SHG	Federation SHGs*	Non-federation SHGs (control group)
0–2 years	44	32
2–4 years	81	66
>4 years	88	75
Combined average	**76**	**61**

*Also includes credit linkage with MFIs as in case of GMSS, SNAKS and JMVP.
Source: Compiled.

Note: Figures in percentage of SHGs.

As on the date of data collection (during February–April 2010), it was observed that 76 per cent of federation SHGs were credit linked as against only 61 per cent of non-federation SHGs. This clearly brings to fore the useful role played by federations in enabling groups to access external funds.

Repeat bank linkages

The data relating to extent of repeat bank linkage (in terms of number of times bank has provided credit to groups) of SHGs, of both categories, have been shown in Table 8.17.

On an average, for all the groups taken together, SHGs had got cash credit limit sanctioned by banks more than two times during their entire period of existence. The federation SHGs, on an average, could manage to get cash credit limit sanctioned 3.2 times by banks as against only 1.9 times by non-federation SHGs. This further confirms the beneficial role played by federations in helping SHGs to access bank credit more frequently.

Cumulative amount of credit sanctioned by banks

The data relating to cumulative amount of credit sanctioned by banks to SHGs, of both categories, have been shown in the Table 8.18.

An analysis of cumulative amount of loan sanctioned by banks to credit-linked SHGs indicate that banks, on an average, sanctioned an amount of Rs 65,655 to federation SHGs and for non-federation SHGs this amount stands at Rs 51,140. This clearly established that presence of federations facilitates groups to access more credit from banks.

Table 8.17 Number of times SHGs accessed credit from banks

Age of SHG	Federation SHGs	Non-federation SHGs (control group)
0–2 years	1.8	1.2
2–4 years	2.8	1.6
>4 years	3.6	2.2
Combined average	**3.2**	**1.9**

Source: Compiled.

Table 8.18 Cumulative amount of credit sanctioned by banks (in Rs)

Age of SHG	Federation SHGs	Non-federation SHGs (control group)
0–2 years	18,330	14,685
2–4 years	66,450	50,625
>4 years	84,610	66,180
Combined average	**65,655**	**51,140**

Source: Compiled.

Table 8.19 Group members benefitting from credit sanctioned by banks (%)

Age of SHG	Federation SHGs	Non-federation SHGs (control group)
0–2 years	36	22
2–4 years	58	43
>4 years	64	48
Combined average	**62**	**44**

Source: Compiled.

Group members benefitting from credit sanctioned by banks

The data relating to percentage of members of SHGs, of both categories, benefitting from bank linkage have been shown in the Table 8.19.

It is evident from Table 8.19 that while 62 per cent of SHG members of federation SHGs could get the benefit of loan accessed from banks, the same stood at only 44 per cent in case of non-federation SHGs. This indicates that presence of federation helps more SHG members to get the benefit of external credit. It was also observed that the average amount of loan availed by a group member (including internal loan) stood at Rs 5,833 for federation SHGs while the same stood at Rs 4,271 for non-federation SHGs.

Educational level of SHG members

In order to study the percentage distribution of SHGs by literacy level of the members of the groups, the SHGs were divided into three categories:

1   those in which all the members of the group are literate
2   those in which more than 50 per cent of the members were literate

3   those in which less than 50 per cent of the members were literate

The data relating to literacy levels of members of SHGs, of both categories, benefitting from bank linkage have been shown in the Table 8.20.

It was observed that the literacy level was higher in non-federation SHGs as compared to federation SHGs. One of the reasons for this was that most of the non-federation SHGs did not have the support of federation for writing books of accounts and, therefore, they were encouraged by SHPI to learn writing their books themselves.

Quality of bookkeeping

The quality of maintenance of books in respect of both categories of SHGs has been summarised in Table 8.21.

It was observed that in case of federation SHGs, books of accounts (minutes book, attendance register, members pass book, etc.) were written by *Samooh Sakhi* (local resource person) for which he or she is paid by the group. This made the group dependent on out-sider to write their books. In case of non-federation SHGs, groups managed this function on their own. The quality of bookkeeping system in the SHGs of both categories was found to be a matter of concern, as books were available but not updated. In most cases, the minute books were updated every month, while other books like loan register and savings register were updated only when the bookkeepers had sufficient time to update them.

Table 8.20 Educational level of SHG members

Particulars	Federation SHGs	Non-ederation SHGs
All the members of the group are literate	13	19
More than 50% of the members are literate (excluding groups having all literate members)	23	31
less than 50% of the members are literate	64	50
Overall percentage of literate members	63	68
Percentage of SHGs reporting increase in number of literate members since formation of group	61	78

Source: Compiled.

Note: Figures in percentage of SHGs.

Table 8.21 Maintenance of books of accounts

Books of accounts written by	Federation SHGs	Non-federation SHG
A literate member of SHG	22	46
Representative of federation/NGO	14	12
Person employed by SHG (local resource person)	42	4
Any other (relatives, friends)	22	38
Without outside assistance	22	46
With outside assistance	78	54

Source: Compiled.

Note: Figures in percent ageof SHGs

Table 8.22 Rotation of leadership

Age of SHG	Federation SHGs	Non-federation SHGs (control group)
Groups in which leadership was changed even once since inception	06	21

Source: Compiled.

Note: Figures in percentage of SHGs.

Governance of SHGs

The information regarding rotation of leadership in respect of both categories of SHGs has been given in the Table 8.22.

Only 6 out of 100 federation SHGs reported change of leadership, even once during the entire lifetime of the SHG. In case of non-federation SHGs, the incidence of changes in leadership was much higher at 21. During the field study, it was observed that in many of the SHGs, the members wanted and preferred the highest educated among them to be the leader since a large number of members were illiterate. Further, it could be also in the interest of the federation/NGO to appoint a capable as well as literate member of the group as the leader so that the running of the SHG is smooth. The concern for smoothness in day-to-day operations could be an important reason for persistence with the same group leaders over a period of time.

Summary of comparison

SHG federation members are SHGs, and they are the purpose for the federation to exist. Hence the performance of the SHGs is very important in assessing the overall performance of the federation. In this section, quality of SHGs in terms of a number of parameters has been analysed and the summary of the same is given in the Table 8.23.

Table 8.23 A comparative analysis of quality of groups

S. No.	Parameter	Federation SHGs	Non-federation SHGs
1	BPL members as a percentage of total members of SHG	No difference	
2	Frequency of meetings	No difference	
3	Attendance in meetings of SHGs	Higher	
4	Level of awareness about functioning of SHGs among members	Higher	
5	Average monthly savings of SHG members	Higher	
6	Annual savings per member in terms of age of SHGs	Higher	
7	Cumulative savings of the group	Higher	
8	Utilisation of groups' savings for internal lending	Higher	
9	Interest rate charged on lending by groups	No difference	
10	Percentage of group members benefitting from internal lending	Higher	
11	Percentage of SHGs credit linked	Higher	
12	Number of times SHGs accessed credit from banks	Higher	
13	Cumulative amount of credit sanctioned by banks	Higher	
14	Percentage of group members benefitting from credit sanctioned by banks	Higher	
15	Educational level of SHG members		Higher literacy level
16	Maintenance of books of accounts		Less dependence on outsider
17	Rotation of leadership		More frequent

Source: Compiled.

Conclusions

It is concluded that federations are engaged in undertaking socially meaningful tasks. They are essentially serving the unserved and meeting the credit needs of some of the most vulnerable sections of population. Considering this facet of their work, their operations may need to be financially supported/subsidised in the short or even the medium term. Further, our field studies revealed that one of the major benefits of federations is that federations could become alternative source of credit to SHGs. Such an alternative is essential because, in several regions of the country, banks' attitude towards SHGs is still not conducive for large-scale delivery of credit to poor.

As regards the impact of federations on SHGs, it clearly emerges that the quality of federation SHGs on parameters related to financial management (savings, inter-lending, bank linkage, amount of credit from external sources, etc.) is better as compared to the non-federation SHGs. On parameters related to general management practices (frequency of meetings, level of attendance, level of awareness regarding objectives of SHGs, availability of written rules and regulations, etc.) both categories of SHGs were found to be more or less similarly placed. In terms of governance (rotation of leadership) and writing of books of accounts, non-federation SHGs exhibited better quality as compared to federation SHGs. Therefore, it can be argued that presence of federation has indeed helped SHGs to manage their financial operations better as compared to non-federation SHGs.

Acknowledgement

The author acknowledges the support received from Centre of Microfinance Research at Bankers Institute of Rural Development, Lucknow, which sponsored a comprehensive study on SHG federations. The present chapter draws heavily from the above study report.

Notes

1 Harper, Malcolm, (2003), Do We Really Need SHG Federations? (Ten Commandments), available at http://www.ruralfinance.org/fileadmin/templates/rflc/documents/Do__we__really__need__SHG__Federations_pdf.pdf
2 Nair, Ajay, (Feb 2005), 'Sustainability of Microfinance Self Help Groups in India: Would Federating Help?', World Bank Policy Research Working Paper 3516.

3 7. MYRADA, (Nov 1999), 'Impact of Self Help Groups (Group process) on the Social/Empowerment status of Women members in Southern India', Paper Presented at the Seminar on SHG-bank Linkage Programme at New Delhi.

4 Sa-Dhan, (Sept 2006), 'Side-by-Side: A Slice of Microfinance Operations in India', New Delhi.

5 Reddy, C.S., (2004), 'SHG federations in India – A Status Report', APMAS.

6 Rajagopalan, Shashi, (Jun 2006), 'Designing Secondary Institutions of Self Help Groups – A Paper for Discussion', APMAS.

7 MYRADA, (Nov 1999), 'Impact of Self Help Groups (Group process) on the Social/ Empowerment Status of Women Members in Southern India', Paper Presented at the Seminar on SHG-bank Linkage Programme at New Delhi.

8 Tamil Nadu Corporation for Development of Women Ltd., (1999), A Guide to SHG Federations.

9 Dhan Foundation, (2004), Annual Report, Available at http://www.dhan.org/Downloads/AN-RE-04.pdf

10 Moyale, T., M. Dollard, and S.N. Biswas, (2006), 'Personal and Economic Empowerment in Rural Indian Women: A Self- Help Group Approach, *International Journal of Rural Management*, 2 (2): 245–66.

References

APMAS, (2007), 'SHG Federations in India', www.apmas.org, www.shg-gateway.in, Accessed on 17 July 2009.

DWCD & CIDA, (2000), 'Strengthening Primary Institutions So That They Become Socially and Economically Independent'.

Fernandez, A.P., (2001), 'Putting Institutions First- Even in Micro Finance: MYRADA'.

Ministry of Rural Development, (30 May 2008), 'National Workshop on SHG Workshop (Agenda Material)', Vigyan Bhavan, New Delhi.

Chapter 9

Do SHPIs play a role in credit access among SHGs? experiences from the SHG–Bank Linkage Programme

Veerashekharappa

Despite the vast expansion of the formal credit system in India, the dependence of the rural poor on informal credit institutions continues in some areas, especially for meeting the emergent credit requirements. Such dependence is pronounced in the case of most vulnerable sections, particularly in the resource-poor areas. As the credit needs of these sections are determined in a complex socio-economic milieu, it is difficult to adopt a project-lending approach as followed by banks, and the dividing line between credit for 'consumption' and 'productive' purposes is blurred. It is in this context that people's participation in development process assumes significance. The participatory approach brings out the mutual trust and overcomes the asymmetric information between the members, which is necessary for initiating banking relationship based on trust and confidence.

The credit programmes introduced and expanded by non-governmental rrganisations (NGOs) under self-help groups (SHGs) could reach poorest of the poor as these groups work on the lines of mutual trust as well as equal participation. These groups have comparative advantages over other constituents of the formal credit system in reaching the rural poor due to the following:

1 Propagator of voluntarism
2 Practitioner of mutual help and cooperative principles
3 Promoter of thrift and savings
4 Provider of timely emergency loans and purveyor of development credit
5 Participative lending methodologies.

National Bank for Agriculture and Rural Development (NAB-ARD) promoted and encouraged this concept to function as financial intermediaries to flow funds to the micro-entrepreneurs. Later, it evolved mechanism to integrate the SHGs with formal banking institution through SHG–Bank Linkage Programme (SBLP). This has brought out a major change in accessing credit from formal institutions and invited attention of many, including policy makers, donors, NGOs and academicians. In this context, an academic exercise is attempted to examine the growth, function and operation in the state of Karnataka, India, with the following specific objectives:

1　To examine the performance of SBLP across self-help promoting institutions (SHPIs)
2　To identify and analyse the reasons including various policies and strategies adopted by different SHPIs
3　To examine the impact of linkage programme on the performance of SHGs in enhancing the outreach and improving the access of poor to livelihood programmes.

Data and methodology

The secondary and primary data are being used for analysis purpose. The secondary data are collected mainly from the Reserve Bank of India (RBI) and NABARD and through other published information. Discussions with district development manager, lead bank manager, district rural development agency, and other main banks officials including managing director of regional rural banks (RRBs) and cooperative banks and the major NGOs were recorded and used. For collection of primary data, multi-level sampling method was adopted. First, the density index was developed with the help of two concentration ratios based on secondary data. The ratios were: (a) SHGs linked per villages and b) SHGs linked per formal financial institutions commercial banks (CBs) RRBs and district central cooperative banks (DCCBs), spread in rural areas in the district. Based on this index, Karkala taluk in Udupi District was selected. Within the taluk, we distributed total sample SHGs among the financial institutions (RRBs, DCCBs and CBs) according to the ratio of outreach of SHGs. On the basis of these, a list of villages was made and from that, villages were chosen randomly. In each selected village, all SHGs were interviewed till the target was achieved. From each group, three individuals are selected for further interactions. This chapter is presented in five sections: section two documents the advantages of group lending, section three examines the growth and expansion of SBLP in Karnataka, fourth section brings out contribution of SHPIs in promotion SBLP, fifth section examines whether SHGs members have had capital gains and the last section provides suggestions based on conclusions.

Importance of credit

Financial systems have been described as a vital for economic development in both developed and developing countries. Normally, the type financial systems vary across countries, depending on the nature of country's economy. The writing of various scholars emphasises the importance of a strong and efficient financial system in providing growth in developing countries through expansion and deployment of credit. Credit enables a person to extend his control as distinct from his ownership on resources; in fact, 'credit' represents the savings' transformation into capital. The extension of credit is important and necessary for the expansion of investment for small farmers and entrepreneurs. But, the credit from formal credit institutions is constrained due to collateral requirement, and often policies are substantially biased in favour of political groups. Further, due to information asymmetries, moneylender continues his dominance in credit market, which will have adverse impact on raising the interest rates or demand for higher collateral.

In India, unlike other countries, the banking system is largely state induced and its operations and functions are integrated with the national objectives. To achieve the national objectives, priority sector lending is made mandatory among the banks. The priority sector lending approach, and subsequent developments, has led to the expansion of the geographical and functional reach of commercial banks, RRBs and cooperative credit institutions. Though the policies on institutional credit have increased the volume of credit across the sectors, it did not produce the desired results in covering of marginal and vulnerable sections.

Nevertheless, with the onset of economic reforms in the early 1990s, there is a distinct shift in the banking policy. The focus of

Table 9.1 Commercial banks' credit to weaker sections

Year	Public sector bank (in Rs in crore)	Percentage of net bank credit	Private sector bank (Rs in crore)	Percentage of net bank credit
1991	10,260	9.7	246	5.2
1992	10,881	9.7	269	4.5
1993	11,865	8.9	283	4.0
1994	12,779	9.1	300	3.1
1995	13,918	8.2	339	2.5
1996	15,579	8.4	381	2.1
2001	24,899	7.2	959	1.7
2002	28,974	7.3	1,142	1.8
2003	32,303	6.7	1,223	1.5
2004	41,589	7.4	1,495	1.3
2005	63,492	8.8	1,913	1.2
2006	78,373	7.7	3,909	1.6

Source: Chavan (2007).

the banks, during the reform periods, has been on enhancing the efficiency and profitability of the banks. As a result of this, many of the regulations that were applied on the banking system, during the pre-reform period, have been relaxed in order to allow a market-based and more liberalised operation for the banking system. This has led to the exclusion of most of the vulnerable group from formal financial system.

As a result of the banking sector reforms, and the new policy changes, the advances to the 'weaker sections' as percentage of net bank credit show a disturbing trend during the reform period of 1990s and later (Table 9.1). Domestic commercial banks, which were mandated to direct at least 10 per cent of their net credit to these sections, were not able to meet this target. Moreover, the gap between target and achievement continued to be widening over the years.

The advantage of group lending approach

The informal credit market in India is not a homogeneous entity. However, in recent years, the traditional landlords and moneylenders are fading away, and over time, a new class of lenders, who are the dealers of working capital, has emerged. These informal lenders have local knowledge and information, and thus do not encounter asymmetric information and lend to the risky borrowers. The informal groups known as SHGs are emerging as self-financers; the SHG is an informal group, whose members pool savings and re-lend within the group on need basis. The group lending movement has made inroads around the world, including India. Considering the strength of the groups, a proposal is made to link them with formal banking institutions. The SBLP is being implemented all over India by NABARD. The primary objective of SBLP is to expand the outreach of the formal banking system and help banks to overcome the problem of high transaction cost by passing on some responsibilities of banks to SHGs, such as loan appraisal, follow-up and recovery. A partnership between these two (SHGs and banks) would seek to make optimal use of the strengths of each in sustaining the collaborative effort, in addition to the set following objectives:

1   As moneylender – provides quick, small emergent loans, but without charging exploitative rate of interest
2   As development banker – provides small production and investment credit to the poor for their economic development but without going through thelong procedures, documentation, security requirements and so on, at lesser transaction cost
3   As a cooperative – adopts participation approach of mutual cooperatives and joint pressure without the ills of self-interest, interference of politicians/government department officials
4   As voluntary agency – helping each other through their common efforts, and for bringing economic and social enlistment among the poor people.

Growth and expansion of SBLP

The SBLP has shown a significant growth over the years; the number of savings accounts from SHGs have increased from 4.16 million in 2007 to 5.01 million in 2008 and further to 5.99 million in 2009. In fact, the amount saved by SHGs has increased from Rs 35.12 billion in 2007 to Rs 37.85 billion in 2008 and further to Rs 54.47 billion in 2009; the incremental growth in 2009 over 2008 was a phenomenal growth of 44 per cent. The average saving per SHGs, across sponsored agencies, is Rs 7,810 (CBs), Rs 12,400 (RRBs) and Rs 8,420 (DCCBs). The credit linkage, which started

Table 9.2 All-India cumulative progress of SBLP (March end)

Year	No. of SHGs financed	Average loan per SHG	Average loan per family
1992–93	255	11,765	692
1993–94	365	9,863	580
1994–95	1,502	11,917	701
1995–96	2,635	13,700	806
1996–97	3,841	15,048	885
1997–98	5,719	20,843	1,226
1998–99	18,678	17,828	1,049
1999–00	81,780	16,618	978
2001–02	197,653	27,601	1,624
2003–04	361,731	36,180	2,412
2005–06	482,598	64,155	4,277
2008–09	1,609,586	76,108	5,436

Source: NABARD.

with 255 SHGs and an advancement of Rs 30 lakh, has shown a phenomenal growth. Table 9.2 presents year-wise achievement; according to it there was unprecedented increase in 1999–2000; this was attributed for considering these loans as part of priority sector by RBI. The total loans disbursed by banks to SHGs in 2008–09 were Rs 12,707 billion, out of which 59 per cent was shared between two states – Andhra Pradesh and Tamil Nadu. The average loans disbursed to SHGs in aggregate is Rs 74,000, while in Haryana, Uttar Pradesh (UP) and Uttarkhand, it is exceeded Rs 100,000; in Maharashtra, it was just Rs 31,300.

The linkage is provided through following three models:

1   Banks lend directly to the ultimate borrowers without having NGOs or SHGs as intermediaries.
2   Banks lend directly to the ultimate borrowers, and NGOs and SHGs are involved as non-financial intermediaries.
3   Banks use SHGs as financial intermediaries to lend the credit to the borrowers, with NGOs as non-financial intermediaries.

Of the three models, the second one is relatively popular (75 per cent of linkages), across regions: the southern region has a higher share, followed by eastern region and the lowest here is observed

Table 9.3 SBLP region-wise in percentage, March 2009

Region	No. of SHGs linked	Cumulative loan disbursed (Rs in million)
Northern	6.5	4.7
North-eastern	3.2	3.1
Eastern	17.3	7.9
Central	11.6	7.4
Western	7.7	4.5
Southern	53.1	72.4
Total	**100 (1,609,586)**	**100 (1,225,351)**

Source: NABARD, SHG–Bank Linkage 2009.

Table 9.4 Distribution of SBLP by southern states, 2009

State	Commercial banks	RRBs	Cooperative banks	Total
Andhra Pradesh	73.3	26.1	1.6	100 (1280900)
Karnataka	34.8	36.2	29.9	100 (457,389)
Kerala	78.8	8.0	13.2	100 (358,863)
Tamil Nadu	74.0	10.1	15.9	100 (730,092)
Total	**67.5**	**21.2**	**11.4**	**100 (2827244)**

Note: Figures in parentheses are numbers.

in north-eastern region (Table 9.3). This trend is been seen ever since the programme has been implemented. Within Southern region, the Andhra Pradesh is first place, followed by Tamil Nadu and Karnataka. The rank at all India level show that after Andhra Pradesh, Orissa, Karnataka, Tamil Nadu and Himachal Pradesh in descending order. Across the state, the better performance is being attributed for better NGO networking and their involvement in promotion of lively hood programmes.

Within southern region, the share of SBLP is high in Andhra Pradesh (45 per cent), followed by Tamil Nadu and Karnataka. Across credit agencies, large proportion of SBLP is held by commercial banks, followed by RRBs and cooperatives. In Karnataka, the share of linkage is evenly distributed across credit agencies. This is due to NGOs spread across the states, as well as the credit agencies coming forward in providing linkages, to fulfil priority sector lending target. In addition, most of the SHPIs provide credit plus services.

SBLP expansion in Karnataka

As mentioned earlier, the cause for success of SBLP depends largely on the strategies adopted by promotional institutions in linking up livelihood programmes. The SHPIs can be classified into three, based on constitution and activities. They are:

1 **NGOs including religious/charitable foundation:** Shri Kshetra Dharmasthala Rural Development Project (SKDRDP), TRDF, Normal

  Federation, Bellary Diocesan Development Society, etc.

2 **Banking institutions:**

  a RRBs (Cauvery Garment Bank, Mysore)
  b Cooperative Bank (The Bidar DCCB)
  c Village Volunteer Vahini clubs SHPI (Gulbarga)
  d Canara Bank, Vijaya Bank, etc.

3 **State as SHPI:**

  a Zillah Pantheist (Sill Pantheist, Belgaum)
  b Department of Agriculture (Danish International Development Agency, Women and Youth Training Extension Project)
  c Karnataka Milk Federation
  d Department of Women and Child

The multiple agencies' involvement has contributed for expansion of SBLP and also contributed in upgrading skills of SHGs in maintenance of records, bank transactions and identifying income-generating activities, as couple of SHPIs are functioning as resource centres. However, within the state, the number of SHGs promoted across district varies (Table 9.5). The highest number of linkages is observed in Dashina Kannada district. This has attributed for the presence of large number of SHPIs as well as involving in developmental work.

Table 9.5 Density of SBLP by district (SHGs per 1,000 households)

Good		Moderate		Low	
District	SHGs	District	SHGs	District	SHGs
D. Kannada	116	Chamarajanagar	62	Haveri	49
Udupi	96	Davanagere	61	Bangalore (U)	47
Shimoga	87	Hassan	61	Bijapur	45
Chikamagalur	83	Gadag	61	Belgaum	45
Gulbarga	80	Tumkur	59	Bagalkot	35
U. Kannada	79	Kolar	57	Koppal	33
Dharwad	79	Bellary	55		
Kodagu	79	Raichur	54		
Bidar	78	Bangalore (R)	51		
Mysore	72				
Chitradurga	70				
Mandya	69				

Features of the selected district

The selected district, Udupi, has a good banking network with 230 branches (CBs, RRBs, and DCCBs and primary cooperative agriculture and rural development banks). The high density of banking network has contributed to less population per branch and less distance in location of branches. Because the large number of branches also contributed for better business development, this has contributed to an increase in aggregate credit deposit ratio, compared to other districts, as well as state average.

The Southern District Credit Cooperative Bank has also initiated group formation under title of 'Navodaya Self Help Groups'; later groups are linked to the bank, and for this an exclusive cell has been created. The NABARD has identified three NGOs as resource centres with financial assistance for skill enhancement of SHG personnel (SKDRDP, NST and Jeevandhara). The SKDRDP is involved in various rural development activities and also has a well-established resource centre. Similarly, the NST and Jeevandhara have also made their space in the district by promoting various activities of SHGs.

Features of the selected sample

Based on methodology mentioned earlier, forty SHGs have been selected; these involved different SHPIs, such as government organisations, NGOs and banks. Of the selected groups, eighteen were formed by NGOs, followed by eighteen state departments and four cooperative banks. The SKDRDP has a monopoly in this area, as no other NGO is operating in these villages.

Normally, the SHG size is expected to be fifteen to twenty members, but among the sample, the strength varies across promoted institutions. The NGOs and state-promoted groups have the size between eleven and fourteen; bank groups' size is nine to ten members. The variation is attributed for two reasons – lack of sufficient eligible members and the scattered nature of villages – which will have negative effect on the attendance in the meeting, which are usually held in the evenings.

Linkage by banks

The selected groups were in existence for more than six years. Normally, groups are eligible for deposit linkage after six months of formation. For the selected samples, on an average, there is a two-year waiting period for linkage (Table 9.6). Across credit agencies, the waiting period was less for cooperatives, followed by CBs and RRBs. The delay in linkage was attributed to failure of groups in achieving the prescribed score in grading and also lack of sufficient staff at bank to follow up the work.

The number of linkages by credit agencies shows that the CBs and RRBs had equal numbers (13 each) and remained groups are

Table 9.6 Time gap in linkage across banks and agencies

Year	Formal credit agencies (%)			Self-help promoting institutions (%)			Total (%)
	CBs	RRBs	Coop.	NGO	State	Coop. Bank	
One	0.0	15.4	28.6	0	13	100	15
Two	53.8	30.8	57.1	83	25	0	47
Three +	46.2	53.9	14.3	17	62	0	38
Total	100 (13)	100 (13)	100 (14)	100 (18)	100 (18)	100 (4)	100 (40)

Table 9.7 Per capita savings (in percentage) of SHGs by SHPIs

SHPIs	Amount saved by SHGs (Rs in thousand)					Total
	>2	2.1>3	3.1>5	5.1>10	10.1>	
NGOs	0	45.3	7.3	17.3	30	100(150)
State	21.5	78.5	0.0	0.0	0.0	100(189)
Cooperatives	100.0	0.0	0.0	0.0	0.0	100(38)
Total	19.4	55.7	6.1	6.9	11.9	100(377)

linked to cooperative banks. All groups formed by organisations are financed by credit agencies; however, the cooperative bank–sponsored groups have received finance exclusively from cooperative banks.

Savings of the group

The per capita savings of groups varies due to number of factors, such as weekly savings and age of the group. Among the sample selected, on an average, per capita savings is Rs 4,500; 75 per cent of members had per capita savings less than Rs 3,000 and the rest had savings of more than Rs 3,000 (table 9.7). About 12 per cent members had per capita savings of more than Rs 10,000.

Credit accessibility

The SHGs access credit formally from two sources: first from their internal savings and second from banks under SBLP. The rate of interest charged by banks to these groups is around 10 to 12 per cent. But cooperative banks have slashed their interest rates to the groups from 10 to 6 per cent, so these rates are much lesser than what is charged by the microfinance institutions (MFIs) or professional moneylenders. The groups, in turn, charge 12 to 13 per cent interest from their members; the surplus is kept within the groups for internal lending.

The frequency of borrowing depends on the need of the members. According to Table 9.8, 10 per cent of total members never borrowed, 18 per cent borrowed one time, the rest borrowed two and more times; this includes both internal and external sources. Across groups, the number of those who have never borrowed is

Table 9.8 Number of times internal loans obtained

SHPIs	No. of loans borrowed by the members						Total
	None	Once	Twice	Thrice	Four+	Five+	
NGOs	3.3	10.7	24.0	16.7	19.3	26.0	100(150)
State	11.0	21.5	19.6	13.5	14.7	19.6	100(189)
Coop.	34.2	36.8	26.3	0.0	2.6	0.0	100(38)
Total	9.8	17.8	21.5	14.6	15.6	20.7	100(377)

high among the cooperative and state group members. This was due to lack of large savings and monitoring of the group's activities. The frequency of borrowing is high among the NGO-SHG groups – 25 per cent of NGO-SHGs have borrowed five times and only 3.3 per cent have never borrowed. If one relates the borrowing pattern with the socio-economic background of the members, we find inverse relationship with landholding; the landless and members with very little land borrowed more number of times than the landholders and higher castes.

The main objective of SBLP is to have capital accessibility by SHG members for investments: timely and adequate, at affordable cost. The pre-linkage and post-linkage scenario shows that after linkage, the number of group members, who have borrowed large amounts, invest in income-generating activities (IGAs).

The post-linkage scenario shows a very positive trend – more than five members in four groups (twenty members) have taken up food-processing units. Each member has borrowed Rs 20,000 from the bank by creating sub-group (within group), with the endorsement of all the group members. The activities taken by the groups vary. Most of the state group members have taken up dairy while the cooperative group members have taken up trading activities. These activities have been taken up due to encouragement of respective promotional institutions. The group members, during group discussions, expressed that the guidance and motivation from SHPIs is a must to take up livelihood activities; for example, due to NGOs' motivation and providing linkages to members, many members have taken up livelihood activities. The intervention at functional monitoring and frequent training has helped NGO-SHGs accessing capital for better investment.

Credit within group

It was observed that in nineteen groups, sub-groups were formed considering their homogeneity in skills and willingness to take up a particular activity. Across the groups, the NGO sub-groups have borrowed bulk loan frequently for investing in IGAs. However, the amount borrowed per SHG is high among the Swarnajayanti Gram Swarozgar Yojana (SGSY) groups (Table 9.9). The per capita amount borrowed by members, on an average, is Rs 13,600. Across groups, the average borrowing is high among the SGSY, followed by NGO-SHGs. Each group has a specific advantage in its affiliation with SHPI. For instance, NGO-SHGs get knowledge support in accessing raw materials and marketing their product, whereas state-affiliated groups get the benefit of rotating fund and accessing poverty alleviatiation programmes, and the cooperatives-affiliated groups get loans at lower cost and also within a short time.

Table 9.9 Borrowing from formal credit institutions by purpose

Agencies	NGO	DWC	SGSY	Coop. bank	Total
CBs	14	7	2	0	23
RRBs	4	9	0	0	13
Cooperatives	0	0	0	4	04
Total	18	16	2	4	40
SHGs taken more than one loan	11	7	0	0	19
Total amount borrowed	1,881,601	1,146,542	800,000	159,000	4,905,601
Per SHG amountt borrowed	104,533	71,658	400,000	3,975	122,640
Per capita amount borrowed	15,945	11,875	17,391	8,833	13,600
Interest charged (FI to SHGs)	11	11		6	
Interest (SHGs to members)					
12	4	0		4	9
24	2	6		0	8
36	5	0		0	5
Repayment of loan (months)	12 to 36, 60	12–36, 60		12, 60	0

Table 9.10 Purpose of borrowing

Amount borrowed (Rs)	Purpose of borrowing				Total
	IGA	Housing and infrastructure	Marriage and health	Old loan repaid	
>25,000	25.7	33.9	21.1	19.3	100(139)
25,001–50,000	25.4	34.1	19.1	21.4	100(173)
500,001–750,000	15.0	21.7	26.7	36.7	100(60)
75,000>	20.0	40.0	40.0	0.0	100(5)
Total	**23.6**	**32.0**	**21.3**	**23.1**	**100(377)**

The utility of loan is shown in Table 9.10. Of the total loans availed (377), 32 per cent were borrowed for house construction or repair, followed by 24 per cent for business, 9 per cent for repayment of old loans and 13 per cent for the marriage purpose. Across the loan size, the smaller loans were taken for the purpose of repayment of loans; larger loans were availed for business, construction of houses and buying household essentials. The two SGSY groups have borrowed for dairy activity but each member has used his share of the borrowed money for other purpose than dairy. Thus, the SGSY amount is being misused.

The relation between amount borrowed and purpose show that higher amount borrowed is spent on asset creation and social functions such as house repair and marriage rather than IGA. For instance, of the total five loans, each of Rs 75,000, two have been for marriage and house construction Table 9.11.

The borrowing sources are from three credit agencies: CBs, followed by RRBs and cooperatives. However, there is variation across purpose of borrowing; for example, the amount borrowed from CBs and RRBs was used for productive purpose, and cooperative borrowings were used to meet marriage expenses and repayment of loans. The CBs are strict in sanctioning of loans. These banks extend loans normally for income-generating purpose rather than for social functions. Cooperative banks do not insist on purpose borrowing. As long as the repayment schedule is met, they do not bother on the purpose of borrowings.

From Table 9.12, it can be observed that the rate of interest paid by the members is independent of the credit agencies. The groups charge interest around 24 to 36 per cent. Although the re-lending

Table 9.11 Source of borrowing by purpose

Amount borrowed (Rs)	Purpose of borrowing				Total	
	IGA	House repair	Marriage and health	Old loan repaid	Number	Per centage
CBs	20.3	42.2	12.5	19.3	100(181)	43
RRBs	66.7	33.3	0.0	21.4	100(136)	40
Cooperative banks	23.0	21.3	29.5	36.7	100(60)	17
Total	23.6	32.0	21.3	23.1	100(377)	100

Table 9.12 Source of funds and the interest paid by borrower

Banks	Interest rates (percentage)				Total
	12	18	24	36	
CBs	53.8	6.2	33.8	6.2	100(181)
RRBs	33.3	0.0	66.7	0.0	100(136)
Cooperatives	24.6	0.0	62.3	13.1	100(60)
Total	28.5	1.2	47.6	22.8	100(377)

has to be made with marginal addition of the extra interest, in fact the actual amount paid is more than what has to be paid. The group members do agree that, while calculation, the interest rate really paid is high, because it is calculated on daily basis. The total amount charged by the banks also cost more than what is to be paid as interest; for instance, a RRB has collected Rs 1,200, as inspection charges, which is in addition to interest amount..

The SBLP provides not only accessibility and adequate credit to the members but also credit plus services, such as awareness training on various activities, expose to IGAs and health insurance.

Conclusion and suggestions

The SBLP has attempted to promote SHGs as an adaptive institutional mechanism under which formal agencies can deal with the poor to deliver savings and credit without being constrained by consideration of physical collateral and cost of handling smaller transactions. No doubt, the SBLP has given a fillip to the formation of a large number of SHGs, with involvement of state, banks and NGOs. However, banks have not taken much initiative in the formation of SHGs and the SHGs promoted by NGOs seem to be displaying relatively better qualities.

The SHPIs have tried to ensure to a large extent the features commonly expected of a typical SHG. The size norms of the SHGs under SBLP are not followed due to location constraints. The current size of SHGs varies from place to place and eligible population within the location.

The study identified some potential strength of groups in providing access to savings and credit facilities. Despite disadvantage at household economy, the SHGs have been able inculcate regular savings habits among the members to mobilise fair amount of savings, individually and collectively. The savings are helping SHGs to develop a safeguard mechanism against any possible loan default. On credit, while most SHGs have taken up internal lending, majority of them were yet to pursue lending based on external funds. The intermediation of SHPIs and high awareness of members and the voluntarism by banks in extending credit to the SHGs have contributed to the gaining of capital for the investment in IGA.

Regarding the interest rates on loans, the SHGs seem to have adopted a kind of via media between the rates prevailing in the informal and formal markets in the district. The interest rate charged to the ultimate member has been above the rate (12–36 per cent per annum) at which the SHGs have obtained external funds and generally lower than the rate prevailing in the informal sector. As financial intermediaries, the SHGs are expected to bring down the cost of transaction to the members. The experience shows that as the SHGs mature, the rate of interest charged by them tends to come down to some extent. About the impact of SHGs, it could be observed that in SHGs which have taken up lending, a significant proportion of their members are found accessing them. The members are finding SHGs to be a useful source for meeting their smaller credit needs. The loans are being taken for various production, consumption and social purposes, a pattern commonly expected under most microfinance interventions. Although the SGSY programme has identified group activity for sanctioning of loan scheme, once the amount is released, the members claim their due amount and use the money as they wish; sometimes this could be against the basic purpose of sanctioned loan.

Based on the above findings, the following policy implications may be drawn about the SBLP and the role of SHGs in it. A key requirement in achieving the goals of SBLP is the successful formation and nurturing of SHGs. Given the nature, any large-scale formation of SHGs would require emergence of good SHPIs. The SHGs' sustainability, to a large extent, depends on the promotional activities carried out by SHPIs. The accesses of capital from the SBLP by SHGs largely depend on critical minimum development theory. For instance, the SHGs of NGO-SHPI group have gained due to their critical minimum development achieved due to continuous monitoring. The groups are managing their own on getting raw material and marketing of their goods independently or through tie-up arrangement with the SHPIs.

References

Allen, F., and D. Gale, (1995), 'A Welfare Comparisons of Intermediaries and Financial Markets in Germany and the US', *European Economic Review*, 39, pp. 179–209.

Belshaw, H., (1931), 'The Provision of Credit with Special Reference to Agriculture', *Auckland University College Text*, No. 1, Cambridge.

Chathukulam, J., (2003), 'Poverty Reduction through Social Capital Formation: The Case of Women's Self Help Groups in Kerala', *Man and Development*, 25(2), June, pp. 67–90.

Chavan, P., (2007), 'Access to Bank Credit: Implications for Dalit Rural Households', Available at http://www.agrarianstudies.org/userfiles/file/chavan_access_to_bank_credit.pdf

Deb, S., (2003), 'Credit Flows and Agricultural Growth: An Inter-Block Study of Institutional and Non-Institutional Finance in Hooghly District', Unpublished thesis, Jadavpur University, Kolkata.

Griffin, K., (1976), 'The Political Economy of Agrarian Change: An Essay on Green Revolution', *Macmillian*, London.

Hoff, K., and J.E. Stiglitz, (1990), 'Introduction: Imperfect Information and Rural Credit Markets – Puzzles and Policy Perspective', *The World Bank Economic Review*, 4(3), pp. 235–250.

Lipton, M., (1976), 'Agricultural Finance and Rural Credit in Poor Countries', *World Development*, 4(7), pp. 543–553.

McKinnon, R.J., (1973), 'Money and Capital in Economic Development', *Brooking Institution*, Washington.

NABARD, (1989), 'Studies of Self-Help Groups of the Rural Poor', Bombay.

National Bank for Agriculture and Rural Development, (1992), 'SHG-Bank Linkage Programme', Bombay.

Padmanabhan, K.P., (1988), 'Rural Credit: Lessons for Rural Bankers and Policy Makers', *Intermediate Technology Publications*, London.

Patrick, H.T., (1983), 'Financial Development and Economic Growth' in Von-Pischke, Adams, Donald (ed.) Rural Financial Market in Developing Countries, *The John Hopkins University Press*, London.

Rajeev, M., and S. Deb, (1998), 'Institutional and Non-Institutional Credit to Agriculture: A Case Study on Hoogli district of West Bengal', *Economic and Political Weekly*, XXXIII (47&48), pp. 2987–2995.

Shetty, Naveen K., and Veerashekharappa, (2009), 'The Microfinance Promise in Financial Inclusion: Evidence from India', *ICFAI Journal of Applied Economics*, 8(6), pp. 174–189.

Shylendra, H.S., (2004), 'The SHG-Bank Linkage Programme: An Assessment and Future Strategies', *Journal of Rural Development*, 23(4), pp. 411–433.

Srinivasan, N., (2009), 'Microfinance India: State of the Sector Report 2009', *Sage Publication, Pvt.*, New Delhi.

Stiglitz, J.E., and A. Weiss, (1981), 'Credit Rationing in Markets with Imperfect Information', *The American Economic Review*, 71(3), pp. 393–410.

Veerashekharappa and Chandrashekhar, (2008), 'Impact Evaluation of SGSY Programmed in Tumkur District', Siddaganga Institute of Technology and MYPSED of State Bank of Mysore, Tumkur.

Veerashekharappa, Shylendra, H.S. and S. Guha, (2009), 'Has the SHG-Bank Linkage Helped the Poor Gain Access to Capital? A Comparative Study between Karnataka and Gujarat', Memograph, *Institute for Social and Economic Change*, Bangalore.

Chapter 10

The role of NGOs, SHGs and international financing agencies in the reconstruction of tsunami-hit Karaikal

Suraj Theruvath and Swetha Muralidharan

Microfinance is all about delivering financial assistance to low-income groups which would include not only credit but also other offerings like savings, fund transfer and insurance. One such case of microfinance can be observed through the works undertaken by various non-governmental organisations (NGOs) in the reconstruction of various tsunami-hit coastal areas of India. Studying the works of all the NGOs in the reconstruction and upliftment of the affected areas would be exhaustive. Hence, efforts have been made to restrict the study of works undertaken in the reconstruction of areas in and around the coastal town of Karaikal.

Karaikal

Karaikal is one of the four French establishments constituting the union territory of Pondicherry. It is situated at a distance of 9 km south of Tharangambadi and 16 km north of Nagapattinam. It comprises the following panchayats of Karaikal: Kottuchcheri, Nedungadu, Thirunallar, Niravi and Thirumalarajanpattinam. As per the 2001 census, the population of Karaikal was projected at 170,640, with an area of 161 sq. km (Table 10.1).

Karaikal is one of the most scarcely populated regions of Pondicherry with the least number of houses per square kilometre. The population is characterised by more number of women than men. Since, Karaikal is situated in the state of Tamil Nadu, majority of people speak Tamil. Karaikal has three major communities: Hindus, Christians and Muslims. Hindus form the majority of population with a proportion of 76.23 per cent, as per the census of 2011, Christians 9.19 per cent, and the rest are Muslims.

Table 10.1 Population of Karaikal

Year	Population	Men	Women
2001	1,70,640	84,365	86,275

Source: Census, 2001.

Fishing community of Karaikal

The coastal zones act as a means of livelihood in many ways to a majority of the population residing in it. Most of the livelihood works that are undertaken include fishing, fish drying, coastal agriculture, salt extraction and production and shell collection. Most of the coastal communities depend on variety of natural resources like fish, shrimp, plants and minerals and corals. The fishing community of Karaikal predominantly consists of middle-level boat owners and numerous labourers. Coastal Karaikal consists of eleven fishing villages, ranging from very small ones to the biggest being the village of Karaikalmedu. Of the many issues affecting the coastal community of Karaikal, two are important: one is the issue relating to indiscriminate shrimp farming which started in Tamil Nadu two decades ago and the second is the great Asian tsunami, which rendered to rubbles the coastal Tamil Nadu, with the most affected area being Nagapattinam. After facing the various challenges of life, and seeing death with its utmost fury, the fishing community of Karaikal leads life with elan and dignity, which indicates a stronger heart within, not commonly seen amongst others.

Aftermath of tsunami

The tsunami which occurred in the Indian Ocean on 26 December 2004 brought in the wrath of Mother Nature on the unexpecting people dwelling on the coastal areas. This event resulted in the initiation of one of the greatest humanitarian aids undertaken by human kind.

Development Alternatives (DA), an organisation which over the past 20 years has been providing assistance to all major disaster-hit communities of the Indian subcontinent, approached Swiss Solidarity and Swiss Red Cross (SRC) for resources to undertake reconstruction and rehabilitation in three villages of Karaikal District in Pondicherry. The objective behind these three organisations associating with each other was to cater to the absolute need of rehabilitation and reconstruction of the affected communities.

As an encouragement to the efforts of DA to create model settlements, the Government of Pondicherry (GoP) formulated a memorandum of understanding (MoU) for the rehabilitation of Kottucherrymedu, Kilinjalmedu and Karaikalmedu. Importance was given to design structurally safe houses as per the cultural preferences of the villages, and at the same time giving importance to modern-looking societies.

Profile of the three villages

Kottucherrymedu is a part of Kottucherry commune in the Karaikal District. Karaikal town is 6 km away while Kottucherry is the nearest town at a distance of 3 km. Kilinjalmedu is situated towards the south of Kottucherrymedu and Mandapathur is towards the north. Population of Kottucherrymedu is 743, of which 65.39 per cent are below the age of 15.

Of the 190 houses in the villages, 77 houses were completely destroyed by the impact of tsunami and the remaining houses suffered varying degrees of damages. The tsunami claimed sixteen lives, out of which were ten children, five women and one man.

The twin settlements of Kilinjalmedu and Karaikalmedu are divided by a common road. The population of Kilinjalmedu is 2,034 of which 58 per cent are above 15 years of age. Tsunami took the lives of 33 people of which fifteen were children, twelve were women and six were men.

Karaikalmedu is situated 3 km from Karaikal town and 20 km from Nagapattinam. It is a cyclone-prone area with a population of 2,861 of which 34 per cent are below 15 years of age. Totally 289 houses were affected in this village while 146 houses were partially damaged and 143 completely destroyed. A total of fifty-one people in the village lost their lives of which twenty-four were males and twenty-seven females. It is interesting to note that a total of 340 fishing boats were damaged.

Reconstruction of tsunami-hit Karaikal: the project

The joint venture of DA with SRC and GoP zeroed down on 1,175 of the 1,200 houses for construction. Maharashtra government and Salvation Army too wanted to take part in the initiative. Due to

Table 10.2 Situation at three selected villages

Village	Total families as per panchayat list	Total families as per government list	Shelter loss	Total relocation (by DA)
Karaikalmedu	730	550	181	430(525)*
Kilinjalmedu	636	500	94	320(500)*
Kottucherrymedu	165	150		9(150)*

Source: DA, Delhi.

Note: Figures in brackets are proposed number of shelters; figures outside the brackets are the shelters actually constructed.

Table 10.3 Final picture of house construction in the three selected villages

Village agencies	Kottucherrymedu	Kilinjalmedu	Karaikalmedu
Development Alternatives	158 + 1	320	430
Salvation Army	0	100	0
Government of Maharashtra	Info not available	80	120
Honeywell Foundation	0	Info not available	0

Source: DA, Delhi.

price constraints, DA, in consultation with SRC and GoP, revised the number of houses to be constructed to 909. Maharashtra government took up the task of constructing 200 and Salvation Army took up 100 houses.

The sustainable reconstruction initiative in tsunami-affected villages of Karaikal was designed to provide an appropriate response to the reconstruction and rehabilitation needs of 909 families in Karaikalmedu, Kottucherrymedu and Kilinjalmedu.

Needs of the affected villages

The identified priority needs of families in the affected villages were:

1 redeveloped village settlements with community facilities and infrastructure;
2 reconstructed houses with basic amenities;
3 economic opportunities and incomes;
4 knowledge and skills regarding safe and sustainable building construction practices.

Phase I

The main criterion of the project was to reconstruct houses with basic infrastructure and amenities spread across three villages in Karaikal region of Pondicherry. In addition to building houses, the project also focused at improving the living conditions with regard to water and sanitation and also generation of livelihood opportunities to ensure sustainable growth environmentally, socially and economically.

Approach

The project took into consideration the views and needs of the village community through participatory processes. It introduced alternatives for construction technology and services. The affected families were exposed to alternative construction systems and building materials in order to aid in the selection of the best possible approach in the construction of the houses. The guidelines of GoP were followed with regard to house size, house design, standards, cost of construction, sanitation, landscape development, roads, water and electrification. Regular reporting mechanism was put in place as a monitoring tool. The project reported not only to the funding agency, the SRC, but also to the local community and the GoP.

The construction process

The project was initiated in June 2005 and completed in October 2008. A total of 150 houses for Kottucherrymedu village and 380 houses for the villages of Kilinjalmedu and Karaikalmedu were constructed and handed over to GoP in October 2007 and January 2008, respectively.

The cost incurred for the construction of one house was initially slated to be Rs 167,000 but due to the escalation of costs of cement, steel, bricks, sand and aggregates, the cost went up to Rs 239,000. The total amount spent for the construction of 909 houses, spread across the three settlements, was Rs 263,259,000.

The project asked the families occupying the houses to contribute 50 per cent of the cost of the grills in their houses which amounted to Rs 1,500. Each family was asked to pay a sum of Rs 400 for meter installation by electricity department. The water supply deposit money was paid by commune panchayat to Karaikal Planning

Table 10.4 Synopsis of activities undertaken

Aims	Community mobilisation	Support to village institution	Capacity building of stakeholders	Livelihood creation
Occupation of houses and asset management	• Participatory design for settlement and house management and speed management • VRCs and panchayats involved in quality management • Maintenance cell	• Formation of VRC (village resource centre) • Baseline survey for beneficiary assessment • Continuous dialogue with panchayats for allocation process • Disabled persons support	• Orientation of VRC and panchayats in technical assets managed. • Nursery managed and plantation by women of Karaikalmedu	
Improvement in quality of life	• Water and sanitation surveys and involvement of women and youth • Nursery raising for greens • Playground	• Engaging with local schools for continuing water quality testing • Key women form SHGs for sanitation training	• Water quality assessment • Sanitation habits training • Nursery training and kitchen garden training • Schools linked up for regular water testing	• Solid waste management as an economic activity • Vermicompost training using village waste
Knowledge and skills in safe construction practices	• Cross-site exposure of women's groups and youth	• Training resource centre (TRC) creation and training • Technical orientation of VRC and panchayats	• Training to supervisors and head masons at TRC	• Trained masons and contractors who can pursue new techniques
Long-term economic benefits	• Business orientation workshops. • Career counseling of youth	• Supporting SNEHA and SHGs to engage in economic activity of nursery.	• Training of enterprises • TRC as an anchor of fly ash production	• Production opportunities • Local enterprise creation • Training in construction-related trades of youth • Support to enterprises

Note: VRC, village resource centre.

Authority. Taps and hand pumps have now been installed and there is water supply in the villages. Today, all the houses and streets are fitted with lights which illuminate the village. A playground for children and a volleyball court have been set up in each village.

Phase 2

Income-generation techniques

1   A total of seventy artisans were trained by the project in safe and sustainable construction techniques.
2   The project helped in the establishment of five fly ash brick-manufacturing units which would be run by the villagers. One of this is run by women's group of Kottucherri village.
3   The project took care of capacity building of over twenty-five local engineers, seven local civil contractors and eighteen young electricians and plumbers and placed them with local contractors.
4   Local masons were used for the construction of houses, which in turn resulted in employment generation.
5   In addition to this, seventy masons were trained and benefitted from the opportunity to work for the reconstruction process.
6   Few women's groups were given the task of managing the village nurseries, which resulted in e income generation for their families.
7   The youth of these villages educated to an extent and looking for jobs were provided English language training by Kamarajar Institute of Karaikal.
8   Each fisherman who lost his boat or livelihood in tsunami was given a seed capital of Rs 3,000 to restart his occupation by the NGO Social Need Education and Human Awareness (SNEHA).
9   Loans at very low interests were also provided to the affected, based on their needs by various NGOs like SNEHA.

Achievements

The project was started in June 2005; since then its achievements are as follows:

1   Three new village settlements have been designed and developed in association with village communities.

2 House designs have been developed in a participatory manner in response to people's needs and cultural requirements, incorporating structural and safety features.

3 Community facilities such as childcare and community halls were designed.

4 The project has trained over seventy artisans working under the local contractors in safe and sustainable construction techniques. In addition, it also trained twenty-five local engineers and seven local civil contractors in safe construction practices, and eighteen youth were trained as electricians and plumbers and were placed with local contractors.

5 The project has linked up with the local building centre to provide training to new entrepreneurs and artisans in future.

6 It took cognizance of the health and hygiene needs of the village settlements.

7 It also addressed the concerns of physically challenged people in the villages.

8 It has set up systems for long-term management of the new assets so created.

Sequence of events

1 26 December, 2004: Tsunami struck
2 January 2005: Assessment mission
3 February–March 2005: Feasibility studies
4 April–July 2005: Discussions with GoP, design development
5 August 2005: Project sanctioned by SRC
6 September 2005: MoU with GoP
7 October–November 2005: Designs approved by GoP
8 November 2005–January 2006: Floods in Karaikal
9 January 2006: Pilot phase initiated and construction work commences
10 February–October 2006: Land filling by GoP
11 January–April 2007: Rescheduling of work amongst the contractors
12 August–September 2007: Rescheduling of work at Kottucherrymedu
13 October 2007: Handing over of 150 houses at Kottucherrymedu
14 January 2008: Handing over of 380 houses at Kilinjalmedu and Karaikalmedu

15 January 2008: Handing over of keys by GoP to residents in Kottucherrymedu and initiation of the maintenance cell
16 April 2008: Electrical connections, roads and infrastructure completed in Kottucherrymedu – families start to move in with technical support from DA for modifications, painting and rectifications
17 July 2008: Handing over of remaining initiated houses at Kilinjalmedu maintenance cell
18 October 2008: All houses of Karaikalmedu completed

SNEHA (NGO)

SNEHA was the initiative of Christy, an educated member of the fishing community, who ventured to work for the oppressed fisher people in the coastal areas of Nagapattinam and Karaikal Districts. SNEHA is a registered society under Societies Act with nineteen general body members of whom six are women and nine managing committee members out of which three are women. SNEHA began in 1984 with very few villages and staff and has established its presence among the fishermen community.

The various strategies employed by SNEHA for the upliftment of fishermen are as follows:

1 Focus on empowerment of fishing community, especially the women in the community
2 Education of children of fishing community
3 Emphasis on protection of the coastal environment.

In 1986, as a part of its economic programmes, SNEHA established self-help groups (SHGs) called 'Sangams' in villages. Each Sangam consisted of twelve to twenty members. Thus, each village would consist of more than one Sangam. SNEHA has, as of June 2003, established 232 Sangams in 51 villages, with the total membership of 4,141, out of which 111 are males and 4,030 are female members. Post-tsunami, it has 639 women Sangams in 51 villages with 11,519 women members.

Each Sangam would open two or three accounts in a bank and contribute an amount of Rs 100 per member per month. The amount thus collected would be used for giving subsidised loans at a rate of 1–2 per cent to the members of the corresponding Sangam.

Table 10.5 Total funds contributed within all Sangams in Karaikal

Number of Sangams	110
Number of villages	10
Total number of members	1,800
Contribution of each member per month	Rs 100
Time period	1990–2009 (19 years)
Funds mobilised	Rs 40,219,200

The focus of this study is on the activities of Sangams in villages of Karaikal. SNEHA coordinates the activities of these Sangams in and around Karaikal. The Sangams coordinated by SNEHA are mainly comprised of women, since men are most of the times not available due to the nature of their work. There are 110 Sangams (SHGs) in Karaikal distributed amongst ten villages. From each village, a member is selected to represent the respective Sangam and all such members would form a 'Village Coordination Sangam' (VCS) which would concentrate on the issues of the entire village. Again, three members from each VCS and one member from each Sangam would be selected to represent the VCS and Sangam, respectively, in the 'District Fisherwomen Federation'. Thus, the District Fisherwomen Federation of Karaikal consists of 140 members in total (10 × 3 + 110 = 140).

Post-tsunami, the fishing community was hesitant to venture into sea for a period of six months. SNEHA encouraged the fishermen by giving a seed capital of Rs 3,000 to women and Rs 2,000 to men. Women of Karaikal are mostly involved in fish vending. Hence, the seed capital helped them in restarting their business and also, at times, in the purchase or repairs of the fishing boats of their family members.

SRC and 'Action Aid' provided funds to SNEHA, which in turn were utilised for the construction of District Fisherwomen Federation building (for occasional meetings and activities of members of the federation) and a flour mill, both together costing Rs 1,000,000. An additional amount of Rs 1,800,000 was spent in the construction of four dry fish platforms. The funds spent included the sum received from SRC and Action Aid and also the funds collated within the Sangams.

Funds were also spent in the purchase of auto carriers (TATA ACE), each costing Rs 175,000, for the conveyance of fish-vending women of the villages to fish-vending sites. The Sangams spent

Rs 150,000 per village for the purchase of cooking vessels which could be rented to the members of the village for personal use and during functions. The auto carriers were also hired by outsiders. These two initiatives would ensure regular flow of funds for the Sangams.

Apart from the internal loans given and managed within the Sangams, the State Bank of India gives subsidised loans to the villagers for amounts up to Rs 2 lakh. SNEHA monitors the management of revolving funds given to Sangams on a regular basis. Revolving funds are allotted to each Sangam in the village on a rotating basis (for example, if one Sangam gets the fund this time, the fund would be given to another Sangam the next time). Hence, the fund revolves within the Sangams from time to time.

SNEHA has also introduced insurance schemes through Life Insurance Corporation of India (LIC) for the villagers. It paid the premiums for the insurance policies of the villagers for the initial three years after which the villagers have started paying Rs 100 per year apart from Rs 50 each being paid by the government and Rs 50 being borne by the insurance company. Hence SNEHA has been instrumental in insuring the lives of the people in the fishing community.

SNEHA was also instrumental in the introduction of scholarship programme, through LIC, for the children of the fishing community studying in the government and other aided schools. The programme gives a scholarship of Rs 1,200 to children studying in standards IX to XII.

SNEHA, on 8 March 2010, was successful in registering a 'Mutual Benefit Trust' at each taluk level. All the Sangams would be the direct members of it. The Mutual Benefit Trust would look after the financial aspects of the Sangams and do periodic audits of the spendings and other financial activities of the Sangam. The other objective of the Mutual Benefit Trust is also to mobilise funds from external sources by reflecting to them the success of Sangams in managing the funds internally.

SNEHA is presently in talks with the women of the villages and is encouraging them to begin small-scale businesses like pickle making, tea powder production, osoap oil production, rice, sauces and incense stick making. It would give loans to women based on their feasibility and ability to begin a particular business. It has also promised to market the products manufactured by the women in areas in and out of Karaikal.

Conclusion

The purpose of this study was to focus on the microfinancial efforts undertaken by the NGOs and international funding agencies in the reconstruction and rehabilitation of the hapless people affected by the peril of tsunami and the efforts of the NGO SNEHA in the upliftment of the people of the affected fishing community, especially women, through introduction of various schemes and activites undertaken within the Sangams (SHGs). SHG concept is a unique way of developmental activity, especially in India. SHGs form the connecting link between the government and the non-governmental organisations. The rise of loan schemes from SHGs has made women's income a permanent component of household income and weakened the women's dependency on men as providers. The usage of funds collected within the Sangams, in terms of giving out loans to Sangam members, and other activities discussed earlier serve as best examples for the functioning of SHGs. It is imperative that the system of microfinance be further strengthened in the country especially credit, savings and insurance for the weaker sections of the society. The number of poor in the country is so large that the efforts of the various banks are not able to meet the credit needs of the poor. Hence, it is essential that the growth of SHGs and NGOs be encouraged. The rise and future of such SHGs and NGOs in the future looks bright, looking at the kind of cooperation and participation that has been observed in the case of SNEHA and the Sangams coordinated by it.

References

Renukarya, C. K., (11–14 July, 2004), 'Integrated quantitative analysis to assess the performance of SHGs in India', *ISTR Sixth International Conference Toronto*, Canada.

Social Need Education and Human Awareness (SNEHA, NGO), (2008), 'Voices of the marginalised'.

Tesoriero, F., (2006), 'An evaluation of women's self help groups (SHGs) in South India', *Community Development Journal*, Vol. 41, No. 3, pp. 321–33.

Zeenat, N., and A. Roy, (2008), 'Sustainable reconstruction initiative in Karaikal', *Development Alternatives*, Delhi.

Chapter 11

Microfinance for poverty alleviation

Analysis of clients' perspectives and changes in their lives in the state of Manipur, India

Melody Kshetrimayum

Microfinance has become an important sector in developing countries for providing financial services to the poor people. It helps the poor to increase their income, increase savings and build assets through various income-generation and productive activities. 'Microfinance is defined as the provision of thrift, credit and other financial services such as money transfer and micro-insurance products for the poor, to enable them to raise their income levels and improve living standard' (Karmakar 2008). The financial services of microfinance also include investment credit and need for skill up-gradation and entrepreneurial development that would enable the poor to overcome poverty. Microfinance has been accepted as the most effective means to alleviate poverty in many developing countries like India, where the central issue of the government is poverty alleviation (Nair 2001).

Poverty alleviation programmes in India

Poverty is a persistent problem caused due to the lack of financial resources to generate livelihoods and income-generating activities. It is a multidimensional phenomenon encompassing lack of access to various basic necessities, such as nutrition, health, education, housing, security and opportunity for future development (Banerjee et al. 2006). It involves not only the lack of well-being but also the denial of opportunities for living a tolerable life (Sinha 2003). According to the Government of India, 29 per cent of the total population of India is poor. In 2001, there were nearly 220 million people living below poverty line, indicating that nearly 21.1 per cent of the entire rural population and 15 per cent of the urban population of India live in poverty (Economic Watch 2009). In

India, poverty is widespread in rural areas and characterised by low income levels which are inadequate to ensure a quality life. Rural India, which encompasses three-fourths of the country's population, lives in poverty.

The government had implemented many poverty alleviation programmes in the last thirty years. Integrated Rural Development Programme was started as the self-employment programme in 1978 in order to enhance employment and income of the rural poor sufficiently, especially the small farmers and landless labourers (Sinha 2000). It seeks to raise the incomes of rural poor to a level above the poverty line by requiring the banks to extend loans to them for the purchase of assets, and by subsidising 25 to 50 per cent of the cost of the assets. Three support programmes were linked with the implementation of Integrated Rural Development Programme for the purpose of enhancing earning capacities of burrowers: (1) Training of Rural Youth for Self-Employment – to provide technical skills to young people in rural areas for self-employment; (2) Development of Women and Children in Rural Areas – to provide women with skills and support (e.g., childcare and nutrition for children) for economic activities so as to enable them to generate income through group entrepreneurship; and (3) infrastructure – 10 per cent of the government funds were allocated to provide support facilities at the district level such as shop buildings, feeder roads, electric lines, common deep bore wells and milk collection vans, which help the borrowers realise the potential of their income-generating activities (Yesudian 2007). Other poverty alleviation programmes includes National Rural Employment Programme (NREP) and Rural Landless Employment Guarantee Programme (RLEGP) to provide employment opportunities to the rural unemployed and underemployed youths, which were merged in 1989 into more well-known Jawahar Rozgar Yojana (Lalitha 2004). Public distribution system and the midday meal scheme started as food safety programmes which aimed at providing food for poor people all over the country and children suffering from malnutrition because of lack of food and nutrients. Then, National Social Assistance Programme came into effect in 1995 as a social security programme to extend financial assistance to old persons having little or no regular means of subsistence, to households living below the poverty line in case of death of the primary breadwinner and to pregnant women of households below poverty line up to the first two live births.

Limitations of poverty alleviation programmes and significance of microfinance

The government had taken up various interventions to alleviate poverty. The Integrated Rural Development Programme launched by the government had not achieved the expected results due to the attempt to develop entrepreneurs out of unskilled landless labourers and corruption on the part of lower-level functionaries, bank staff and borrowers themselves. Other anti-poverty programmes like Jawahar Rojgar Yojna also declined due to lower allocation of funds for this programme during the Ninth Plan period. The poverty alleviation programmes of India launched by the central government did not yield the expected result. The major cause was the provision of subsidised credit central to these programmes. Despite the reduction in the incidence of poverty since the mid-1990s, a large proportion of Indian population is still below the poverty line. The poor performance of the anti-poverty programmes of India and failure of delivering credit to the poor seeks for a new and viable institutional structure (Umdor 2007). If the challenge of poverty has to be taken up, microfinance has a major role to play in providing financial services to the poor as well as empowering the poor. The government started promoting microfinance as it gained significance as a tool of poverty alleviation in many developing countries where there is an immediate need of credit among the poor. The logical foundation of promoting microfinance, mainly in the non-financial sector in India, rests on the apparent failure of state-owned credit institutions, including the cooperatives, to reach out to the poor and the 'disappointing' performance of government programmes of poverty alleviation that were meant to enable the poor to earn supplementary income from self-employment (Nair 2001). Microfinance significantly prevents people from extreme poverty through financial assistance, productive activities and training programmes. It provides credit needs of poor, generates income through income-generation activities, and also provides basic banking services to the poor.

Microfinance initiatives in India

In 1992, the National Bank for Agriculture and Rural Development (NABARD) initiated the self-help group(SHG)–Bank Linkage Programme (SBLP) to include the poorest of the poor inside the formal banking system. NABARD had already initiated certain research projects on SHGs as a channel for delivery of microfinance such as 'Savings and Credit Management of SHGs' which threw encouraging possibilities to initiate the SBLP (Satish 2005). Under the SBLP, the SHGs are formed and trained for six months and then linked to the banks to avail loans. The emphasis of this programme was on improving access to microfinance rather than just microcredit. It became a means to improve the access of existing banking network to the poor people. The government also started new anti-poverty programmes to provide credit to poor people, which also promote microfinance. Swarnajayanti Gram Swarozgar Yojna (SGSY) was launched in 1999 to organise the rural poor to form SHGs), capacity building and building up of infrastructural facilities, technology, credit and marketing. Among the non-governmental organisations (NGOs) in India, Mysore Resettlement and Development Agency (MYRADA) and Professional Assistance Development Action are the pioneers in microfinance. MYRADA started savings and credit scheme targeting the rural poor living below poverty line, and under this scheme, the members of the SHG must compulsorily save a considerable amount in order to be eligible for credit. The beneficiaries are encouraged to save, and with the savings habit, they are taught to cultivate the habit of thrift which helps them cut down unnecessary expenditure and develop their savings.

Under SBLP, three models have emerged:

Model-1: NABARD–Bank–SHG (with NGO acting as facilitator)
Model-2: NABARD–Bank–NGO–SHG (with NGO acting as facilitator and financial intermediary)
Model-3: NABARD–Bank–SHG (without the facilitation of NGO)

In Model-1, the NGOs form the SHGs and nurture and facilitate them. The bank provides financial assistance to the NGOs to further lend to the SHGs. The process of the formation of SHGs is same in all the models but NGOs facilitate the group formation in the first two models. In the second model, both facilitation and financial intermediation are done by NGOs. In the third model, the banks form the groups and provide financial assistance to the SHGs without the facilitation of the NGOs.

Poverty, poverty alleviation programmes and microfinance in north-eastern region of India

The north-eastern region (NER) of India consists of eight states – Assam, Meghalaya, Sikkim, Tripura, Manipur, Arunachal Pradesh, Mizoram and Nagaland – which are extraordinarily diverse, colourful and mysterious because of their different cultures. The region remained relatively backward for a long time and suffered from lack of infrastructure in various sectors of communication, technical expertise, development and transportation. In all NER states, centrally sponsored programmes have been under implementation from Sixth Plan onwards. Integrated Rural Development Programme was able to alleviate 15 per cent to 20 per cent of the poor above poverty line (Borah 2009). Capacity building mostly remained women-centred in the trades like tailoring, knitting, embroidery and weaving. Though the self-employment programme through SGSY promoted SHGs, it did not yield expected results as it failed to involve NGOs participation in the process. However, the approach of State Institute of Rural Development, Assam, is worth mentioning. It adopted social mobilisation followed by capacity building, credit linkage to SHGs and their schemes, linkage to market and repeated financing in stages. According to the summary report of National Institute of Rural Development (National Institute of Rural Development 2009), on wage and infrastructure development programmes reveals that the implementation of all the previous programmes like NREP, RLEGP and Sampoorna Grameen Rojgar Yojna except National Rural Employment Guarantee Programme were able to provide wage employment in the range of 20–35 person days, per worker family, per annum. Involvement of panchayats and local-level institutions in the planning and implementation of the programme was very low except in Tripura and Nagaland.

The microfinance movement in the NER started in Assam in the late 1990s and has been dominated by the SBLP initiated by NABARD. Since then, the programme spread through the region and the linking process had been taken up by many NGOs. Microfinance is considered as a means of employment generation and a strategy for poverty alleviation in the region. According to Singh (2008), as of 2006, Assam contributed 56,499 SHGs out of 62,517 SHGs linked in the region. Tripura, Manipur, Mizoram, Meghalaya, Nagaland and Arunachal Pradesh together account for only 6,018 SHGs, which is only 9 per cent of the SHGs linked in the NER states. The distribution of the SHGs that have been credit linked to banks during 2002–06 in NER indicates that microfinance under the SBLP has not developed in the NER states except Assam which contributes 91 per cent of the total SHGs linked. Looking at the context of the NER, banks and finance institutions do not come forward in a proactive manner to cater to the needs of the poor because of the law and order situation, insurgency and social tension in the region (Bera 2008).

Poor people are largely excluded from the microfinance programmes in rural areas and from the facilities provided by the microfinance institutions. Banks and microfinance institutions consider them as non-bankable. Besides, high operation cost to deliver to distant villages and hilly areas is also one of the reasons that the microfinance programmes do not reach the poorest of the poor (Mohanty 2009). As a result, the distribution of the SHGs linked in the NER is very poor. This is also because of the fact that NGOs in the region, which act as microfinance institutions, are not professionally managed. However, the Institute of Integrated Resource Management, Asomi, Young Mizo Association, Rural Development Organisation (RDO), Human Resource Development Organisation (HRDO) and Youth Volunteers Organisation are some of the leading NGOs in the region which are undertaking microfinance activities. These NGOs provide financial services and training programmes to enhance microfinance activities in the region. They facilitate and promote the SHGs under SBLP. The NGOs, which act as microfinance institutions, provide financial assistance to poor people for taking up income-generation activities. They nurture SHGs and supervise the SHG members to undertake microfinance activities. Funding agencies like Rashtriya Grameen Vikas Nidhi, Small Industries Development Bank of India, Friends of Women's World Banking, North Eastern Development Finance Corporation Ltd and NABARD provide financial assistance to the NGOs which carry out financial and social intermediation in the region.

Objectives and methodology

The objectives of the chapter are:

1 to understand the meaning of poverty perceived by the clients
2 to understand the contribution of microfinance in poverty alleviation.

Research setting

Manipur that covers a geographical area of 22,327 sq. km. is one of India's economically and infrastructurally backward states located in the extreme north-eastern corner. It has nine districts, of which four – the Imphal East, Imphal West, Bishnupur and Thoubal – are located in the valley and the remaining five – Churachandpur, Chandel, Ukhrul, Senapati and Tamenglong – are located in the hills. The total population of Manipur is 2,293,896 according to the census of the year 2011. Imphal is the capital of Manipur but the district was divided into Imphal East and Imphal West in the year 1997. The literacy rate, according to 2001 census, is 79.8 per cent, out of which the male literacy rate is 86.49 per cent and female literacy rate is 73.17 per cent. It can be noted that Manipur is ranked tenth in the country by the literacy rate. The sex ratio is 987: 1,000. Manipur state is connected to the rest of the country though national highway Nos. 39, 53 and 150.

In Manipur, people are deprived of basic facilities including drinking water, electricity, communication, banking system, opportunities and other material and non-material resources. In short, people are deprived of development. While poverty declined in most of the states in the country in the last decade, Manipur is one of the five states where poverty rate increased by 9.2 per cent between 2004–05 and 2009–10 and 12.5 lakh of the total population are still below poverty line in 2009–10 (Dey 2012). Poverty is one persistent problem here that people become adjusted and adapted to vulnerability and lack of resources. The accessibility and the use of resources are limited. The condition is worsened by frequent adverse economic conditions like economic blockades, strikes and bandhs.

The main credit delivery methodologies of Manipur include microfinance, banking and informal credit institutions. There were seventy-seven scheduled commercial banks as on 31 March 2007, and the average population per bank offices of the state was 38 per thousand (Economic Survey 2007–08). The number of banks increased to eighty-one in the year 2009 (Economic Survey 2010–11). However, a large section of households is still not covered by a bank and most of them are outside the formal financial sector. Moreover, poor people hardly avail loan from bank as banks consider them as non-bankable and not trustworthy. A large section of the population is not aware of the savings facilities provided by formal financial institutions as there is absence of these institutions in the remote areas.

Four NGOs undertaking microfinance activities were selected from the list of NGOs in Manipur that are undertaking microfinance activities. The NGOs were RDO, Women Voluntary Organisation, HRDO and Weaker Section Development Society. The research study was conducted in Imphal East, Imphal West, Thoubal and Senapati Districts of Manipur where the NGOs effectively formed and supervised groups of women. The two branches of RDO are taken as two different NGOs as they are managed and operated by different functionaries in different places.

Data collection and analysis

The study covered twenty groups which were promoted and facilitated by the above NGOs. Three members from each group, who had been involved in microfinance activities for at least two years prior to the time of data collection, were selected. There were altogether sixty participants selected from the groups. Interviews were conducted with the participants to gain comprehensive insights and capture field reality from them. All the participants were contacted, appointments for interviews were fixed according to their convenient time and consent was taken before their respective interviews began. They were informed clearly about the purpose of the study before the interviews.

Structured interviews were conducted in Manipuri language to collect primary data from the respondents. Face-to-face interaction with the clients helped in finding out their anti-poverty perspectives, change brought by their participation in microfinance and their problems even after getting involved in microfinance activities. Observation during the interaction also helped in the analysis of primary data. Pamphlets, reports and handbooks provided by the NGOs were used as secondary data. The analysis of data was done by using statistical parameters that included frequency.

Clients' perception on reasons of being poor

Figure 11.1 shows that 45 per cent believe that they are poor because they have inadequate money. Having inadequate money leads to inability to start income-generation activities, meet the emergency needs or avail education and medical facilities. Twenty-five per cent

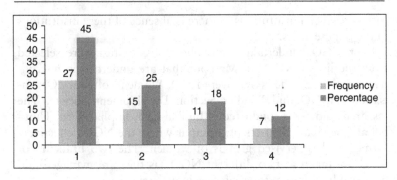

Figure 11.1 Clients' perception on reasons of being poor

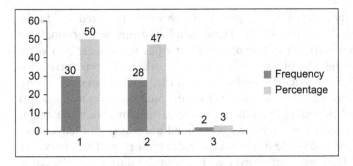

Figure 11.2 Clients' perception on ways to come out of poverty

felt that uncertainty of income is the reason of being poor. They have the view that irregularity in income makes people more vulnerable to financial shocks and emergency needs. Eighteen per cent of the clients think that landlessness is the main cause of poverty, and for them, having land is the biggest asset in life. Twelve per cent of clients considered inadequate skills or education as the main reason of being poor. Thus, the survey showed that different people have different outlook on how poverty persists in their lives.

Clients' perception on ways to come out of poverty

As seen in Figure 11.2, half the number of clients said that increasing employment opportunities will help them to overcome poverty.

Participants remain idle as they are not given employment opportunities and depend on petty business for a living. They also said that many educated youths of the area remain unemployed. Thus, the participants believed that increasing employment opportunities will make them self-reliant and hence can contribute to the economic development of society. Forty-seven per cent of women want to avail loan to start business and income-generating activities which will eventually enable them to come out of poverty. They need capital to make money from their business and income-generating activities on a sustainable basis. They are not able to start earning money as they do not have the capital. Only 3 per cent of clients said that they want to educate their children to overcome poverty. Educating children is their biggest asset which will help them to come out of poverty.

Income-wise clients' perception on ways to come out of poverty

Participants who earn different amount of income had 'different ways to overcome poverty'. Their resolution to overcome poverty depends on their past experiences and attempts to alleviate deprivation with the amount of income they earn.

Twenty-five per cent clients, who have the lowest income level, Rs 401–800, consider that increasing employment opportunities will help to come out of poverty whereas 75 per cent of clients in

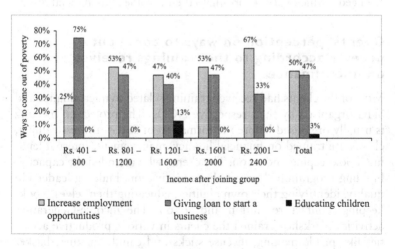

Figure 11.3 Income-wise clients' perception on ways to come out of poverty

the same income group think that giving loan to poor to start a business is a better option to come out of poverty (Figure 11.3). Fifty-three per cent of clients in the income group Rs 801–1,200 said that increasing employment opportunities helps people to come out of poverty and 47 per cent of them said providing loan will help poor people. Fifty-three per cent in the income group Rs 1,601–2,000 said that increasing employment opportunities will help poor to overcome poverty and remaining 47 per cent stated that providing loan will help poor to start new income-generating activities. Forty-seven per cent of the clients in the income group Rs 1,201–1,600 are of the opinion that increasing employment opportunities is the better option to come out of poverty. Forty per cent of clients in the same group said that providing loan to start a new business will probably help poor while remaining 13 per cent expressed that educating their children will help them to come out poverty in the long run. Sixty-seven per cent of clients in the income group Rs 2,001–2,400 said increasing employment opportunities is best option to overcome poverty and 33 per cent of clients opined that providing loan will help the poor to come out poverty.

Among the lowest income group (Rs 401–800), majority of clients said that giving loans to start a business will help them to come out of poverty. But in all other income groups, majority of clients said that increasing employment opportunities is the better option to overcome poverty. This shows people's different priorities and felt needs, which vary according to their income and financial needs.

Clients' perception on ways to come out of poverty according to the trainings received on microfinance

Most of the clients had received training related to microfinance and SHG organised by their respective NGOs. The projection meeting is usually organised before the formation of SHGs. In this training, clients are trained on financial literacy, management, internal lending, bookkeeping and so on. The clients who attended the capacity-building programme learned about motivation, building leadership quality, identifying their own abilities, educating themselves, bookkeeping, conflict resolution and so on. The income-Generation activities workshop trained the clients in various productive activities like pickle making, incense sticks and candle making, basket and handicrafts and other traditional food making.

Thirty-three per cent of the clients who attended projection meeting said increasing employment opportunities will help people to come out poverty through which they can increase their income (Figure 11.4). But 67 per cent of them were of the opinion that poor people should be given loans to start their own business which they can easily handle and also make money out of it. Eighty-three per cent of them said increasing employment opportunities will help them to overcome poverty. The remaining 17 per cent are of the opinion that people should be given loans to initiate their own productive activities. Among the clients who took part in capacity-building programmes and income-generation activities workshops, 70 per cent of clients stated poor should be given employment opportunities and the remaining 30 per cent told that poor people should avail loans to start a business. Twenty clients have taken part only in income-generation activity programmes to earn their living. Half of the clients said that increasing employment opportunities is the only way to overcome poverty and it is sustainable for a long-term basis. Forty per cent of clients told providing loan to poor people will be advantageous for them to come out of poverty. The remaining 10 per cent of them said educating children will definitely help them to come out of poverty.

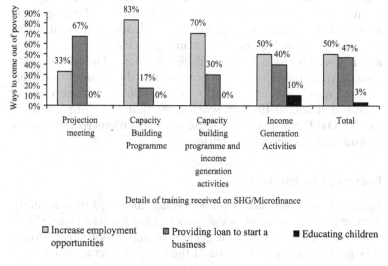

Figure 11.4 Clients' perception on ways to come out of poverty according to training received on microfinance

A majority of clients who attended projection meeting said that availing loans to start a business will help them to overcome poverty whereas all clients who attended capacity-building programme and income-generation activities told increasing employment opportunities is the better option to come out of poverty. Their perception differs according to the type of training received. The projection meeting trained them about financial literacy and bookkeeping before joining the group. However, capacity-building programmes and income-generation activities workshops enhanced their capabilities and helped them to learn different skills which gave them more scope and options. This makes them think about options other than getting loans for income generation.

Participation in paid work and other projects

Paid work refers to any economic activity through which women can earn income and other projects include activities that enhance women's skills to undertake economic activities. Due to lack of financial assistance and non-availability of capital, the participants could not carry out economic activities which could provide them economic independence. With participation in SHGs through small savings, women received lump-sum amount and this helped them 'engage in self-employment activities'. Such economic activities include lending business, tailoring, charcoal, groceries, road-side hotel and other petty business such as poultry farming, pickle and incense stick making which could be carried out at home. The participants also participated in other projects such as the capacity-building programmes, skill up-gradation workshops, projection meetings and financial literacy workshops that were organised by the NGOs. Participation in these projects enhanced their skills to undertake economic activities.

Increase in income

Each and every member of the SHGs had increased their monthly income through microfinance activities. All of them had started and invested in their own income-generating activities from the loans they get from the group. Some of the income-generation activities include piggery, livestocks, vegetable farming, weaving and working as vendors. All the clients have succeeded in increasing their income irrespective of the type of income-generation activities involved. All participants said that they achieved economic independence through the income-generation activities they started.

Increased social network

Being a member of groups itself is to be a part of an extended social network of friends and neighbours who trust and cooperate with each other. During group meetings, women work together to save, carry out group procedures and make resolutions. While they engage in such activities, they interact to share ideas and put forward their knowledge and experiences that help them bond together. When interpersonal conflict arises due to different opinions, women solve it by cooperating and adjusting to one another's requirements. The social network of friends provides emotional support and widens economic opportunities to women that contribute to their financial and overall well-being.

Acquisition of literacy

The SHG members who were illiterate before joining the group have learned simple numeracy skills. They no longer need to place a thumb impression. Bookkeeping about the financial transaction of the group is taught by their respective NGO field workers. Group activities like documentation of the minutes of meetings are done by all the SHG members together.

Asset building

Ninety-two per cent of clients have succeeded in building household assets, (Figure 11.5). Eight per cent of clients were able to buy land, which they think as the biggest property earned in life through microfinance. It means that almost everybody was able to build assets through participation in microfinance activities.

Decision making in the family according to training received on microfinance

For this study, 'decision making' was defined as identifying and choosing alternatives based on the values and preferences of the decision maker, leading to the selection of a course of action. It

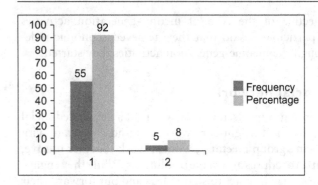

Figure 11.5 Assets built after joining the group

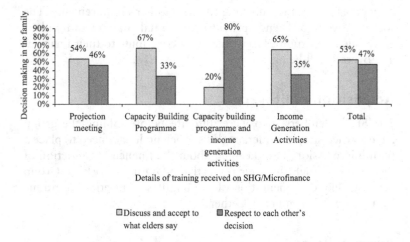

Figure 11.6 Decision making in the family according to training received on microfinance

includes participation of the clients in the decision making of the family regarding education of children, business, family expenditure on food and clothes, assets and financial issues. Financial issues refer to issues relating to women's income, savings, investment and sustainability of their income-generating activities.

Fifty-four per cent of clients who had participated in the projection meeting said that they do not have control over the decision making in their families while 46 per cent of them said they participate in the decision making in the family (Figure 11.6). Sixt-seven per cent of clients who received training on capacity-building programmes said that they do not actively participate in the decision making in their families while 33 per cent of them who also participated in the same training told that they have control over the decision making of their families. Twenty per cent of women who had participated in the capacity-building programmes and income-generation activities workshops said that they accept what other family members say and 80 per cent of them who received the same training said that they actively participated in the decision making in the family. Sixty-five per cent of the clients who received training on IGA said that they discuss and accept what their elders say but do not have control over the decision making, while 35 per cent of them said that they actively participated in the decision-making process.

The decision-making power of the clients in their families is highest amongst clients who attended both the capacity-building programmes and income-generation workshops. These training programmes provided opportunities to the SHG members to interact with each other from different communities, different institutions and other SHG members. The knowledge gained from different training programmes helped them to gain confidence and know their capabilities and consequently increase their decision-making power.

Discussion

In India, poverty is characterised by low income levels which are inadequate to ensure quality of life. Low income affects people's access to various basic necessities such as housing, education, health, nutrition, security and opportunity for future development. The clients perceived poverty as a condition that lacks adequate money to fulfill their needs. The clients perceived poverty depending on their socio-economic condition such as lack of regular income or systematic means of earning. Having perceived poverty as lack of money, the clients engaged in microfinance activities to get access to their financial needs. They engaged in economic activities and paid work with the help of loans provided by the NGOs. The clients also participated in capacity-building programmes and income-generating activities workshops that enhanced their economic skills, which further provides them economic opportunities to engage in varied number of paid work. Engaging in microfinance activities had helped them overcome lack of money and avail economic opportunities. Their participation in capacity-building and related programmes also affected their capability to perceive resources that would provide them opportunities in the future rather than receiving immediate benefits. Microfinance through its various credit and financial services along with capacity-building programmes enabled the clients to raise their income levels and improve their standard of living. It reduced poverty of the clients by providing loans, increasing their income, building assets, upgrading their capacities and economic skills, strengthening their capability as decision maker in their families and increasing their social network. Thus, microfinance integrates people's perspective of poverty in its policy implementation and services.

Conclusion

Knowing people's perspective in alleviating poverty has become an important component as it makes possible to understand the concept of poverty from the perspective of poor people and people who are directly involved in alleviating poverty. In fact, a clear perspective always has a direct impact on the activities. The variation of the views of the clients and their perspectives about poverty help in better understanding the priorities of poor people. The perception on poverty widely differs from culture to culture and community to community. Perceptions and priorities of poor people must be listened to and addressed so that the NGOs involved can make effective policies and programmes accordingly. Understanding poverty from people's perspective help in getting diverse range of information and also create a new relationship between the service provider and the poor. The present study aimed at understanding poverty from clients' perspective and relates their perspective to the services provided by microfinance. It examined whether microfinance services had addressed the needs and priorities of the clients or not. Engaging in microfinance activities had enhanced their income-generation activities, increased income, built assets, extended social network and enhanced their economic skills, thereby reducing their poverty. Microfinance alleviates poverty when it addresses people's needs and priorities which differ from one region to another. In a state like Manipur where poverty is a persistent problem faced by people, microfinance had helped the poor clients of four NGOs mentioned to overcome poverty. It had addressed the clients' needs of credit, training and employment opportunities. Microfinance institutions had incorporated people's perspectives on poverty and their ways to overcome poverty and microfinance has been accepted as the most effective means to alleviate poverty by the clients who avail its services to overcome lack of money.

References

Banerjee, A. V., R. Benabou and D. Mookherjee, (2006), 'Introduction and Overview', in A. V. Banerjee, R. Benabou and D. Mookherjee (eds). *Understanding Poverty*, New York: Oxford University Press, Inc., pp. xiii–lii.

Bera, O., (2008), 'A Great Scope for Microfinance in NER', *Microfinance Focus*, Vol. II, No. VI, p. 23.

Borah, P., (2009), 'NEC and the Development Initiatives in the North East', *Dialogue: A Journal of Astha Bharati*, New Delhi, Vol. 10, No. 3.

Dey, S., (2012), Poverty Increases in Four NE States: Planning Commission, *Business Standard*.

Economic Watch, (2009), *http://www.economywatch.com/indianeconomy/poverty-in-india.html* Accessed on 2 June, 2009.

Indian Institute of Banking and Finance, (2009), *Micro-Finance Delivery Methodologies, Microfinance-Perspectives and Operations*, Mumbai, India: MacMillan.

Karmakar, K. G., (2008), 'Regulatory Framework for Microfinance Institutions in Karnataka', (ed). *Microfinance in India*, New Delhi: Sage Publications.

Lalitha, N., (2004), *Rural Development in India: Emerging Issues and Trends, Vol. I*, New Delhi: Dominant Publishers and Distributers, p. 128.

Mohanty, B., (2009), 'Micro-Finance for Development of the Deprived Section', *Vision: Jaya Prakash Narayan Institute of Economics and Social Studies*, Vol. XXIX, No.1.

Nair, Tara, (2001), 'Institutionalising Microfinance in India', *Economic and Political Weekly*, Vol. 36, No. 4, pp. 399–404.

National Institute of Rural Development, (2009), 'Poverty Eradication/Alleviation in North East India: An Approach', *http://www.esocialsciences.com/data/articles/Document127112008380.8906671.pdf* Accessed on 7 July, 2009.

Satish, P., (2005), 'Mainstreaming of Indian Microfinance', *Economic and Political Weekly*, Vol. 40, No. 17, pp. 1731–39.

Singh, R., (2008), 'Microfinance for Micro Enterprise Development', *DGCCS's Journal of Commerce*, Assam, Vol. V, No. 1, pp. 143–50.

Sinha, R. K., (2003), *Understanding Poverty*, New Delhi: Anamika Publishers and Distributors (P) Ltd.

Sinha, S., J. Samuel and B. Quiñones, (2000), 'Microfinance in India: Adjusting to Economic Liberalization', in Remenyi, J. and M. Quinones (eds). *Microfinance and Poverty Alleviation: Case Studies from Asia and the Pacific*, New York: Pinter, pp. 84–106.

Umdor, S., (2007), 'Microfinance Programme in Northeast India', *Eastern Quarterly, A Journal of Manipur Research Forum*, New Delhi, Vol. 4, No. II.

Yesudian, C. A. K., (2007), 'Poverty Alleviation Programmes in India: A Social Audit', *Indian Journal of Medical Research*, Vol. 126, No. 4, pp. 364–73.

Chapter 12

Microfinance-plus services – from access to impact

Empirical evidence from rural India

Naveen Kumar K

The importance of 'financial intermediation' in attacking poverty has long been accepted. Yet, substantial challenges remain in providing affordable, useful and sustainable financial services. Further, it is now well recognised, that along with financial services, access to non-financial services is necessary for the poor to break away from the vicious cycle of poverty. In this context, the microfinance industry is rapidly transforming, as per the needs of the clients, by delivering not only services, but also (along with credit) non-financial services, generally termed as 'credit-plus services'. The advocates of microfinance argue that the access to credit-plus services can help reduce poverty substantially through increased income and employment.

A large number of studies are available worldwide (Bangladesh, India, Bolivia, China, Guatemala, Indonesia, Zambia, Thailand, etc.), that have assessed the impact of microfinance services on assets, income, employment, food security and empowerment of women. However, the findings vary considerably from study to study, suggesting that the impact of microfinance is highly context specific. Nevertheless, the studies showed that the programme has made a significant contribution to the improvement of the social and economic status of the poor in general, and women in particular. They found that timely access to credit, savings, insurance and entrepreneurial training can contribute to a long-lasting increase in income through several means. Further, housing, health and education are the key areas of the non-financial impact of microfinance at the household level. It has been recorded that the impact of microfinance interventions on housing, health, education and nutritional level of the household member has improved wherever microfinance institutions (MFIs) have been working. The households of microfinance clients have better nutrition, health practices and health education, compared to non-client households. The study by Robinson showed that access to microfinance services has led to an enhancement in the quality of life of clients and an increase in their self-confidence, and has helped them diversify their livelihood security strategies, and thereby increase their income. Thus, regardless of the scale, outreach, location and the type of clients, microfinance interventions have one target in common – human development that is geared towards both the economic and social uplift.

In general, the microfinance programme targets both economic and social poverty of the member households by delivering various 'credit-plus services', like savings, insurance, health services, training and entrepreneurial development. Though several studies have highlighted the impact of microfinance services on the well-being of a household, a limited number of studies have examined the access and impact of credit-plus services on the household economy of the member, particularly in India. In this backdrop, this study examines the level of access and the impact of various credit-plus services in reducing economic and social poverty. In examining this objective, the study tests the hypothesis, that extension of credit-plus services by MFIs will lead to positive welfare changes in member households.

METHODOLOGY

Survey design and data

Generally, the microfinance programmes are to correct market failures in delivering credit and non-credit services to the rural poor. Most microfinance programmes state that their primary goal is to alleviate rural poverty by delivering financial and non-financial services to the poorest households, especially to the women in those households. The data have come from a survey of 318 member households of 106 women self-help groups (SHGs) in ten villages in the state of Karnataka, India, in 2006–07. Five of the villages are supported by Sri Kshethra Dharmasthala Rural Development Project (SKDRDP), Dharmasthala, Dakshina Kannada, and the other five are supported by Sanghamithra Rural Financial Services, Mysore. The rationale behind the selection of Sanghamithra is that it is the only not-for-profit company registered under the Indian Companies Act, 1956, and working in the state for more than ten years, with wide experience in microfinance services in the state of Karnataka. Sanghamithra also extends its microfinancial services in the neighbouring states of Tamil Nadu and Andhra Pradesh. However, the motivation behind the selection of SKDRDP was that it is the largest (by reaching the number of poor people and loan outstanding) NGO-MFI working in the field of microfinance in the state of Karnataka. SKDRDP, an MFI, is also reaching the poor with many non-financial services to the poor, through the development of micro-enterprise units, health care and sanitation facilities, literacy programme and so on.

To study the impact of microfinance-plus services on the welfare of member households of microfinance, a multistage sampling technique was adopted in the selection of the units. Accordingly, at the first stage, Mysore District, from the operational area of Sanghamithra MFI, and Dakshina Kannada District, from SKDRDP MFI, were selected purposively. Selection of the districts was done keeping in view that it should satisfy the two criteria: (i) cover (formed/linked to the MFI) the maximum number of SHGs and rural poor households and (ii) the district should be the first operational area, so that we have matured groups and members for the study. The second stage of sampling was the selection of taluks. There are two taluks: T. Narasipura taluk and Belthangady from Sanghamitra and SKDRDP operational areas, respectively, which were selected using the same criteria as was used for the selection of districts. The third stage of sampling covered the selection of villages. From each taluk, the village list was prepared with a number of SHGs formed/linked to the MFI. Consequently, top five villages, having highest number of SHGs and members, were selected from each taluk. The fourth stage of sampling involved the selection of SHGs. In each selected village, the current MFI-linked SHG list was prepared. Accordingly, from each village, 25 per cent of SHGs were selected, randomly. In all, 106 SHGs (53 SHGs from each taluk) were randomly selected from ten villages. The fifth stage of sampling involved the selection of member households. From each randomly selected SHG's, 25 per cent of the member households were selected randomly. In total, 318 households (159 households, each from Belthangady and T. Narasipura taluk) were selected for the study.

As one of the main objectives was to study the welfare impact of microfinance-plus services, it was decided to fix a minimum time period or gestation lag so that the membership in microfinance would have an impact on the member households. Therefore, the study considered 'new entrants' or 'new borrowers' of two or less than two years' membership in SHGs as a comparison or control group. In the sample, the households having more than two years' membership was considered as member group.[1] The rationale for selecting the new entrants as the comparison or control group was that these households had not availed much benefit (financial and non-financial) from the microfinance groups and they were new to the microfinance sector.[2] Generally, in the first year of group formation, members are trained in various SHG management issues and they start pooling their resources in a savings bank account. Once the group has generated a common fund through compulsory savings, it will start rotating the fund as small loans for a fixed period and rate of interest by the end of first or in the second year. Thus, in the first two years, members of microfinance groups are not exposed to many microfinance services. Hence, their socio-economic condition is comparable with the matured household members of the microfinance group. The members having membership of more than two years in the SHG would have had more access to lots of financial and non-financial services than the new members. Thus, access to higher opportunities or resources enhances economic and social well-being of the long-time members.

Method of data collection and analysis

The primary data were collected through well-designed and pre-tested schedules. The tools employed were direct, personal interviews and focus group discussions with SHG members. The welfare impact of microfinance-plus services are both qualitative and quantitative in nature. As a result, we adopted both qualitative and quantitative variables and indicators to analyse the impact (outcome) of 'microfinance-plus services' on the welfare of member household economy. Further, to study the impact of microfinance-plus services in improving the economic and social well-being of the member households, an attempt was made to assess the economic and social changes in the member households with the help of the log-linear regression model.

Socio-economic profile of the sample households

This study made an attempt to explore the social and economic aspects like age, literacy, family size, caste, marital status, occupation and income of the sample households in Belthangady and T.

Narasipura taluks. In the total sample, 76.4 per cent of the members had a membership of more than two years, while, 23.6 per cent of the members in the study area had joined the programme recently, with a membership of two years or less. In the subsequent sections, the social and economic profiles of the member households are discussed in detail.

Age composition

The empirical results reveal that the average age of member group in Belthangady and T. Narasipura taluks is 37.03 and 36.46 years and 36.21 and 32.37 years for the control groups, respectively. The difference in the mean age across member and control groups is higher in T. Narasipura as compared to Belthangady taluk. Compared to the member group, the age of the control group is lesser; it confirms that in recent years, younger women are attracted to join the microfinance programme. A large percentage of member group households in both the taluks are in the productive age of 30 to 59 years. Further, there are very small percentages of member households in the category of 60 and more years in the study area. In the control group households, larger percentages of the members belong to the age group of 15 to 29 years. It is absolutely clear that, in recent times, younger women are becoming part of microfinance movement.

Family size

It is observed that 43.2 and 34.7 per cent of the member and control group households, respectively, have a family of less than four members. However, 22.6 and 30.7 per cent of the member and control group households, respectively, have a family of seven members and above. This implies that in rural areas the presence of the nuclear family is very much visible and there are some families that are still within the boundaries of the joint family system.

Caste

Caste is one of the imperative characteristics that specify the social status of the households in the society. From the study, it is found that a considerable proportion of the sample households belong to other backward castes (OBCs), scheduled tribes

(STs) and scheduled castes (SCs). In Belthangady taluk, 49.6, 22.4 and 13.6 per cent of member groups belong to OBCs, STs and 'minorities', respectively. However, in the same taluk, 44.2, 29.4 and 23.5 per cent control group households belong to OBCs, SCs and STs, respectively. In T. Narasipura taluk 34.6, 25.4 and 21.2 per cent member households belong to forward classes, STs and SCs, respectively. However, 56.10, 19.5 and 19.5 per cent control group households belong to SCs, forward classes, and STs, respectively. Further, it depicts that the new members, who belong to SCs and STs, are joining the programme, and it is a good sign of social and economic inclusion of the poor in general, and women in particular.

Marital status

Marriage is a social institution and it re-organises society, leading to the formation of kinship ties and membership in descent groups. In the total sample more than 80 per cent of the members (control and member group) are married. Similarly, 6.6 and 9.3 per cent widows joined the microfinance programme from the member and control groups, respectively.

Education

A substantial percentage of the respondents had no formal education. In the total sample, 39.9 and 44 per cent of the member and control groups, respectively, were illiterate. The illiteracy rate was higher in T. Narasipura taluk, that is, 52.5 and 51.2 per cent of the member and control group members were illiterate compared to 28 and 35.3 per cent member and control group members in Belthangady taluk, respectively. Educational development in Belthangady taluk was comparatively better than in T. Narasipura taluk and it has reflected in the study. The level of education can positively influence the impact of banking literacy, group management and decision to take up self-employment.

Occupation

The microfinance programme in the study areas has diversified the occupation of the member households. The opportunity for self-employment has improved in the study area. In the total sample,

56.7 per cent members in the control group depend on agricultural and non-agricultural wage labour as an occupation and 21.3 per cent were unemployed, while 37.9 per cent of the member groups were self-employed in petty business, dairy, poultry, sheep rearing and so on. It was observed that 19.3 and 24.3 per cent of member group and control group, respectively, had diversified their occupation – wage employment with self-employment and cultivation with self-employment.

Access to microfinance-plus services

Before assessing the impact of credit-plus services, this study attempted to explore the access to various credit-plus services by the member households. It will explain the magnitude of credit and non-credit services accessed by the members 'before' and 'after' joining the microfinance programme. In this context, pre- and post-scenario of microfinance members were analysed. Further, the impact of the programme was analysed through using the control and member group households of two or less than two years and more than two years membership in the microfinance programme, respectively.

Access to savings services

The study shows that the members made regular savings and accumulated a considerable amount of money individually and collectively compared to their abilities to save. It is developing the habit of saving that is much more important than the amount of savings among low-income households. We asked the households if they had ever saved money in a financial institution before joining a microfinance programme. Among those who are members of MFIs at present, 93.7 and 98.1 per cent in Belthangady and T. Narasipura taluks, respectively, indicated that they did not have any institutional savings prior to microfinance membership.[3] However, the scene has changed dramatically in the post-microfinance programme period by bringing all the members (100 per cent) under the umbrella of formal savings. The programme inculcated the habit of savings among the members in a commendable manner and it works as an insurance (collateral) against the loan.

Access to credit services

Accesses to credit for women will bolster household development through enhanced decision making in spending on food, health and education. However, in practice, for poor women accessing credit services is a nightmare. In the study area, there were 92.4 and 98.8 per cent of the households outside the scope of access to formal credit. Nevertheless, the microfinance programme has given new hope for the poor households to access credit for productive and non-productive purposes.

Access to insurance services

People belonging to rural areas, with lower income, are more prone to risks and uncertainties. Similarly, the access to insurance services in rural areas is negligible. Prior to microfinance programme, 91.8 and 92.4 per cent of the members in Belthangady and T. Narasipura taluks, respectively, did not have any type of insurance coverage. However, the innovations of microfinance have promoted the access to micro-health insurance in the study area. At the time of the survey, 100 and 53.4 per cent members in Belthangady and T. Narasipura taluks, respectively, were accessing micro-health insurance services to cover various health and other risks.

Access to training and awareness

It was observed that prior to the microfinance programme none of the members had access to any type of training from any agency in Belthangady and T. Narasipura taluks. However, post-microfinance programme, 100 and 57.2 per cent of the members in Belthangady and T. Narasipura taluks, respectively, accessed training from different agencies. The members in both the taluks had training on SHG management, income-generating activities (IGAs), health care, nutrition and sanitation. The access to training and awareness programme in the study area has widened and encouraged the social and economic development of the poor.

Access to health care services

The poverty and vulnerability of the poor hindered their access to health care services in the pre-microfinance programme. It was observed from the focus group discussion that many of the rural people in T. Narasipura taluk were not able to bear the cost of private health services and the public hospitals were too far to cater to their needs. Thus, they took small amounts of credit from informal sources to avail private health services. The external borrowings and bad health condition amplified their vulnerability. However, microfinance intermediaries like SHGs, SHG federations, MFIs and self-help promoting institutions (SHPIs) extended easy access to credit with various types of health care services. It was reported from the field that in post-microfinance programme, 78.6 and 42.8 per cent members in Belthangady and T. Narasipura taluks, respectively, accessed various types of health care services (preventive, promotive and curative).

Access to social networks

The social network plays a pivotal role in improving the economic, social, political and psychological life of the poor. In Belthangady and T. Narasipura taluks, 81.8 and 90.6 per cent women members, respectively, had not networked with any formal or informal institution in the study area. However, in the post-microfinance programme, 85.5 and 52.2 per cent of the members in Belthangady and T. Narasipura taluks, respectively, had networked with various local institutions.

Access to micro-enterprise services or self-employment

Prior to the microfinance programme, only 6.3 and 3.8 per cent members in Belthangady and T. Narasipura taluks, respectively, had access to micro-enterprise or self-employment. However, in the post-microfinance programme, 73.6 and 61.6 per cent of the members in Belthangady and T. Narasipura taluks, respectively, had joined various types of micro-enterprise or self-employment programmes. In Belthangady and T. Narasipura taluks, 27 and 30.2 per cent members, respectively, had access to 'micro-enterprises' activities in the study area.

Impact of microfinance-plus services

The present study examines the welfare impact of credit-plus services on the social and economic changes of the member household.

We will begin with the 'economic' impact of credit-plus services, and subsequently, we will look at the 'social' impact.

Economic impact of microfinance-plus services

To assess the economic impact of microcredit-plus services on the member households, the changes in economic variables like household income, employment, assets, housing condition and household expenditures will be observed.

1. *Change in household income and employment:* The impact of credit-plus services on the income of the member households is represented in Table 12.1. In Belthangady taluk 34.4 and 47.2 per cent of the member households belonged to the fourth quartile (more than Rs 37,001) and third quartile (Rs 28,001–37,000), respectively, of the net annual income of the household. In the same taluk, 82.35 per cent of the control group households belonged to the net annual income of less than Rs 19,000 (first quartile). In T. Narasipura taluk, 22.03, 44.07 and 33.05 per cent of the member households belonged to the income group of fourth, third and second quartiles while 90.24 per cent of the control group households belonged to the first quartile. Hence, it is apparent that, in total,

Table 12.1 Net annual household income (in Rs)

Net annual household income Rs (quartiles)	Belthangady (N=159)		T.Narasipura (N=159)		Total (N=318)	
	Control group	Member group	Control group	Member group	Control group	Member group
Less than Rs 19,000	28 (82.4)	2 (1.6)	37 (90.2)	1 (0.8)	65 (86.7)	3 (1.2)
Rs 19,001 to Rs 28,000	5 (14.7)	21 (16.8)	4 (9.8)	39 (33.1)	9 (12.0)	60 (24.7)
Rs 28,001 to Rs 37,000	0	59 (47.2)	0	52 (44.1)	0	111 (45.7)
More than Rs 37,001	1 (2.9)	43 (34.4)	0	26 (22.0)	1(1.3)	69 (28.4)
Number of observations	34	125	41	118	75	243

Source: Primary Survey.

Note: Figures in parentheses denote percentage to the total number of households in the particular sample group.

more than 73 per cent of the member group households had higher net annual income of more than Rs 28,000, and 86.67 per cent control group households had a net annual income of less than Rs 19,000. Therefore, microfinance services have played a positive role in improving the household income and enhancing the welfare of the households.

2. *Change in household employment:* Large numbers of member households are self-employed in various income-generating activities. In Belthangady and T. Narasipura taluks, 37.6 and 38.1 per cent member households, respectively, are self-employed as compared to 5.9 and 0 in the control group households. In Belthangady taluk, out of total self-employed (47 members), 92.6 per cent are self-employed in SIRI micro-enterprises.[4] They are producing more than seventy-five items like chemical items, food products, readymade garments, pickles, areca leaf cups, fancy items, condiments, agarbatthis, squashes and vermicompost, and another 7.4 per cent are self-employed in dairy, tailoring, petty shop and so on. In T. Narasipura taluk, out of 38.1 per cent of the self-employed, majority are engaged in dairy (55 per cent), floriculture (16 per cent), petty shop (14 per cent) and tailoring (11 per cent). The study also reveals that in the member groups, the wage labourers and cultivators also opted for various types of self-employment with their prior occupation. This shows that microfinance had diversified the employment of the members. In Belthangady, 16.8 and 28.8 per cent member households and in T. Narasipura taluk, 22.0 and 19.5 per cent member households are engaged in wage labour with self-employment (dairy, floriculture and petty shop) and cultivation with self-employment (dairy, floriculture, and petty shop), respectively.

The magnitude of agricultural and non-agricultural wage is very high in the control group households – 35.3 and 73.2 per cent in Belthangady and T. Narasipura taluks, respectively. It is also evident that increased number of years of membership in microfinance has decreased the dependency on wage labour and increased diversification of employment of the rural women. The microfinance programme has improved the employment opportunity for the member households over the years. In total, only 6.6 per cent member groups and 21.3 per cent of control group members are unemployed. Therefore, it is clear that the employability through credit-plus services has improved in the member group households as compared to the comparison group. The focus group discussion with the members of microfinance revealed that most of the members, prior to joining the microfinance groups, were either unemployed or homemakers. Microfinance has created optimism in the lives of poor women and released them from poverty by improving their employment opportunities.

3. *Change in household assets*: The microfinance programme has created the habit of thrift and savings among the members of microfinance. Prior to microfinance membership, only 6.3 and 1.9 per cent of the households had formal saving in Belthangady and T. Narasipura taluks, respectively. However, in the post-microfinance programme, all the members had compulsory savings accounts. In the total sample, per capita annual savings was Rs 1,710.53 for the member group and Rs 642.40 for the comparison group. There was Rs 1,854 and Rs 764.71 per capita annual savings for the member group and control group, respectively, in Belthangady taluk. In T. Narasipura taluk, the per capita annual savings was Rs 1,579.75 for the member group and Rs 540.98 for the comparison group. It is clear that microfinance membership has improved the per capita annual savings in the member group as compared to the comparison group.

Table 12.2 presents the possession of physical assets by the member households as against the comparison households. There is a marginal difference in the average landholdings between the member groups and the control group households. The average value of the landholdings is higher in the member group. This difference has emerged due to the investment on improvement (irrigational development and fencing) in the landholding by the member households. The possession of livestock is comparatively higher in the member group. In Belthangady and T. Narasipura taluks, 69.6 and 64.4 per cent of the member groups, respectively, had livestock, while in the control groups, it was 20.6 and 7.3 per cent. The average value of livestock was more than Rs 25,000 for the member group households as compared to around Rs 15,000 for the control groups. The possession of electronic articles also plays pivotal role in the households. It is obvious from Table 12.2 that a large number of member households possessed electronics goods. The average value of electronic appliances is higher for the member households (Rs 7,947.96) as compared to the control households (Rs 4,136.39). Similar changes in the household assets were seen in the obtaining of gold ornaments and other assets by the member households. It was observed during the focus group discussions that a majority of the SHG members use microfinance loans to buy gold jewellery either for themselves or for their children. They feel that posses sion of gold ornaments or some physical assets instills a symbol of prestige and social status in society and provides security (protects) at times of risk or emergency. In some villages, it was observed that microfinance loans were effectively used for the development of dairy or sheep rearing by purchasing livestock. As a result, it has enhanced the employment and savings and increased consumption of milk products in the member households.

4. *Increase in household expenditure*: Household expendi- ture is another important indicator of welfare. It indicates the level of expenditure of the household for various productive and non-productive purposes. It was observed that member house- holds have increased their expenses on education, housing appli- ances and repairs, clothing and health through the borrowings from the microfinance groups. Table 12.3 shows the annual household expenditure on education, food, cloth, household appliances, hous- ing repair, health, electricity, telephone and other expenses by the households. Generally, the major share of the household income is spent on food. It is obvious from the table that member households spent, approximately, an average of Rs 19,302.40 and Rs 19,060.17 on food in Belthangady and T. Narasipura taluks, respectively. The control group households, however, spent only Rs 10,747.06 and Rs 10,775.61 in the respective study taluks. The expenditure on hous- ing (repair) was more for the member group households than that of the control group (Rs 14,627.57 and Rs 1,133.33, respectively). The expenditure on education in the total sample was Rs 4,144.85 for the member households and Rs 1,468.63 for the control group households. It is clear from the table that, in all cases, the house- hold expenditure was higher for member households than the control group households. Therefore, it is apparent from the above discussion that household expenditure has improved or increased over the years of membership in the microfinance group. The enhanced household expenditure will lead to improvement in the household welfare of the members.

5. *Change in housing condition*: The housing condition shows the social and economic status of the member in the society. The type of the dwelling and access to facilities in the household like water, toilet, electricity, fuel and telephone are the major determi- nants of housing condition. The credit-plus services have facilitated considerable changes in the quality of housing in the study area. The

Table 12.2 Possession of physical assets by the households

Types of physical assets possessed by the households		Belthangady (N=159)		T. Narasipura (N=159)		Total (N=318)	
		Control group	Member group	Control group	Member group	Control group	Member group
Land holdings							
Possessing land (%)	No	12 (35.3)	49 (39.2)	35 (85.4)	60 (50.8)	47 (62.7)	109 (44.9)
	Yes	22 (64.7)	76 (60.8)	6 (14.6)	58 (49.2)	28 (37.3)	134 (55.1)
Average acres of land		1.26	1.64	0.95	1.68	1.12	1.66
Average present value (Rs)		53,333.33	95,681.82	60,909.00	94,500.00	33,121.17	95,090.91
Livestock							
Possessing livestock (%)	No	27 (79.4)	38 (30.4)	38 (92.7)	42 (35.6)	65 (86.7)	80 (32.3)
	Yes	7 (20.6)	87 (69.6)	3 (7.3)	76 (64.4)	10 (13.3)	163 (67.1)
Average present value (Rs)		16,142.86	25,258.95	10,166.67	25,451.00	13,154.77	25,354.98
Electronics							
Possessing electronic goods (%)	No	26 (76.5)	11 (8.8)	32 (78)	29 (24.6)	58 (77.3)	40 (16.5)
	Yes	8 (23.5)	114 (91.2)	9 (22)	89 (75.4)	17 (22.7)	203 (83.5)
Average present value (Rs)		4,645.00	7,973.00	3,627.78	7,922.92	4,136.39	7,947.96
Vehicles (2- and 4-wheelers)							
Possessing vehicles (%)	No	34 (100)	101 (80.8)	41 (100)	110 (93.2)	75 (100)	211 (86.8)
	Yes	0	24 (19.2)	0	8 (6.8)	0	32 (13.2)
Average present value (Rs)		0	35,000	0	40,000	0	37,500
Tools and equipments							

Possessing tools and equipments (%)	No	32 (94.1)	93 (74.4)	40 (97.6)	101 (85.6)	72 (96)	194 (79.8)
	Yes	2 (5.9)	32 (25.6)	1 (2.4)	17 (14.4)	3 (4)	49 (20.2)
Average present value (Rs)		13,000.00	33,500.00	3,500.00	7,500.00	8,250.00	20,500.00
Others (gold, petty shop)							
Possessing other articles (%)	No	27 (79.4)	21 (16.8)	34 (82.9)	24 (20.3)	61 (81.3)	45 (18.5)
	Yes	7 (20.6)	104 (83.2)	7 (17.1)	94 (79.7)	14 (18.7)	198 (81.5)
Average present value (Rs)		11,034.48	14,500.00	10,642.86	13,975.00	10,838.67	14,237.50
Number of households		34	125	41	118	75	243

Source: Primary Survey.

Note: Figures in parenthesis denote percentage to the total number of households in the particular sample group.

Table 12.3 Annual household expenditure across the taluks

Particulars of household expenditures (per annum)	Belthangady (N=159)		T. Narasipura (N=159)		Total (N=318)	
	Control group	Member group	Control group	Member group	Control group	Member group
Education	1,651.85	4,555.34	1,262.5	3,557.64	1,468.63	4,144.85
Food	10,747.06	19,302.40	10,775.61	19,060.17	10,762.67	19,184.77
Cloth	1,166.18	2,508.40	1,373.17	2,094.07	1,279.33	2,307.20
Household appliances	1,283.82	2,848.00	926.83	1,922.03	1,088.67	2,398.35
Housing	1,764.71	20,996.00	609.76	7,881.36	1,133.33	14,627.57
Health	566.18	998.40	353.66	628.39	450.00	818.72
Electricity and phone bills	896.67	1,942.67	923.53	1,537.63	910.94	1,732.23
Others	508.82	1,301.20	343.90	574.58	418.67	948.35
Number of observation	34	125	41	118	75	243

Source: Primary Survey.

Note: Figures in parenthesis denote percentage to the total number of households in the particular sample group.

dwelling conditions of the member group households were much better than that of the control group households. It is apparent from Table 12.4 that a large number of control group households in T. Narasipura taluk had either *kutcha* or semi-pucca houses. It was also observed that dwelling conditions of the member group was superior in Belthangady as compared to T. Narasipura taluk. Even some of the new entrants to microfinance had better dwelling conditions in Belthangady taluk, due to the SKDRDP's Swagraha Yojana (own house) housing development programme. However, in the total sample, the dwellings of the member group households were comparatively better than that of the control group.

It is also evident, from Table 12.4, that the member and control group households mainly used either their own or public sources of water for drinking purposes. Hence, there was not much difference in using of water sources across the member group and control group. In Belthangady taluk, a large numbers of households had their own source of water, while in T. Narasipura taluk, households mainly depended on the public water supply. The focus group discussion with the members in T. Narasipura (Vatal village) revealed that the quality of drinking water (adequacy, timely and clean) had improved after the interventions of SHG members in the village local administration.

The households with access to electricity revealed qualitative changes in the standard of living. In the total sample, 91.9 per cent of the member group households (73.7 per cent own and 17.2 per cent Bhagyajothi connections) had electricity connections as compared to only 69.3 per cent in the control group. In Belthangady and T. Narasipura taluks, only 8.8 per cent and 9.3 per cent of the member households and 29.4 per cent and 31.7 per cent of the control group, respectively, had no power connection. There was not much difference in the usage of fuel by the households across the member and comparison groups. In general, the connectivity of telephone across the sample households was very scanty. In the member group households, 23 per cent had phone connection; in the control group, it was 9.3 per cent. In Belthangady and T. Narasipura taluks, 26.4 and 19.5 per cent member households and 17.6 and 2.4 per cent comparison group households, respectively, availed phone connections. In the study area, 72.8 per cent households in the member group and 45.3 per cent in the control group had toilet facility. In Belthangady and T. Narasipura taluks, respectively, 98.4 and 45.8 per cent of the member households and 85.3 and 12.2 per

Table 12.4 Housing condition of the households

Characteristics	Belthangady (N=159)		T.Narasipura (N=159)		Total (N=318)	
	Control group	Member group	Control group	Member group	Control group	Member group
Type of dwelling						
Pucca	16 (47.1)	93 (74.4)	1 (2.4)	28 (23.7)	17(22.7)	121 (49.8)
Semi-pucca	12 (35.3)	31 (24.8)	11 (26.8)	76 (64.4)	23 (30.7)	107 (44)
Kutcha	6 (17.6)	1 (0.8)	29 (70.7)	13 (11)	35 (46.7)	14 (5.8)
Rented	0	0	0	1 (0.8)	0	1 (0.4)
Main source of drinking water						
Own	23 (67.6)	104 (83.2)	5 (12.2)	61 (51.7)	28 (37.3)	165 (67.9)
Public	6 (17.6)	18 (14.4)	34 (82.9)	57 (48.3)	40 (53.3)	75 (30.9)
Other	5 (4.7)	3 (2.4)	2 (4.9)	0	7 (9.3)	3 (1.2)
Electricity						
Yes, having electricity connection	15 (44.1)	86 (68.8)	17 (41.5)	93 (78.8)	32 (42.7)	179 (73.7)
Bhagyajothi	9 (26.5)	28 (22.4)	11(26.8)	14 (11.9)	20 (26.7)	42 (17.2)
No connection	10 (29.4)	11 (8.8)	13 (31.7)	11 (9.3)	23 (30.7)	22 (9.1)
Fuel used for cooking						
Gas	0	0	0	5 (4.2)	0	5 (2.1)
Kerosene	0	0	0	1 (0.8)	0	1 (0.8)
Firewood	34 (100)	125 (100)	41 (100)	112 (94.9)	75 (100)	237 (97.5)

Telephone connection						
No connection	28 (82.4)	92 (73.6)	40 (97.6)	95 (80.5)	68 (90.7)	187 (77)
Yes	6 (17.6)	33 (26.4)	1 (2.4)	23 (19.5)	7 (9.3)	56 (23)
Toilet facility						
Yes own	29 (85.3)	123 (98.4)	5 (12.2)	54 (45.8)	34 (45.3)	177 (72.8)
Open	5 (14.7)	2 (1.6)	36 (87.8)	64 (54.2)	41 (54.7)	66 (27.2)
Number of observations	34	125	41	118	75	243

Source: Primary Survey.

Note: Figures in parentheses denote percentage to the total number of households in the particular sample group.

cent of control group households had toilet facility. The SKDRDP has taken initiatives of 'Grama Nairmalya' (village sanitation) by constructing toilets in its project areas. The institution provided the materials and capital assistance for the poor households for the construction of toilets. Hence, in Belthangady taluk, even with less than two years of membership, the households had toilets.

Social impact of microfinance-plus services

Social impact of the credit-plus services on the household economy was examined through the development of *human* and *social capital*. The development of *human capital* was examined through indicators like education of the children, access to health care services, improvement in the level of confidence and development of skills of the women. On the other hand, the development of *social capital* was studied through the extension of networks and memberships in various institutions across the member and control group members of microfinance.

1. *Educational development:* At the household level, education creates choices and opportunities, reduces the burden of poverty and builds empowerment. The benefits of microfinance reach beyond the member; it could increase the educational opportunities of the client's children. Appendix A12.1 reveals that the non-enrolment and dropout of children in the age of group 6 to 14 years were very less for both the member and control group households. However, the number of dropouts was very high for the control group members in the age group of 15 to 18 and 19 to 21 years, in both the taluks. Very high rate of enrolment with very low rate of dropout of the students was recorded for the member households in all three age groups for both the taluks. Majority of the members of microfinance group opined in the focus group discussions that they were able to send their children to the schools/colleges after joining the microfinance programme. The member group households were spending more on children's education (average of Rs 4,144.85) compared to the control group households (average of Rs 1,468.63).

2. *Health care services – micro-health insurance:* Poverty and ill health have a two-way relationship. Poverty aggravates physical living conditions, poor sanitation, poor hygiene and insufficient nutrition. Given the economic status of the poor, they are more vulnerable to many risks in their lives. These risks prevent them

from breaking the vicious cycle of poverty. Insuring against these risks is considered as one of the risk management strategies for the rural households. In this context, micro-health insurance is considered as one of greatest innovations to reach the low-income people who are vulnerable to plenty of risks. In delivering micro-health insurance the 'partnership model' was found to be more convenient and cost-efficient because it works in a structural arrangement where the genuine win-win-win scenario will benefit the insurers, MFIs and their clients, especially with regard to price and product design. This study has looked at two 'partner-agent micro-health insurance models' that are actively involved in the delivery of micro-health insurance products in Karnataka. SKDRDP and ICICI Lombard and Karuna Trust and the National Insurance Company are the two agents and insurers in the provision of micro-health insurance.

Table 12.5 depicts the accessibility of micro-health insurance across the two study taluks. It is clear that in Belthangady taluk, the entire member and control group households obtained micro-health insurance. However, in T. Narasipura taluk, only 7.3 and 55.9 per cent of the control and member group households, respectively, availed micro-health insurance. In Belthangady and T. Narasipura taluks, 17.7 and 66.6 per cent control group households, respectively, claimed their insurance. However, the percentage of claims in the member group is also high, that is, 20.8 and 31.8 per cent in Belthangady and T. Narasipura taluk, respectively. It is apparent that a large number of poor households are benefitting from the micro-health insurance. During the focus group discussion, many of the members opinioned that health insurance had saved their money and assets (with no insurance, they have to mortgage their assets) in times of their illness.

3. *Improvement in skill and the level of confidence*: Generally, the rural poor woman lacks skills and knowledge. It was also observed that majority of the rural women did not have mobility and lived within the four walls of their homes, taking care of their children and the household. However, participation in the microfinance programme encouraged them to participate in various socio-economic activities. The training imparted by different institutions and individuals opened up new avenues and encouraged them to take up different self-employment activities in the locality. In the focus group discussions, a majority of the women said that prior to microfinance programme they lacked basic banking knowledge

Table 12.5 Access to micro-health insurance services

Do you have micro-health insurance services?	Belthangady (N=159)		T. Narasipura (N=159)		Total (N=318)	
	Control group	Member group	Control group	Member group	Control group	Member group
Yes	34 (100)	125 (100)	3 (7.3)	66 (55.9)	37 (49.3)	191 (78.6)
No	0	0	38 (92.7)	52 (44.1)	38 (50.7)	52 (21.4)
Did you make any claims against the insurance premium?						
Yes	6 (17.7)	26 (20.8)	2 (66.6)	21 (31.8)	8 (21.6)	47 (24.6)
No	28 (82.3)	99 (79.2)	1 (33.4)	45 (68.2)	29 (78.4)	144 (75.4)
Average number of members insured in the family	1.59	5.02	1.11	4.15	1.35	4.72
Average amount of insurance premium (Rs)	620.88	644.72	123.11	174.33	439.21	574.59

Source: Primary Survey.

Note: Figures in parenthesis denote percentage to the total number of households in the particular sample group.

(banking literacy). However, continuous intervention by the MFI/ NGO through the groups improved their skills and knowledge.

The microfinance programme, in the study area, has made considerable impact on skill enhancement and in building the level of confidence of the members through participation in various training programmess and awareness and knowledge-enrichment activities. In Belthangady taluk, all the members of the microfinance programme had received some training or another. However, in T. Narasipura taluk 75.6 per cent of the control group members did not have any training as against only 31.4 per cent in member group. Appendix A12.2 depicts that 95.2 per cent of the member households were trained in various IGAs, as against 52.9 per cent of the control group households in the same taluk. In T. Narasipura taluk, 9.8 per cent control group households were trained on various IGAs as against 63.6 per cent in the member group households. It is obvious from the table that a large number of the member group households benefitted from various training programmes of microfinance as compared to the control group households. A short duration of membership also leads to less opportunity to avail benefits of training through the microfinance programme. Therefore, it is apparent from Table A12.2 as well as from the focus group discussions with the members that microfinance has provided various types of exposure to the external world and added a new dimension to employment, management of household, health and sanitation, children's education, thrift and savings.

4. *Development of social capital*: The term 'social capital' found its way into economic analysis only recently, although for long various elements of the concept have been in existence under different names. It refers to features of social organisation such as networks, norms and social trust that facilitate coordination and cooperation for mutual benefits. It is a set of 'horizontal and vertical associations' between the people and various institutions. In microfinance, people form the groups vertically link with MFIs/NGOs/banks and horizontally link with the members of same group or with their peers. Associations (microfinance groups) and institutions (MFIs, SHGs) provide an informal framework to organise information sharing, coordination of activities and collective decision making.

Table 12.6 clearly represents the networks/membership that has increased through the microfinance programme. The development of networks was associated with the member group households in both the taluks. Exactly 42.4 per cent of the member group in

Table 12.6 Number of members having different networks or membership with local institutions

| Network/membership or association with various institutions in the study area | Belthangady (N=159) | | T. Narasipura (N=159) | | Total (N=318) | |
	Control group (N=34)	Member group (N=125)	Control group (N=41)	Member group (N=118)	Control group (N=75)	Member group (N=243)
1[a] With only one institution	4 (11.8)	0	14 (34.1)	4 (3.4)	18 (24.0)	4 (1.6)
2[b] With two institutions	20 (58.8)	18 (14.4)	19 (46.3)	18 (15.3)	39 (52.0)	36 (14.8)
3[c] With three institutions	9 (26.5)	44 (35.2)	7 (17.1)	56 (47.5)	16 (21.3)	100 (41.2)
4[d] With four institutions	1 (2.9)	53 (42.4)	1 (2.4)	34 (28.8)	2 (2.7)	87 (35.8)
5[e] With five institutions	0	10 (8)	0	6 (5.1)	0	16 (6.6)

Source: Primary Survey.

Notes: (i) Figures in parenthesis denote percentage to the total number of households in the particular sample group. (ii) 1=Banks/MFIs/Post office/cooperative banks; 2 =Enterprise units (SIRI, milk cooperative); 3 = Women associations (Mahila Mandal's); 4 = Political association (Panchayat) and 5 = Others (network with other institutions) (1[a] =1); (2[b] = 1+2); (3[c] = 1+2+3); (4[d] =1+2+3+4) and (5[e] = 1+2+3+4+5).

Belthangady taluk has membership or association with four institutions compared to only 2.9 per cent of the control group members. In T. Narasipura taluk, more than 75 per cent of the members have membership in more than three institutions. Thus, it is obvious that the microfinance programme has encouraged building up of social capital through a network/association with various institutions.

To sum up, it is evident from the above analysis that credit-plus services have improved the economic and social conditions of the member households in the study area. However, to strengthen these empirical findings, we have applied an econometric model to examine the welfare impact of credit-plus services through change in per capita income (PCI) of the member households.

Econometric model

Access to credit-plus services from the microfinance groups enabled the members to undertake income-generating activities and diversify their occupation. As a result, the income of the member household increased. To test the relative importance of the factors that determine the household income of the microfinance member households, a log linear regression model was estimated by using the ordinary least square method.

The access to credit-plus services from the microfinance groups enabled the members to undertake income-generating activities and diversify their occupation that increased the household income. The PCI of households among the member group was higher at Rs 8,863.65 as compared to Rs 3,954.44 among the control group. Similarly, the PCC accessed from the microfinance programme was Rs 22,108.20 and Rs 5,730.96 among the member and control groups, respectively. To test the relative importance of the factors that determine the household income of the microfinance members, a log linear regression model was estimated by using the ordinary least square method. We found that the semi-log functional form was better than the non-log form to estimate the determinants of household income. In order to justify the semi-log specification, we tested the distribution of residuals for normality. The validity of the T-test and F-test also depended upon a norm distribution. In the normal probability plot, we found that the residuals were more close to the normal probability curve in the case of semi-logarithmic specification than the non-logarithmic specification. Therefore, the results support the assumption an appropriate

Table 12.7 Measurement and descriptive statistics of main variables

Variable	Description of the variables	Expected sign	Mean	Standard deviation
PCI	PCI of the household (Rs)		7705.82	3947.21
PCC	Per capita credit (PCC) accessed from SHGs (Rs)	+	18245.64	15371.79
Lhold	Land holdings (in acres)	+	0.51	0.50
Occp	1 = Individuals having self-employment; 0 = otherwise	+	0.47	0.50
MFIs	1 = SKDRDP Project area; 0 otherwise	+	0.50	0.41
Memgroup	1 = Member group; 0 = otherwise (control group)	+	0.76	0.43
Edn1	1 = Primary education (1 to 5th std); 0 = otherwise	+	0.23	0.42
Edn2	1 = Secondary education (6th std & above); 0 = otherwise	+	0.36	0.48
Marriage	1 = Married; 0 = otherwise	+	0.90	0.29
SC	1 = Individual belongs to SC; 0 = otherwise	+	0.22	0.41
ST	1 = Individual belongs to ST; 0 = otherwise	+	0.23	0.42
OBC	1 = Individual belongs to OBC; 0 = otherwise	+	0.37	0.48
N	Number of observations		318	

regress and are natural logarithm of PCI of the household. In this model, PCI of the household is the dependent variable and per capita loan amount, land holdings, occupation, project areas of the MFIs, member group, education of the members and caste are the explanatory variables.

The estimated equation is as follows

$$ln\,PCI = \beta_1 + \beta_2 PCC + \beta_3 Lhold + \beta_4 Occp + \beta_5 MFIs$$
$$+ \beta_6 Memgroup + \beta_7 Edn1 + \beta_8 Edn2 + \beta_9 Marriage$$
$$+ \beta_{10} SC + \beta_{11} ST + \beta_{12} OBC + ui$$

The results on determinants of household PCI are presented in the Table 12.8. The results show that the independent variable

Table 12.8 Determinants of household income: OLS estimates

Variable	Co-efficient	Std. error #.	t-Statistics
Per capita credit	0.000008964 *	0.0000015	6.023491
Land holding	0.188751147 *	0.036115	5.226438
Occupation	0.314094704 *	0.041399	7.586939
MFIs	0.150946878 *	0.046585	3.240244
Member group	0.161124342 *	0.064714	7.645285
Education 1	−0.03876493	0.04637	-0.83598
Education 2	0.109201556 **	0.042886	2.546295
Marriage	0.161124342 **	0.064714	2.489801
SC	−0.109536238 ***	0.058377	-1.87636
ST	−0.110073374 ***	0.057782	-1.90498
OBC	−0.112876631 ***	0.058023	-1.94538
Constant	0.7955 *	0.0101	0.78459
R^2	0.54		
Durbin Watson	1.657		
F – statistics (11–306)	50.09 *		
N	318		

Notes: (i) OLS, ordinary least squares.
(ii) # White Heteroskedaticity-Consistent Standard Errors and Covariance.
(ii) *, ** & *** Significant at 1, 5 and 10 per cent level, respectively. Dependent Variable = log per capita income (ln PCI)
SC, ST and OBC denote caste-based reservation in India.

PCC is positive and significant at 1 per cent. The access to loan provides income-generating capacity to the household; thus, the variable was expected to influence the household income positively. This a priori expectation corroborates with the result obtained in this model. In the model, the size of land holdings is positive and significant at 1 per cent. Ceteris paribus, higher the size of land holdings, higher will be the income of the households. This coincides with our results. The occupation is positive and significant at 1 per cent. It indicates that the members who are self-employed have 31 per cent more income than members with occupations like cultivation and wage employment. The variable MFI is positive and significant at 1 per cent. This indicates that the households from the SKDRDP (Belthangady taluk) project area had 15 per cent more income compared to those from Sangham-ithra (T. Narasipura taluk). The coefficient of the member group is positive and significant at 1 per cent. This reveals that having more years of experience in microfinance is likely to increase the PCI of household by 16 per cent. The coefficient of (Edn2) sec-ondary education and beyond is positive and significant at 5 per cent. It can be argued that members having secondary education and more had 11 per cent more income than the people who had only primary education and members who had no formal educa-tion. This can be attributed to the fact that secondary education provided better information about the microfinance programme to access the credit-plus services and their benefits. The coefficient of marriage is positive and significant. This suggests that members who were married had 16 per cent more income than the unmar-ried members of microfinance. The coefficient of caste variables negatively influenced household PCI. This result deduces that the forward caste members availed larger benefit of microfinance than the SC, ST and OBC members. This further implies the preva-lence of social exclusion even in the microfinance programme. The R-square value was 0.54, which means that 54 per cent of the variations in the household's PCI were explained by the variables included in the model.

Conclusion and policy implications

Microfinance is not a panacea to all problems of poverty. How-ever, it is considered as a vital tool to break the vicious circle of poverty which is characterised by low incomes, low savings and low investment. In order to generate higher incomes, more sav-ings and more investment, there is a need to inject capital in the form of microfinance. Correspondingly, for optimum utilisation of resources available to fight poverty, the poor require access to various non-financial services. In recent years, numerous experi-ments were conducted in the field of microfinance. One such experiment was the delivery of credit-plus services to improve the standard of living the poorest of the poor. In this context, the present study has tried to examine the access to various credit-plus services and its welfare impact on the member households. The study showed that microfinance intervention has contributed in widening the access to credit, savings, micro-health insurance, self-employment and micro-enterprise development, and provided training and awareness in the member group as compared to the control group households.

In evaluating the extent to which credit-plus services of micro-finance has made an impact on member households, the present study concentrated on economic and social dimensions of the changes in the households. On the economic front, credit-plus services, in general, enabled the households to improve their income, assets, expenditure, employment, and housing conditions. However, the magnitude of impact varies across the member and control group households. For example, large numbers of member group households had a very high net annual household income in third and fourth income quartiles. A large number of control group households were in first and second quartiles. This confirms the fact that a large number of member group households accessed credit-plus services and used it for income-generating activities or building their asset bases. The credit-plus services have also enabled the households to improve their housing conditions, which was particularly true for member group households in the study area. Furthermore, the empirical result reveals that credit-plus services have supported small-scale self-employment or micro-enterprise development among the member households.

It is important to note that the innovation in microfinance has played a crucial role in inculcating savings and thrift habits among their members, particularly poor women. A significant proportion of member households had no savings in any formal institutions before joining the microfinance programme. It is also true in the case of access to credit services. On the impact of credit-plus services in reducing vulnerability to risks faced by households, micro-health insurance has been widely used a major coping mechanism by the member households. The study finds that participation in the microfinance programme also resulted in various skill enhancement trainings and awareness programmes, networking with various institutions of poor women. Further, all these non-financial services helped the poor households to soften their welfare path. Thus, we can conclude that the credit-plus services of MFIs not only uplifted the poor from 'income poverty' but also from 'knowledge poverty'.

Appendix

Table A12.1 Enrollment and dropout of students at various levels of education

Educational level	Bethangady (N=159)						T.Narasipura (N=159)						Total (N=318)					
	Control group			Member group			Control group			Member group			Control group			Member group		
	a	b	c	A	b	c	a	b	c	a	b	c	a	b	c	a	b	c
Illiterate	0	1	2	0	0	0	3	1	2	0	1	2	4	2	4	0	1	2
Primary education	10 (1)	0 (4)	0 (4)	57 (2)	0 (0)	0 (2)	23 (4)	0 (11)	0 (1)	49 (0)	0 (4)	0 (2)	33 (5)	0 (15)	0 (5)	106 (2)	0 (4)	0 (4)
Secondary education	6 (2)	0 (2)	0 (4)	25 (0)	0 (1)	0 (2)	5 (1)	0 (5)	0 (1)	13 (1)	0 (2)	0 (2)	11 (3)	0 (7)	0 (5)	38 (1)	0 (3)	0 (4)
High school and PUC	6 (0)	5 (0)	0 (1)	30 (0)	45 (0)	0 (0)	1 (0)	0 (0)	1 (1)	24 (0)	32 (1)	0 (1)	7 (0)	5 (0)	1 (2)	54 (0)	77 (1)	0 (1)
Degree and beyond	0 (0)	5 (0)	2 (0)	0 (0)	22 (0)	49 (0)	0 (0)	4 (0)	0 (0)	0 (0)	9 (0)	13 (0)	0 (0)	9 (0)	2 (0)	0 (0)	31 (0)	62 (0)
Other	0 (0)	0 (0)	0 (0)	0 (0)	0 (0)	1 (0)	0 (0)	0 (0)	0 (0)	0 (0)	0 (0)	0 (0)	0 (0)	0 (0)	0 (0)	0 (0)	0 (0)	1 (1)
Total	22 (3)	10 (7)	2 (11)	112 (2)	67 (1)	50 (4)	32 (8)	4 (17)	1 (5)	86 (1)	41 (8)	13 (7)	54 (8)	16 (22)	7 (12)	198 (3)	109 (8)	65 (9)

Source: Primary Survey.

Notes: (i) a = children in the age group of 6 to 14 years (1 to 8th standard); b = children in the age group of 15 to 18 years (9th to PUC/equivalent education) and c = c in the age group of 19 to 21 years (degree education/equivalent). (ii) Figures in parentheses indicate the number of students dropped out or discontinued from particular educational level.

Table A12.2 Participation of the member in training and awareness activities

Training on skill and confidence development	Belthangady (N=159)				T. Narasipura (N=159)				Total (N=318)			
	Control group (N=34)		Member group (N=125)		Control group (N=41)		Member group (N=118)		Control group (N=75)		Member group (N=243)	
	Yes	No	Yes	No	Yes	No	Yes	No	Yes	No	Yes	No
Number of members participated in any of the training/awareness/orientation/exposure programmes	34 (100)	0	125 (100)	0	10 (24.4)	31 (75.6)	81 (68.6)	37 (31.4)	44 (58.7)	31 (41.3)	206 (84.8)	37 (15.2)
Training in management of group and confidence building	34 (100)	0	125 (100)	0	10 (24.4)	31 (75.6)	81 (68.6)	37 (31.4)	44 (58.7)	31 (41.3)	206 (84.8)	37 (15.2)
Training on IGAs and skill improvements	18 (52.9)	16 (47.1)	119 (95.2)	6 (4.8)	4 (9.8)	37 (90.2)	75 (63.6)	43 (36.4)	22 (29.3)	53 (70.7)	194 (79.8)	49 (20.2)
Training on health and nutrition	16 (47.1)	18 (52.9)	125 (100)	0	9 (22)	32 (78)	82 (69.5)	36 (30.5)	25 (33.3)	50 (66.7)	207 (85.2)	36 (14.8)
Training on household management	30 (88.2)	4 (11.8)	116 (92.8)	9 (7.2)	10 (24.4)	31 (75.6)	96 (81.6)	22 (18.4)	40 (53.3)	35 (46.7)	212 (87.2)	31 (12.8)
Other trainings and exposure programmes	3 (8.8)	31 (91.2)	27 (21.6)	98 (78.4)	1 (2.4)	40 (97.6)	6 (5.6)	112 (94.4)	4 (5.3)	71 (94.7)	33 (13.6)	210 (86.4)
Has the training improved the skill/knowledge and awareness in the member?	13 (38.2)	21 (61.8)	118 (94.1)	7 (5.9)	7 (17.1)	34 (82.9)	74 (62.7)	44 (37.3)	20 (26.7)	55 (73.3)	192 (79.0)	51 (21.0)
Was the training helpful in taking the IGAs?	17 (50)	17 (50)	106 (84.8)	19 (15.2)	2 (4.9)	39 (95.1)	54 (45.8)	64 (54.2)	19 (25.3)	56 (74.7)	160 (65.8)	83 (34.2)
Has the training resulted in increase in income of the member?	7 (20.6)	27 (79.4)	105 (84)	20 (16)	2 (4.9)	39 (95.1)	65 (55.1)	53 (44.9)	9 (12.0)	66 (88.0)	170 (70.0)	73 (30.0)

Source: Primary Survey.

Note: Figures in parentheses denote percentage to the total number of households in the particular sample group.

Notes

1 The microfinance programme in the selected taluks (villages) was extensively developed. As a result, finding the (eligible) household/s that is/are not a part of microfinance programme as a control group was difficult task. Therefore, in this study we have considered the new entrants into the microfinance programme with the membership of less than two years as a control group (even finding a meaningful control group of less than one-year membership was also difficult).
2 Care has been taken to avoid the selected households that are having dual membership – more than one SHG membership and many members from the same households are having membership in the same SHG.
3 The poor have no access to formal financial institutions due to their poverty and high transaction cost for the banks to handle the very small amounts of money.
4 'Shree Dharmasthala SIRI Gramodyoga Samsthe' is a company under Section 25 of Companies Act with share capital from SHGs, which provides forward and backward linkages to the SHG members for taking up income-generation activities.

References

Armendariz, B., and J. Morduch, (2005), The Economics of Microfinance, Cambridge, MA: *MIT Press.*

Edgcomb, E., and L. Barton, (1998), Social Intermediation and Microfinance Programs: A Literature Review, USAID: *Microenterprise Best Practices.*

Godquin, M., (2004), Microfinance Repayment Performance in Bangladesh: How to Improve the Allocation of Loans by MFIs, *World Development,* 32 (11): 1909–26.

Hossain, M., (1988), Credit for Alleviation of Rural Poverty: The Grameen Bank in Bangladesh, Washington, DC: *IFPRI.*

Littlefield, E., J. Morduch and S. Hashemi, (2003), Is Microfinance as Effective Strategy to Reach the Millennium Development Goals, CGAP Focus Note 24, Washington, DC: *CGAP.*

Morduch, J., (1999), The Microfinance Promise, *Journal of Economic Literature,* 37 (4): 1569–614.

Otero, M., and E. Rhyne (eds), (1994), The New World of Micro-Enterprise Finance: Building Healthy Financial Institutions, West Hartford, CT: *Kumarian Press.*

Rajasekhar, D., and S. Madeshwaran, (2005), Economic and Social Benefit of Microfinance Programme: An Econometric Analysis, In Bhattacharya, B.B. and A. Mitra (eds.) *Studies in Macroeconomics and Welfare,* New Delhi: *Academic Publication.*

Robinson, M., (2001), The Microfinance Revolution: Sustainable Finance for the Poor, Washington, DC: *The World Bank.*

Zeller, M., and R.L. Meyer, (2002), The Triangle of Microfinance- Financial Sustainability, Outreach and Impact, Washington IFPRI and Baltimore, MD: *The Johns Hopkins University Press*.

Zohir, S., S. Mahmud, B. Sen, M. Asaduzzaman, J. Islam and A. Al-Mamun, (2001), Monitoring and Evaluation of Microfinance Institutions, Final Report, Mimeo, *BIDS*, Dhaka.

Chapter 13

Financial inclusion

Technology, institutions and policies[1]

Raghuram Rajan

Distinguished members of NASSCOM and distinguished guests: Thank you for inviting me to speak here today. The Indian information and communications technology industry that you represent has a proud history of accomplishment. You have done India great service, not just by creating a world class industry but also by showing the rest of us what is possible. I am hopeful that financial firms can join hands with you to build a technology-enabled financial sector that can reach every nook and cranny of India, and even across borders, to foster growth. This will entail new, uniquely Indian models, much as you have developed in software or in mobile communications. The Dr Nachiket Mor Committee Report has given the RBI much food for thought on these issues. I want to reflect on the recommendations, even while putting some additional issues on the table.

Financial inclusion is about (a) the broadening of financial services to those people who do not have access to financial services sector; (b) the deepening of financial services for people who have minimal financial services; and (c) greater financial literacy and consumer protection so that those who are offered the products can make appropriate choices. The imperative for financial inclusion is both a moral one and one based on economic efficiency. Should we not give everyone that is capable the tools and resources to better themselves, and in doing so, better the country?

Last week, I met with some members of Ela Bhatt's Self-Employed Women's Association. In a room full of poor but confident women entrepreneurs, I asked how many borrowed from moneylenders before they came to SEWA. About half the women raised their hands. When asked how many thought of approaching a regular bank before they came to SEWA's cooperative bank, not one raised her hand. Interestingly, many of them said that the loan from SEWA freed them from the moneylender's high interest rate, which gave them enough to service SEWA's loan fully even while focusing on other productive activities. I have heard this from other micro-entrepreneurs – the highest return initial investment is often to free oneself of the clutches of the moneylender. Despite this high return from the delivery of credit to the poor, and despite much of our financial inclusion efforts being focused on credit, we still reach too few of the target population. So there is much more to be achieved.

We have tried to effect inclusion in the past through mandates – whether it be through direction on branch opening or on lending to priority sectors. That we are still far short of our goals has led some critics to suggest we should abandon mandates because the market will take care of needs; If the poor have demand for financial services, the critics say, providers will emerge to supply it. Markets do respond to need, and competition is a very healthy force for improvement, but market functioning can be impeded by poor infrastructure, uneven regulation, natural or regulatory monopolies, and even cartelisation.

While enlisting competitive forces wherever possible to compete for the bottom of the pyramid's business, as a development central bank we also need to offer a supportive hand. By putting in place the right infrastructure and enabling regulation, we have to encourage the development of the products, institutions, and networks that will foster inclusion.

Let us start with products. We have been trying for decades to expand credit. We have focused much less on easing payments and remittances or on expanding remunerative savings vehicles or on providing easy-to-understand insurance against emergencies. Perhaps we should try to expand financial inclusion by encouraging these other products, and allow credit to follow them rather than lead. Indeed, many successful organisations working with the poorest of the poor try to get them to put aside some money as savings, no matter how little, before giving them loans. Some of our self-help groups (SHGs) work on this principle. Not only does the savings habit, once inculcated, allow the customer to handle the burden of repayment better, it may also lead to better credit allocation. With the power of information technology, perhaps the analysis of the savings and payment patterns of a client can indicate which one of them is ready to use credit well.

One roadblock to access, even to something as simple as a universal basic savings account, is know your customer (KYC) requirements. Experts have emphasised the need to make it far simpler to open basic accounts, and have suggested minimising the required documentation. In an effort to do so, the Dr Nachiket Mor Committee recommends requiring proof of only a permanent address. This is nevertheless more onerous than current RBI norms, which allow an applicant to self-certify her address and other details for accounts below Rs 50,000. But despite the RBI's exhortations, few banks have reduced their demand for documentation – they fear that they will be held responsible if something goes wrong, no matter what the regulatory norms are. The acceptance of third-party KYC certification is particularly difficult.

Today, stringent KYC norms keep too many out of the banking system, and lead to unnecessary harassment for others. Banks may adopt these norms more because of regulatory or legal liability than to safeguard against true criminal or terrorist activity. Can't we do better? Some bankers suggest that by monitoring activity patterns in accounts carefully, even while putting some limits on basic accounts (such as holding a large-value cheque for a few days before it is cashed), much of the suspicious activity can be detected and stopped. Could we allow a commercial bank some regulatory dispensation in case there is minor mischief in some low-value accounts, provided the bank has a reliable system in place to detect greater mischief? Could the gains in easing widespread access to safe accounts outweigh the costs of minor fraud? How can we get entities within the system to rely on each other's KYC, without the process having to be continuously repeated? How can technology assist in effectively addressing the above issues? These are questions we have to examine and address.

The broader issue is whether through sophisticated state-of-the-art technology, we can offer customers products that are simple, low cost, and easy to use. We have done this with mobile phones; can we do it with banking? Payments may be another obvious product. I should note that our payments infrastructure in India is very advanced. We have three large RBI technology centres devoted to supporting payments. For large-value transactions, we have a state-of-the-art real time gross settlement system. In the national electronic funds transfer system, our flagship retail funds transfer system, we have near-real-time transaction processing – we continuously send messages to banks even though net settlement takes place at hourly intervals. We also send a positive confirmation to the remitter after the funds have been credited to the beneficiary's account.

We have introduced an additional factor of authentication for all e-commerce transactions, and are swiftly moving to Chip and PIN technology for credit card transactions. SMS alerts for bank and credit card transactions are a welcome advance relative to even the United States, where thieves find it easy to bill thousands of dollars to your credit card even before you know it is stolen. All this means that we have the infrastructure to provide cheap and safe payments and remittances. What we need are non-governmental players to utilise this infrastructure to provide the products and access that people want.

A lot is already happening. Real-time funds transfer through the immediate payment service (IMPS) put in place by National Payments Corporation of India has contributed significantly towards growth of mobile banking. The Aadhaar Payment Bridge System allows government benefits to be transferred through the use of unique identification number given to the citizens. But we are still not where we should be, either on mobile payments or on direct benefit transfers.

With over 900 million mobile phones, the potential for mobile banking as a delivery channel for financial services is a big opportunity in India. We have consciously adopted the bank-led model for mobile banking, while the non-banks, including mobile network operators, have been permitted to issue mobile wallets, where cash withdrawal is not permitted as of now. The key to cheap and universal payments and remittances will be, if we can find a safe way to allow funds to be freely transferred between bank accounts and mobile wallets as well as cashed out of mobile wallets, through a much larger and ubiquitous network of business correspondents. The Nachiket Mor Committee suggests the creation of payment banks as a step towards this goal. Other suggestions include interoperable business correspondents who will get the scale economies to serve in remote locations, and the usage of NBFCs as banking correspondents. We will examine all this.

In the meantime, interesting solutions are emerging. Cashing out is important for remittances, because we have a large recipient population in the country, most of whom do not have access to formal banking services. We have recently approved the in-principle setting up of a payment system which will facilitate the funds transfer from bank account holders to those without accounts through ATMs. Essentially, the sender can have the money withdrawn from his account through an ATM transaction. The intermediary processes the payment, and sends a code to the recipient on his mobile that allows him to withdraw the money from any nearby bank's ATM. The system will take care of necessary safeguards of customer identification, transaction validation, velocity checks and so on. We need more such innovative products, some of which mobile companies are providing.

In India, despite the high mobile density, it is also a reality that most of the handsets are very basic ones and many of the mobile connections are prepaid subscriptions. These are important constraints. The RBI's Technical Committee on Mobile Banking has recommended, among others, the need for a standardised and simplified procedure for registration/authentication of customers for mobile banking services, a cohesive awareness programme to be put in place, the adoption of a common application platform across all banks to be delivered to the customers independent of the handset being used, along with use of SMS and USSD technology for providing necessary level of security (through encryption) for such transactions. The Telecom Regulatory Authority of India (TRAI) has prescribed optimum service parameters, as also a ceiling on charges for provision of USSD services by telecom operators to the banks and their agents. We have a great opportunity for banks and telecom service providers to come together to deliver mobile banking services of all kinds in a seamless and secure manner to their customers. In the next few months, we will accelerate the dialog between key players.

Technology can also be used to facilitate credit, a product I started the talk with. MSMEs get squeezed all the time by their large buyers, who pay after long delays. All would be better off if the MSME could sell its claim on the large buyer in the market. The MSME would get its money quickly, while the market would get a claim on the better rated large buyer instead of holding a claim on the MSME. The large buyer could get a better price for his purchases. All this requires setting up a trade-receivables exchange, which the RBI has been discussing with market participants. Once again, the key is to reduce transaction costs by automating almost every aspect of the transaction so that even the smallest MSMEs can benefit.

One of the difficulties the poor and small businesses have in accessing credit is the lack of information about them, both upfront as they are being evaluated for credit, and after lending where the lender has to monitor them. If savings and payments products are sold widely, and information, including payments to mobile companies, utility companies, as well as the government, collected, then the excluded can build information records that will help them access credit. If, in addition, negative information on defaults is shared in a fair and responsible way through the financial network, every individual borrower will have something at stake – their credit history – which can serve to encourage timely repayment. This, in turn, can improve the willingness of banks to lend.

Finally, let me turn to consumer literacy and protection. As we reach more and more of the population, we have to be sure that they understand the products they are being sold and have the information to make sensible decisions. Caveat emptor or let the buyer beware is typically the standard used in financial markets – that is, so long as the buyer is not actively misled, she is responsible for researching her product choices and making purchase decisions. While this puts a lot of burden on the buyer to do due diligence, it also gives her a lot of freedom to make choices, including of course the freedom to make bad choices.

But with poorly informed and unsophisticated investors, we should consider the Dr Nachiket Mor Committee's recommendation of setting some guidelines on what products are suitable for different categories of investors. Broadly speaking, the more complicated the product, the more sophisticated should be the target customer. Should we move to a norm where a suite of simple products is pre-approved for dissemination to all, but as products get more complicated, financial sector providers bear more and more responsibility to show that the buyer was sophisticated and/or appropriately counseled before she purchased?

Of course, the longer run answer is for customers to become savvier. Can the technology sector help educate people in financial matters? After all, finance is not something most people learn in schools, but it is something they encounter every day in the world. Low-cost but high-quality distance finance education is something the country very much needs and we look to entrepreneurs here to think of innovative ways to provide it.

Before I conclude, one caveat. Technology can magnify the reach of finance for bad purposes as well as good. Many of you must receive frequent e-mails, purportedly from me, informing you of a large sum of money that awaits you at the RBI, and urging you to send me your account details so that I can transfer the money to you. Let me assure you that the RBI does not give out money, I do not send these e-mails, and if you do fall for such e-mails, you will lose a lot of money to crooks and be reminded of the adage – if anything looks too good to be true, it probably is not true.

Of course, technology can also offer answers to check fraud. Can we enlist social media in enabling the public to identify fraud and help regulation? How can we do this in a responsible way? Again, these are questions at this point, but I am sure we will find the answers.

Let me conclude. Technology, with its capacity to reduce transaction costs, is key to enabling the large volume low-ticket transaction that is at the centre of financial inclusion. By collecting and processing large volumes of data easily, technology can also improve the quality of financial decision making. When products have network effects, technology can ensure not just interoperability, key to obtaining the benefits of networking, but also security, key to maintaining the confidence of people and preventing them from withdrawing from the formal financial system once again. Can the successful ICT industry partner with the finance industry to revolutionise financial inclusion in this country? I sincerely hope you will.

Note

1   Keynote address delivered by Dr Raghuram Rajan, Governor, Reserve Bank of India, at the NASSCOM India Leadership Forum in Mumbai on 12 February 2014.

Printed in the United States
By Bookmasters